GIANTS

THE 25 GREATEST CENTERS OF ALL TIME

Mark Heisler

TRIUMPH
B O O K S

Copyright © 2003 by Triumph Books

No part of this publication may be
reproduced, stored in a retrieval system,
or transmitted, in any form by any means,
electronic, mechanical, photocopying,
or otherwise, without the prior written
permission of the publisher, Triumph Books,
601 S. LaSalle St., Suite 500, Chicago,
Illinois 60605.

Library of Congress Cataloging-in-Publication Data

Heisler, Mark.
    Giants : the 25 greatest centers of all time / Mark Heisler.
        p. cm.
    ISBN 1-57243-577-1 (hard)
    1. Centers (Basketball)—Rating of—United States. 2. National Basketball
Association—History. I. Title.

GV884.A1H37 2003
796.323´092´2—dc21

2003047332

This book is available in quantity at special
discounts for your group or organization.

For further information, contact:

Triumph Books
601 South LaSalle Street
Suite 500
Chicago, Illinois 60605
(312) 939-3330
Fax (312) 663-3557

Printed in People's Republic of China
ISBN 1-57243-577-1
Interior design by Robert A. Wyszkowski
Contributing writer: Roland Lazenby
Rankings were compiled by an editorial panel in consultation
with Pete Newell, Willis Reed, and Jerry West.

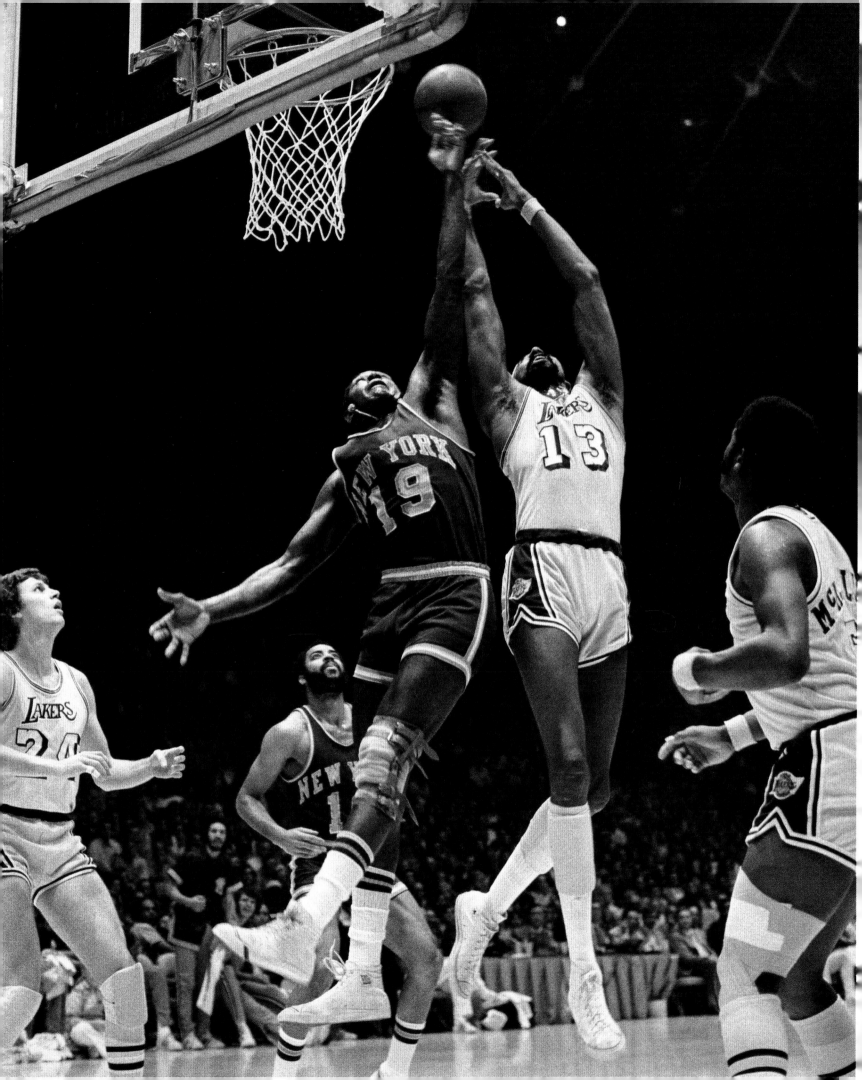

burst of speed. He was easily the quickest 6´9´´, 6´10´´ guy I've ever seen. He caught Bryant that night—just took an incredibly long leap and blocked the shot with his left hand. It was unbelievable. He may have left much of the offense to his teammates, but Russell always got back to the defensive end and prevented teams from scoring easy hoops on his Celtics.

Russell was tough to compete against, but he didn't hesitate to offer his friendship. I was a rookie at the All-Star Game in St. Louis in 1965 when I ran into him on the hotel elevator.

"How ya doin', rookie?" he asked. "Where you going?"

I told him I was going down to have dinner.

"I think I'll go have dinner with you," he said.

It was the beginning of our friendship. There used to be a lot of doubleheaders in Madison Square Garden on Tuesday nights. Often the Celtics would play us in the second game. Most of Russell's teammates would stay in the locker room during the first game, but he'd often come out and watch the other teams. I remember one night early in my career, I asked him what he was doing.

"I like to watch guys and figure out what they do best offensively," Russell told me. "In crunch time, guys always go to their best move."

Russell was making sure he had that knowledge of his opponents. That's how he led his Celtics teams to 11 titles in 13 seasons. He was always learning, and he had a tremendous IQ for the game.

In some ways, Chamberlain and Russell's accomplishments have helped cast the shadow of expectation over the generation of big men that followed. For example, consider Patrick Ewing, whose career is considered flawed by some because his teams didn't win an NBA title. I couldn't carry that guy's jock in terms of being a center. That guy was a workhorse. The Knicks teams I was on won two titles. Patrick didn't win any, but he didn't have Clyde Frazier, Dave DeBusschere, Bill Bradley, and Dick Barnett.

You look at Pat's numbers—that guy has got some numbers. Every night he went to work. He was an All-Star 11 times and his teams were in the playoffs 13 times. None of his teams won because he played during the era of Michael Jordan.

The year the Knicks should have won it, in 1994, they lost because John Starks and Anthony Mason, two of Pat's key teammates, lost focus at a key moment. All they had to do was win one game. Some people have used things like that as a reason not to give Patrick his due. Often that's how expectations work for a big man. They have to lead their teams to championships to be considered truly great. Patrick Ewing was a great center.

Pat and Hakeem Olajuwon enjoyed a great rivalry during their playing days. Patrick won the NCAA title at Georgetown over Hakeem's University of Houston team. But in the pros, Hakeem's Rockets managed the edge. Hakeem was so mobile, so quick. He could go get the ball from guards. They didn't have to necessarily get it to him. He had that footwork, and he could run up and down the floor. Pat didn't have that mobility, but he had a presence and power. Between them they treated us to a great show.

Sometimes winning a championship isn't even enough to earn a guy respect. Take Wes Unseld: despite being small for a center, he deserves a lot

of respect. I introduced Wes at his induction into the Hall of Fame. He's the only center in my era who was shorter than me—except when he was wearing an Afro. When Wes wore an Afro, I couldn't see over it. The rest of the time, though, he made me feel good because I could think, "At least I'm bigger than one guy."

He was a rookie when he was named the league's Most Valuable Player and was first-team All-NBA. That's awesome.

Wes was such an effective player. He did a lot of rebounding and setting up those screens. He had a wide body, almost like a football body. You could hardly get around him, as if he were a tackle. He could really rebound the ball and throw the outlet. He'd get his points, but he'd get the points that nobody else wanted. He'd get the ball off the offensive glass when

Gus Johnson or Jack Marin or Freddy Carter would miss. He'd get the ball and score, or throw it back out and let 'em shoot again.

Another guy I had great respect for was Nate Thurmond, who played with Golden State. Rick Barry became a great, great player because Nate set all those screens for him. Imagine if a team today had a player of Nate's size, with his great scoring ability, plus his defense and rebounding, and that great wingspan that allowed him to change shots on the defensive end.

Would Nate make a team good today? I think so, because that's what great centers do: they make their teams good, or even great. That's why we consider them giants, why we have such great expectations for them. It's also why their presence will always define the game. ∎

PREFACE
By Jerry West

A book like *Giants* is great fun, particularly because it gives me pause to look back over the careers of the huge talents who have played this great game. I was fortunate to have battled with and against many of the players listed here.

In the old days, we didn't have TV coverage of basketball like we do today, so you didn't get much of a look at the really good players until the NCAA Tournament. In 1955, that was where I got my first look at a young, thin player named Bill Russell, a guy who really got a late start in the game.

Even though he was somewhat awkward, you saw something special in Bill. Unlike most players he was almost acrobatic, with this incredible ability to block shots and rebound. You could see that he had changed the way the game was going to be played inside. With the things he was doing, he was totally different from any other player that had ever come along.

Today the pundits look at players and make pronouncements about their greatness, and as a professional observer you often have different opinions about players. A lot of the so-called pundits didn't understand that Bill Russell was different in those early years.

By the time I first played against him in 1960, he had already demonstrated his greatness very effectively by leading the Celtics to three championships. I'll never forget the circumstances when I played against him in 1960 as a rookie with the Lakers. We played them in something like 12 to 14 exhibition games that season, and then in another 10 regular-season games. I had my fill of seeing Bill Russell at an early age. I always

prided myself on the fact that as a player he didn't block very many of my shots.

Some players are more aware of circumstances and other players on the court than others, and I always tried to be aware. That was definitely a challenge against that great Celtics team of Russell's. One of the things they did so well was steering the opposing player who had the ball toward Russell. Then the rest of his teammates covered the passing lanes really well, so that when offensive players encountered Russell and tried to pass the ball, the Celtics would have an excellent chance to steal the pass.

What made them even more dangerous was that Russell didn't block shots out of bounds. He directed a lot of blocks to his teammates, and his teammates were great at getting their running game going off of Russell's blocks. I found that if you didn't get surprised, you could actually shoot the ball against Russell, but you had to have the right angle and you had to know where he was—at all times. He was just so athletic, so supremely competitive, and so smart. The things he did had never been done before, and in a lot of ways, they haven't been done since, either.

When Wilt Chamberlain came along he had a lot in common with Russell. The first time I saw Wilt play was in the 1957 NCAA championship game, when his University of Kansas team lost to North Carolina in three overtimes. Wilt had received a lot of publicity ever since he was a young teenager in Philadelphia. When LeBron James gained so much notoriety as a high school junior it made me wonder what would have happened if Wilt had come of age in 2000 instead

of during the fifties. In this age of sports shows and cable TV, I think today's media would have run out of words trying to talk and write about Wilt.

My first experience playing against Chamberlain came during that rookie season of 1960. What people may not realize is just how athletic he was and what a dominant force he was. We had never seen anything like him. The thing that made him so unique, besides being so big, was that he was very mobile. Despite his size he could run the floor as well as any player in the league.

At that early point in his career, Wilt was shooting the fadeaway with great accuracy and, because of his overwhelming size, that fadeaway was virtually unstoppable. His dunk shot was also a hopeless situation for defenders. With his huge scoring and rebounding totals in those early sixties seasons, his presence had an enormous impact on the NBA. They actually changed the rules when he played, in part to try to lessen his impact. But you really couldn't lessen his impact, no matter what you did or what rules you changed.

Wilt came to the Lakers later in his career, and his first seasons in Los Angeles were an adjustment for us because we had never played with a dominant center. Bill Sharman became our coach in 1971 and immediately asked Wilt to shift his emphasis from scoring to shot-blocking and rebounding. It wasn't an easy sacrifice—Wilt told reporters that asking him not to score was like "asking Babe Ruth not to hit home runs." But he changed his game, and we had a very fine team in 1972.

Among my personal treasures are the memories of the fun relationship I had with Wilt. He was one of the most misunderstood people of all time. He was truly a sensitive, nice person. Because of his size, everybody expected him to be at his best every night—not just at one job, but at every phase of the game. That he was able to endure and succeed despite those impossible expectations says so much about him.

Another of my obvious personal favorites is Kareem Abdul-Jabbar, who I had the challenge of playing against. That was followed by the honor of working with him as a coach and team executive. In my mind there were two distinct phases to his career, the first being those early years in Milwaukee. He was thinner and not very physical, but he had enormous skills and finesse. He entered the second phase as he matured and got bigger. His skyhook was the greatest shot in the history of basketball. It was unstoppable. He could shoot it any time he wanted to. It had this sweeping reach that no one could get to or hinder.

Beyond the shot, Kareem was just so skilled. With his low-key style and his perfect skills he made it look easy. People didn't realize how hard he had worked to perfect his great skill.

Another thing that I'll always appreciate about Kareem was that he was the consummate professional. This guy never missed games, never asked to get out of practice, never complained about money. He just came every day and did his job. As a coach, you love a player like that.

I remember feeling a similar awe the first time I saw Shaquille O'Neal play, and thinking how much fun it would have been to play on a team with a center of that magnitude. Obviously I have a strong personal connection with him. He combines incredible size and strength with the ultimate in athleticism. Then there's his heart: the bigger the game, the better he's going to play.

With his sense of humor and playfulness, Shaq has the perfect mentality for competition. He keeps things loose and relaxed—until the ball goes up. Then he makes things really difficult for any opponent. I don't care what you do: you cannot guard him. His strength and skill are startling to opponents. People don't understand how skilled he is.

Watching him grow and develop has been one of the joys of my professional life. What surprised me during his early days in Los Angeles was how frustrated he got. He was not fun to be around. The shortcomings of our team and his teammates made him angry because he knew he was going to be judged on how much he won.

Once Shaq and his teammates learned how to win championships, that anger subsided. Now he's very confident in his ability to dominate opponents and frustrate any game plans they might have. There's just no answer for him. He's a scary guy to play against, just so physical. Thank God he's a nice guy or he could have killed somebody by now.

Another guy who created dread in opponents was Moses Malone, one of those unsung players. He wasn't one of those classically pretty players to watch, but he had this instinctive ability to rebound the ball and, when he got it, he knew what to do with it. It was no fun to play against him. He just physically wore people down inside with his great energy and his great enthusiasm for playing the game.

Dave Cowens was another of those guys who defined the NBA of the seventies. At 6'8'', he would have to be considered a forward today, but in those days he played center. And he played it with a tremendous competitive spirit. You'd watch him work so hard, so all out, and you'd say, "I don't want to have to play against a guy like that every night."

One of my favorites to come out of that era was Bob McAdoo, who truly was one of the game's great scorers. I've often wondered just how many points he could have scored if he had landed in the right situation early in his career. That didn't happen for him, and by the time Bob came to the Lakers late in his career we had heard all the horror stories about his selfishness and difficult nature. But I loved Bob McAdoo. He is such a good person and so darned competitive. If we hadn't had him in Los Angeles, we wouldn't have won the titles we did. He did an unbelievable job for us, and he did it coming off the bench—which is the toughest job in basketball. We had heard all the negatives about him, but we never saw them. All he did was sacrifice for our team.

Then there's Robert Parish, one of those guys who is like Father Time: every year you expected him to slack off, and yet every year he seemed to come back and deliver again. He was a complementary player, but he too presented a very difficult matchup because of the way he shot the ball way up over his head. It was so hard to block. And then there was his demeanor. You'd look at that guy and ask, "Is he awake?" Then he'd hurt you.

The Chief was paired with another amazingly deceptive player in Kevin McHale. You'd watch him in warm-ups and he wouldn't seem to be a guy who could even play the game. He wasn't sleek, not pretty. But boy could he play. He, too, presented a very different matchup with his long arms and great footwork in the post. He could work you over with those moves inside, but what made him really great was his versatility at the other end. He was able to defend against 6'7'' players just as easily as he could play seven-footers. He didn't get much publicity because he played alongside Larry Bird. McHale probably could have gotten more praise playing somewhere besides Boston, but that combination of McHale, Parish, and Bird was truly great.

Hakeem Olajuwon was a player I greatly admired. I watched him early in his career, and it was obvious that he was a very gifted athlete. With his twirling moves and dancing footwork, he was pretty to watch. His competitiveness really jumped out at you. Of the centers of that era, he's the one who really commanded the respect of the other centers. To this day, they all speak of him with reverence.

Then there's Yao Ming—with him you look back over the past and then try to see ahead; you wonder what lies in store for a guy like him. I don't think anyone knows what his future will be. He's a really gifted kid, particularly in his understanding of the game and how to use his teammates.

Unfortunately, I really don't think his young teammates with the Houston Rockets know how to use him. His shooting and passing skills are so great, and at 7'5'' he also has tremendous presence. His teammates always have a safe place to pass the ball. He's very unselfish, and he knows how to get the ball back to them.

His teammates don't really know yet how to take advantage of all he has to offer. You can only hope that with time they will come to understand what he is. We don't have many of those truly gifted big players. They're so rare. That's just one of the reasons we call them giants. ∎

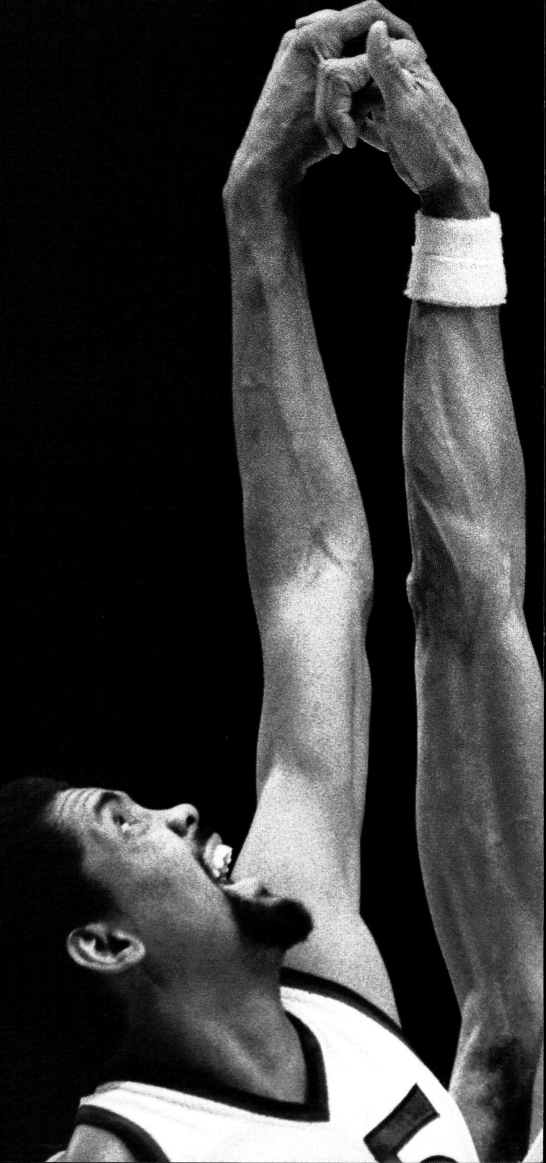

PHOTO CREDITS

Adrees A. Latif/AFP/CORBIS: pg. 132
Adrees A. Latif/Reuters NewMedia Inc./CORBIS: pp. 62 (bottom left),
   111 (bottom right)
AP/Wide World Photos: pp. v, xv, xvi, xviii, 3, 5, 9, 10 (bottom left),
   11 (top right), 14, 20, 25, 29 (top), 29 (bottom), 30, 35 (top),
   35 (bottom), 41, 42, 43 (bottom), 55 (bottom), 56, 58, 60, 63, 64,
   65, 66, 67 (bottom left), 67 (center), 70 (bottom left), 70 (center),
   71 (top), 77, 80 (center), 83 (bottom), 84, 87, 94, 96, 97 (top),
   97 (bottom), 104, 106, 127 (top), 128, 130 (bottom left),
   130 (center), 131 (top), 131 (bottom), 133 (bottom left),
   133 (center), 136 (top), 136 (bottom)
Bettmann/CORBIS: pp. ii, x, xii, xiii, xx, xxii, 2 (bottom), 11 (bottom),
   12, 15, 17 (top), 23 (bottom), 26, 27, 32 (bottom left), 39 (bottom),
   46, 54 (bottom left), 54 (center), 55 (top), 68, 71 (bottom),
   78, 82, 86 (bottom left), 101 (top), 135
Brent Smith/Reuters NewMedia Inc./CORBIS: pg. 114 (center)
Brian Drake/Sportschrome: pp. 44, 49, 86 (center), 90, 98, 102, 109,
   111 (top), 112, 115 (bottom), 134
Brian Spurlock/Sportschrome: pg. 124
CS/Sportschrome: pp. 92 (bottom left), 93 (bottom)
David Liam Kyle/*Sports Illustrated*: pg. viii
DLJ/Sportschrome: 87 (top), 91, 93 (top), 107 (bottom), 113, 119
Hulton Archive/Getty Images: pp. 80 (bottom left), 81, 83 (top)
Ira Strickstein/Bettmann/CORBIS: pg. 99
Jeff Haynes/AFP/CORBIS: pg. 122
Jerry Ward/Bettmann/CORBIS: pg. 96 (center)
John Gress/AFP/CORBIS: pg. 118
John Kuntz/Reuters NewMedia Inc./CORBIS: pg. 123 (bottom)
Kevin T. Gilbert/AFP/CORBIS: pg. 126 (center)
Manny Rubio/Sportschrome: 23 (top), 38 (bottom left)
Mike Blake/Reuters NewMedia Inc./CORBIS: pg. xxiii
Paul Natkin/SportPics: pg. 48
Ray Stubblebine/Reuters NewMedia Inc./CORBIS: pg. 108
Roger Ressmeyer/CORBIS: pg. 73
Sam Mircovich/Reuters NewMedia Inc./CORBIS: pg. 123 (top)
***Sporting News*/Hulton Archive/Getty Images:** pp. 8, 10 (center),
   28 (bottom left), 28 (center), 32 (center), 37, 38 (center), 39 (top),
   40, 43 (top), 59 (top), 59 (bottom), 62 (center), 63 (top),
   72, 76, 92 (center)
Stephen Shaeffer/AFP/CORBIS: pg. 126 (bottom left)
Time Life Pictures/Getty Images: pp. 4, 7, 17 (bottom),
   22, 74, 105, 107 (top), 114 (bottom left), 115 (top), 120, 127 (bottom)
Wally McNamee/CORBIS: pp. 100, 110
Walter Iooss/StocklandMartel.com: pg. 21
Wen Roberts Photography: pp. xiv, xvii, 2 (top), 33, 34, 47, 52, 75

TABLE ABBREVIATIONS KEY

G = Games Played
Min. = Minutes Played
FGM = Field Goals Made
FGA = Field Goals Attempted
Pct. = Percentage Made
FTM = Free Throws Made
FTA = Free Throws Attempted
Off. = Offensive Rebounds
(starting '73–'74)
Def. = Defensive Rebounds
(starting '73–'74)
Reb. = Total Rebounds
Tot. = Total Rebounds
(starting '73–'74)
Ast. = Assists

PF = Personal Fouls
Committed
Dq. = Games Disqualified From
St. = Steals (starting '73–'74)
Blk. = Blocked Shots
(starting '73–'74)
TO = Turnovers
(starting '77–'78)
Pts. = Points Scored
RPG = Rebounds Per Game
APG = Assists Per Game
PPG = Points Per Game
***** = Denotes that a player
led the league in that
particular category

ACKNOWLEDGMENTS

I am indebted to the people who made this project so interesting for me, principally the members of my unofficial ad hoc committee: Hubie Brown, Bob Cousy, Bill Fitch, George Kiseda, Pete Newell, Harvey Pollack, Doc Rivers, Bob Ryan, Jack Ramsay, Gene Shue, Willis Reed, Jerry West, Roland Lazenby, and Bill Walton.

To Tony Cotton, Frank Deford, Hank Hersch, Curry Kirkpatrick, Doug Looney, Leigh Montville, Bruce Newman, Phil Taylor, Rick Telander, and Alex Wolff of *Sports Illustrated*.

To Terry Pluto (author of the remarkable *Loose Balls*), Phil Berger, Merv Harris, Anne Byrne Hoffman, Bob Rubin, and Roland Lazenby for their books on NBA players and history.

To Mitch Rogatz at Triumph Books for hiring me.

As always, to my wife, Loretta, for putting up with me, and to our daughter, Emily, who reminded me to take a break now and then by crawling onto my lap and typing her name on the PC.

INTRODUCTION
LAND OF THE GIANTS

In the eighties, dominated by such relatively medium-sized players as Magic Johnson and Larry Bird, a theory arose that the day of the giant was over in the NBA. This was preposterous, as could be seen every draft day when five or six heretofore anonymous and, often, barely ambulatory seven-footers would be selected in the first round.

It could also be seen on the rosters of the teams that won the titles in the eighties, all of which had a stellar center or two. Johnson's Lakers had Kareem Abdul-Jabbar (and won no more titles after Kareem retired). Bird's Celtics had Robert Parish and Kevin McHale. Julius Erving's 76ers had Moses Malone. Isiah Thomas' Pistons had Bill Laimbeer, a man who was too hated to be remembered as a great player but without whom the Bad Boys would have won nothing.

What did happen in the eighties, nineties, and into the new century, despite all the moaning that there weren't enough good big men to go around, was that there were enough of them to begin canceling each other out. In fact, there were so many that they spilled over into the power forward position, which was becoming indistinguishable from the center position, and even into small forward, where such players as 7´0´´ Kevin Garnett lined up. The skinny Garnett joked that he was 6´12´´ so no one would tell him he had to play center. If he had arrived in 1959, with Wilt Chamberlain, he would have found only two players his size—Wilt and Walter Dukes—and he wouldn't have had a choice.

By the eighties, nineties, and in this new century, too, coaches learned how to defend big players. They double- and even triple-teamed them, subscribing to the universal dictum, "Make the other team beat you from the outside."

LAND OF THE GIANTS

It was relatively easy to double-team a big man who set up under the basket in the heart of the defense. It was more difficult to send two players at Johnson, Bird, or Michael Jordan, who floated around the perimeter. This just made it harder for the big men, who were already carrying a considerable burden of popular expectation, who were often little understood, and who tended to inspire little compassion.

The ground still shook when they walked, though, even if they wished it were otherwise.

The lives and careers of men whose physical stature and skills raise them so far above the crowd have common themes. It's hard to be different. It's especially hard, growing up, to tower physically above the other children who say whatever is on their minds and whose coordination is years ahead.

Any of the men in this book could tell stories of being ridiculed. If they would be envied in later life, they also would still be gawked at. People who would never ask a 300-pound person how it felt to be so fat will walk up and ask how the view is up there, or the weather, or if they are basketball players ("No, I'm a jockey for giraffes").

Some, such as Wilt Chamberlain and Shaquille O'Neal, seemed to glory in it, boasting of heroic

deeds or, as Shaq did, tattooing a Superman logo on one huge bicep. Others, such as Nate Thurmond, who didn't like to dunk, or Artis Gilmore, who took up scuba diving and rejoiced in the serene world under the sea, seemed to shrink from it. All of them had to deal with it.

What they may have missed, especially early in their lives, was the degree to which they embodied shorter people's fantasies about being all-powerful, the degree to which they were admired and envied.

They could not, however, miss noticing how much they also were resented. If one embodies a pleasant fantasy, whether he asked to or not, he also must harvest the disappointment when something happens to prick the popular bubble.

Since the giant is deemed to be all-powerful, he will be held responsible for the shortcomings of those around him. For these men, not winning at least one championship during their careers (or, in the case of Wilt, the most mythic of them all, winning the championship every year) is considered a major shortcoming.

Some were luckier than others, going to teams where their skills and personalities meshed with _____ _____ _____ away from

was 10 on a scale from 1 to 10, he was the right man in the right place at the right time. No one else ever hit it so perfectly, and the rest of them paid a price for that.

In later years, when the NBA ballooned to 29 teams with talent spread more thinly, it got even worse. Such players as David Robinson and Patrick Ewing, the top picks in their classes, were assigned to the worst teams, which had earned their draft position by being so lousy.

While the Spurs and Knicks tried to put together teams worthy of their centers, Robinson and Ewing, early in their careers especially, were criticized for shortcomings that wouldn't have been noticed if they'd been on championship-caliber teams. Both turned inward. Robinson had a religious reawakening. Ewing, a stranger in a strange land in New York, lived in a New Jersey condo and went "home" each summer to Washington, D.C. As both figured out, that was just life.

I did not use a strict methodology in selecting the centers featured in this book, and I assigned them to the decades in which they entered the league (with the exception of George Mikan, who entered during the forties). Few people would be likely to choose the same men. I selected the 25 centers I thought had

had the greatest impact on the professional game, including two, Kevin McHale and Tim Duncan, who were actually forwards. I also chose Bill Laimbeer, who was universally loathed; Ralph Sampson, who never played 30 games in a season after he turned 28; and I've given special mention to a 26th man, Yao Ming, who represents the NBA's global reach and is the first pure, potentially dominant center to enter the game in years.

McHale was a prototype of the modern power forward. At 6´11´´ he was taller than most centers in the fifties and sixties and possessed of a repertoire so varied and refined, he all but redefined low-post offense. And at 7´0´´, though not your prototypical post player, two-time MVP Duncan is arguably the best big man to come along since Shaq.

Laimbeer was the most highly evolved "project"—i.e., side of beef—the game would produce. Sampson was a hard man to pigeonhole and didn't last long, but when he was healthy, people knew he was around.

Of course, some fine players had to be left out of this book: Brad Daugherty, Jack Sikma, Zelmo Beaty, Mel Daniels, Arvydas Sabonis, and depending on how you view the evidence, Walt Bellamy. ∎

RANKINGS

15

10

16

8

9

2

13

5

1

25

20

1. WILT CHAMBERLAIN

No other player in the game has or ever will have the consistent scoring ability that Chamberlain had. Exceptional size and strength enabled him to beat the double-teams he encountered throughout his career, and he still holds multiple scoring and field goal records. He was also a prolific rebounder and shot-blocker, and he actually led the league in assists for one season. Durability is another big factor in his ranking, as he played 48 minutes in every game with very few exceptions. The only area in which he was not consistently dominant was in winning championships, many of which were lost to Bill Russell's Celtics.

2. BILL RUSSELL

Russell won two NCAA championships at the University of San Francisco and then went on to win 11 NBA titles in 13 seasons with the Boston Celtics. He controlled the defensive game more effectively than any other player, and he refined his block by crouching in a set position until the ball left the hands of the shooter. Catlike quickness in his jump almost always allowed him to avoid being faked in the air and, though it wasn't a statistical category when he played, Russell is widely recognized as the best shot-blocker of all time.

3. KAREEM ABDUL-JABBAR

Abdul-Jabbar developed an unblockable skyhook, considered the number one shot in the history of the NBA. Even before perfecting that shot he consistently scored in the 30s, was a tremendous shot-blocker, and had a complete game. He was not physically strong but he was wiry and, as the years progressed, he bulked up and became much stronger. He didn't have a lot of post moves but he used those he had well. He was a tough competitor who knew how to win, as proved by his six championships with the Bucks and the Lakers as well as his three NCAA championships at UCLA. A six-time MVP, Abdul-Jabbar had one of the most remarkable basketball careers of all time.

4. SHAQUILLE O'NEAL

O'Neal still has some playing years left so he suffers a little when compared to the giants of the past, especially in terms of future championships he may yet win. A remarkable player at both ends of the court, he is a great competitor and leader. Offensively he has the quickest feet at the post of any center except Hakeem Olajuwon, and his hands and ability to control the ball in the basket area are outstanding. Considering his sheer size, his speed is exceptional. He also plays 40 minutes a game and rarely gets beat in transition.

Depending on how much longer he plays and what else he accomplishes, Shaq may turn out to be the greatest center of all time.

5. HAKEEM OLAJUWON

Olajuwon was a remarkable athlete and one of the greatest centers the game has ever seen. He had little more than a dunk shot when he came to the NBA, but with his outstanding footwork he developed a more effective back-to-the-basket game than any center—of his time or any other. His quickness and fast feet made him the greatest big man of all time in terms of steals, and his shot-blocking ability puts him high on the list of all-time defensive centers. Playing both ends of the court, Olajuwon led Houston to two straight championships.

6. GEORGE MIKAN

Other than Abdul-Jabbar's skyhook, Mikan's hook shot off the backboard is the best single shot in the history of the game. He released the ball with his wrists turned inward, giving the ball more bite against glass, wood, or tin—the three backboard surfaces to which he had to adjust his shot. He was a leader and a competitive player who knew every trick in the book and raised hell with teammates if he didn't get the ball. He protected the basket area but was not a shot-blocker of Russell, Chamberlain, or Olajuwon caliber. Mikan led the Lakers to five titles in six seasons.

7. MOSES MALONE

A three-time league MVP, Malone was a prolific scorer and rebounder. He was a dominating low-post player who worked hard for 21 seasons after jumping to the ABA directly out of high school. He had a big body and used it well to set up shots, and he had great power moves. Not nearly as much of a defensive threat as the great centers ranked above him, Malone was never a leader in blocked shots. Nevertheless, he had menacing physical presence and offensive energy.

8. BILL WALTON

Walton is hard to categorize because he had only a few full years of play. His big season in Portland when he was healthy revealed his potential ability to control a game, but after winning the championship there he developed foot problems and was never the same. He was not an above-average face-up shooter, but he had a powerful back-to-the-basket game. Before he was hurt Walton was a wonderful post passer, set good screens, rebounded well, and was a very good shot-blocker. His greatest strength was his unbelievable skill in passing to the outlet receiver after a rebound—which he would often do before hitting the floor following a defensive board.

9. DAVID ROBINSON

Like Abdul-Jabbar, Robinson's numbers dropped during the last third of his career; however, in his first few years of NBA play he was a consistent 25- to 30-point scorer. He was also a very bright player with excellent foot speed. His shot-blocking was above average and consistent, but he was not very aggressive physically. He was not a back-to-the-basket center; the face-up shot was his forte. The Spurs' 1999 and 2003 championships helped to secure Robinson's place in history.

10. PATRICK EWING

Ewing was definitely a back-to-the-basket center, but he never developed a total post game. His best shots were facing the basket. He had a very good outside shot, was a good rebounder and a decent passer, but no one part of his game was really well above average. He was a dominating center in the last era that saw a multitude of dominating centers, faring well against many of the players on this list. Ewing played under a great deal of pressure as the appointed "savior" in New York.

11. WILLIS REED

Reed was drafted as a center, won Rookie of the Year, then played two seasons at power forward before moving back to the middle. He was a little undersized for a defensive player, but he was an extremely accurate outside shooter from about 18 feet. He didn't have many post moves but he did have a very good fallback jumper. Reed played both ends of the court well and was a perfect fit for coach Red Holzman's offense and defense on the New York Knicks, with whom Reed won championships in 1970 and 1973.

12. NATE THURMOND

Thurmond developed into a solid post player during his career. He was never a great scorer, but he was consistent. An outstanding defensive force—Abdul-Jabbar often called him the best defender he ever played against—and a popular player who commanded real respect from teammates and opponents alike, Thurmond didn't seem to get the same attention as the superstars he went up against. Nonetheless, many experts felt his offense was superior to Russell's and his defense superior to Chamberlain's, providing one of the most balanced packages in the history of the game.

13. DAVE COWENS

Cowens was small as centers go, but he was a fiery, aggressive player who loved to compete. He was never considered a great scorer but he did earn points consistently. He was a good rebounder for his size. He didn't have a lot of back-to-the-basket moves, but he could really drive. Cowens' career was relatively short, but it included two championships and an MVP award.

14. KEVIN MCHALE

McHale never officially played the center position, but he was the best post player in the league while the Celtics were winning three championships during the eighties. He was all arms: he looked like a windmill when he began his fakes. Few defenders could effectively stop him because of his abundance of post moves. Not a big shot-blocker, pass stealer, or rebounder, McHale's long arms did earn him many easy rebound baskets. He was such an enormous threat that opponents had to double-team him, forcing him to learn to pass from the post.

15. ELVIN HAYES

An extremely talented player who was a thorn in the side for many of the coaches he played for, Hayes had a remarkable outside shot from what was easily as far as the present-day three-point line. He had little back-to-the-basket game and was at best a fair passer, but he could create a shot off the ball over one dribble. An outstanding defensive shot-blocker, Hayes unfortunately didn't defend drives well. He was an exceptional raw talent but never worked to broaden or improve his game.

16. WES UNSELD

Unseld was undersized in height but strong as a bull. He set great screens and, along with Bill Walton, is regarded as one of the best outlet passers ever to have played the game—he had the ability to hit an on-the-run teammate 80 feet away. Never a big scorer and without a real post game, Unseld still gave most teams trouble defensively using his bulk and strength. A very intelligent player, Unseld was greatly respected around the league.

17. ROBERT PARISH

In the same mold as Nate Thurmond, Parish was a great all-around center whose consistent play didn't attract a lot of attention. He could execute the two-man game with a forward as effectively as anyone in the league, and he had a deadly jumper from the 15- to 20-foot range. Parish never developed much of a back-to-the-basket game and was not a big shot-blocker, but he guarded the basket well. He came to play every night, defended Abdul-Jabbar well during the Celtics-Lakers rivalries, and walked away with four championships.

18. TIM DUNCAN

As with Kevin McHale and Robert Parish in Boston through-out the eighties (and, briefly, Hakeem Olajuwon and Ralph Sampson in Houston), Duncan and David Robinson teamed up to give San Antonio a pair of seven-footers on their front line and, in 1999 and 2003, delivered NBA championships. Duncan earned two straight MVPs to round out his first six seasons in the league, in which he primarily played forward to Robinson's center. At age 27, Duncan is almost certain to move into the top 10 or higher by the time his career is over.

19. BOB LANIER

A back-to-the-basket left-hander with a good hook shot and decent range facing the basket, Lanier was not a jumper and his size slowed him down in transition. He could pass from the post, was a decent rebounder, and was always among the top scorers in the league, but he spent most of his career on a weak Detroit team and never had a real championship run.

20. ALONZO MOURNING

With his size more suited to the power forward position, Mourning made up for any physical shortcomings he might have had with strength, intensity, and competitive fire. He routinely blocked more shots than bigger centers, including his chief rival—Shaq—and he was a serious offensive threat facing the basket. Sadly, he lost some of his best years to injury and illness.

21. BILL LAIMBEER

A face-up center with no back-to-the-basket game, Laimbeer set very effective screens for teammates and was a very smart player. Gifted with many tools, he was tough, competitive, and loved contact. Instead of being a scorer, he became an intimidator in the basket area; few opponents would challenge him when he drove to the hoop. His career numbers weren't flashy but he was a huge part of the Pistons' back-to-back championships.

22. RALPH SAMPSON

Another center who was more comfortable facing the basket, Sampson had a decent shot with good range but never took advantage of his height to develop a post game. His scoring and rebounding were very good during his first few playing years until knee problems limited his capabilities. Like Wes Unseld, Sampson was a popular, well-liked player throughout the league.

23. BOB MCADOO

A tall, gangly shooter who played both forward and cen-ter, McAdoo was more comfortable and effective when fac-ing the basket. He was truly a great shooter, but defense was not his strong point—he couldn't handle the big play-ers physically. McAdoo was also a decent rebounder and could block a shot well.

24. DAN ISSEL

Another forward-center type, Issel was not a back-to-the-basket player nor did he have post moves to any extent. But he was a prolific scorer with great range who had some tremendous games. Issel came into the NBA in the middle of his career, having won his only champi-onship alongside Artis Gilmore in the ABA.

25. ARTIS GILMORE

An excellent scorer and above-average shot-blocker, Gilmore was often compared to Chamberlain in terms of size and strength. He never really developed a back-to-the-basket game but he had a fine left-handed shot from 16 feet or more. Gilmore couldn't move very well laterally and his defensive play consisted mainly of blocked shots. ∎

THE FIFTIES

George Mikan

Bill Russell

Wilt Chamberlain

arry Truman was president. The nation was returning to civilian life with a vengeance, creating suburbs, expressways, and an entire industry devoted to leisure. Baseball ruled the sports scene, since the modern era of the National Football League, generally dated from the 1958 title game between the Baltimore Colts and New York Giants, hadn't begun.

Professional basketball was in its Stone Age, as if men were first beginning to walk on their hind legs. Dwarfed even by college basketball, the pro game was considered beneath contempt, a "YMCA sport," by the star sportswriters for the big-city newspapers.

Basketball generally was still in an early stage of development. Before the forties, it had believed itself to be an egalitarian game, as much the province of clever ball handlers running weaves out front as of big, lumbering geeks.

Its illusions would not survive the fifties. A huge, awkward-looking galoot named George Mikan was already at work, bursting the bubbles (also the noses if they got in the way) of little men forever. Mikan was quickly followed by Bill Russell, the first great athlete to play center, who was followed by Wilt Chamberlain, another quantum leap into the future. Suddenly it was a wholly different game. No decade before or since has seen such a dizzying revolution in the style of play.

Mikan, the game's marquee player when the decade dawned, had started in the rival National Basketball League, signing with the Chicago Gears in 1946 for $12,000 a year, more than twice the $5,000 offered by a team from the Basketball Association of America (the NBA's forerunner).

The last thing this upstart sport, barely emerged from its ballroom days, could afford was a bidding war. Mikan had to go to court to collect his money, and when the Gears folded, he signed with the NBL's Minneapolis Lakers in 1947. A year later, the Lakers and five other teams merged with the BAA, and the NBA was born.

In short order, Mikan led the talented Lakers to four titles in five seasons. Opposing coaches began stalling to keep the games close. The 24-second clock arrived in 1954. Russell arrived in 1956.

By the end of the decade, Chamberlain was in his rookie season, the Celtics dynasty was in bloom, and fast-break basketball was in vogue. Mikan had been a force because he scored points. Russell made the Celtics a dominating team by shutting down opponents, blocking their shots, retrieving their misses, and starting wave after wave of fast breaks. Chamberlain dominated any which way he wanted.

After that, the game involved ever more frantic competition for the next great big man. The era of giants had arrived.

50s

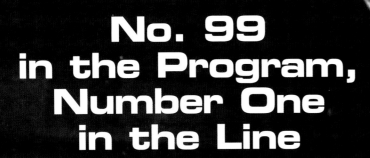

No. 99 in the Program, Number One in the Line

"He could raise that left elbow and move to the basket, and the bodies would just start to fly."

—LAKERS TEAMMATE SWEDE CARLSON

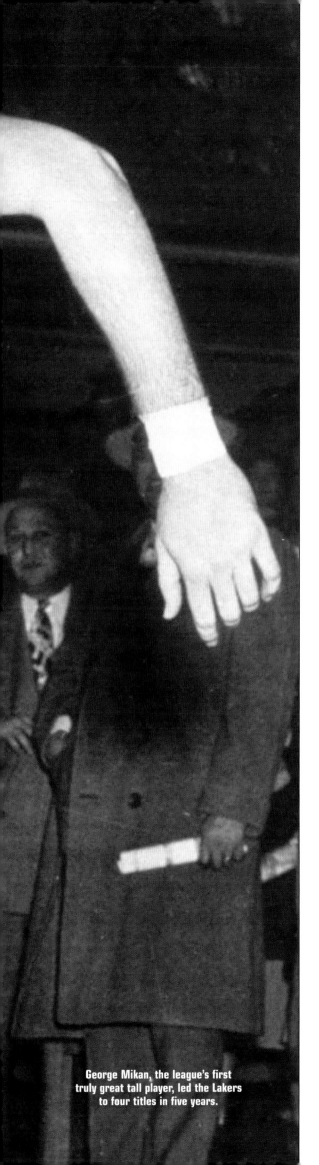

George Mikan, the league's first truly great tall player, led the Lakers to four titles in five years.

GEORGE MIKAN

6

George Mikan was a gentle, intelligent, well-meaning man who had studied for the priesthood. He had wavy hair and thick glasses. He was accomplished at the piano, and he attended law school.

When he lumbered into the Minneapolis Lakers dressing room in Sheboygan, Wisconsin, in 1947, he'd been a star at DePaul University and had signed a mammoth five-year, $62,000 contract with the Chicago Gears in the National Basketball League before it folded. But the Lakers had never seen him, and when they did, they didn't know whether to shake hands or laugh.

"I didn't know what he was like at all," said Jim Pollard, the team's star at a streamlined 6´6´´. "He walked into that locker room at Sheboygan, and I thought that was the biggest-looking dumb character that I'd ever seen for a guy that was barely 23 years old. He had these great big, thick glasses, and he had this homburg hat on.

"I said to myself, 'What the hell's a guy, 23 years old, doing wearing a homburg and a great big storm overcoat?'"

Mikan proceeded to take off the homburg, hang up the overcoat, secure the big, thick glasses with an elastic band, and kick everyone's butt for the next seven seasons. He was not only 6´10´´, he was 265 pounds and, having discovered the joy of competition, anxious to use every inch and pound of it. He wasn't a gazelle, but when he made a move, he led with his off elbow, not shyly, either, and he generally got where he wanted to go.

When he got there, he knew what to do, too. He could hook with either hand, and he had a 77 percent career free-throw percentage. Of the big men in this book, only Kevin McHale had a better mark from the line.

"He was one of a kind," says former Celtic great Bob Cousy. "I remember Ed Macauley, who had the unenviable task of guarding him when we played them. We'd walk through train stations, and he'd walk by one of these huge columns. Macauley had a wry sense of humor and would bump into the column and say, 'Oh, excuse me, George.'

"To Macauley, trying to guard him in the pivot, that's what it seemed like, trying to guard one of these huge columns. Mikan was unmovable. He was so much stronger than anyone in the league at that time.

"He just had his way in those days. The Lakers ran no transition. It wasn't unlike what the Sixers did with Wilt [Chamberlain] after a while. The Lakers simply waited for Big George to get down floor, and then the offense started with him getting it. They'd run some splits and things, but basically he would just overpower you.

"He wasn't clumsy. I say awkward and plodding, and I suppose that implies clumsy, but he wasn't clumsy. But he wasn't agile, either. It was somewhere in between that. He simply was able to go where he chose to go. If he wanted to spin to his right, he would perhaps fake in with a shoulder move. That would do it enough if he just got you leaning a bit."

Mikan was not only effective, he was openly ambitious.

"I always tried to give my best," Mikan said later. "But in pro sports, the better you become, the more you make. So I started trying to score."

He was a quick learner at that. He'd been an awkward youth, cut by his high school team in Joliet, Illinois, because of his poor eyesight. But at DePaul, young coach Ray Meyer put him through agility drills, shadowboxing, and dancing lessons. Meyer taught Mikan to take a position near the basket—the lane was only six feet wide then, although the NBA

- Born: June 18, 1924, in Joliet, Illinois
- College: DePaul
- 6´10´´/265 pounds
- Named first-team All-American by *The Sporting News* in 1944 and 1945
- Scored 1,870 points for DePaul
- Outscored the entire Rhode Island State team with 53 points in the 1945 NIT semifinals
- Averaged 23.1 points and 13.4 rebounds per game in his professional career
- Shot 78.2 percent from the free throw line in the pros
- Member of NBL Chicago American Gears championship team in 1947
- Named NBL Most Valuable Player in 1948
- Led the NBA in scoring from 1948–49 to 1951–52 and in rebounding in 1951–52 and 1952–53
- Made two All-NBL First Teams (1947, 1948), one All-BAA First Team (1949), and five All-NBA First Teams (1950, 1951, 1952, 1953, 1954)
- Named NBA All-Star Game Most Valuable Player in 1953
- Member of six Minneapolis Lakers championship teams: NBL (1948), BAA (1949), and NBA (1950, 1952, 1953, 1954)
- Served as head coach of the Minneapolis Lakers, 1957–58
- Voted the greatest player in the first half-century by the Associated Press
- Member of the NBA 25th Anniversary All-Time Team (1970) and the NBA 35th Anniversary All-Time Team (1980)
- Voted One of the 50 Greatest Players in NBA History in 1996
- Inducted into the Naismith Memorial Basketball Hall of Fame in 1959

"HE WAS ONE OF A KIND. MIKAN WAS UNMOVABLE. HE WAS SO MUCH STRONGER THAN ANYONE IN THE LEAGUE AT THAT TIME."

—BOB COUSY

Mikan had the skills to complement his size, among them a soft hook shot from either side.

would expand it in his honor—so his teammates could pass it in to him.

Mikan did his part, dutifully. It made sense to him. He was big and belonged near the hoop. His teammates were small and should stay the heck outside. If they disagreed, he let them know about it, to the point where it became the stuff of legend.

"I've got a Mikan story for you," says Pete Newell, former University of California coach and big man's guru. "They [the Lakers] had a rookie from Tennessee named Lefty Walther. The kid was a real good player. They're playing a game, and Mikan is in the post and the guy drives right by Mikan, goes in for a layup. Mikan's got his hand up for the ball, he's the top dog. He gets mad and yells at him.

"The next time the kid gets the ball, he drives, and his man and Mikan's man go up to block the shot. The third time he drives, his guy, Mikan's man, and Mikan all go after the shot.

"Mikan's thing was, 'They're paying you $5,000 to play out there and they're paying me whatever to play in there, so when I ask for the ball, darn it, give it to me.'

"The kid was gone in a few games."

It took a while to work things out with Pollard, who wasn't just some kid from Tennessee. There was some argument about who was allowed to drive where until Mikan realized Pollard wasn't throwing him the ball, whereupon they arrived at an accommodation.

Like Bill Russell, the last piece in the Celtics puzzle, Mikan joined a star-studded cast in Minneapolis and turned it into a dynasty. Pollard and the other forward, Vern Mikkelson, would become Hall of Famers, as would Slater Martin, the little point guard who came along in 1949.

But it was No. 99 who was in the spotlight. In one of the first star turns in recorded basketball history,

Collegiate Record

Season	Team	G	Min.	FGM	FGA	Pct.	FTM	FTA	Pct.	Reb.	Ast.	Pts.	Averages RPG	APG	PPG
'41–'42	DePaul					Freshman team statistics unavailable.									
'42–'43	DePaul	24	...	97	...	...	77	111	.694	...	...	271	...	...	11.3
'43–'44	DePaul	26	...	188	...	...	110	169	.651	...	...	486	...	...	18.7
'44–'45	DePaul	24	...	218	...	...	122	199	.613	...	...	558	...	...	23.3
'45–'46	DePaul	24	...	206	...	...	143	186	.769	...	...	555	...	...	23.1
Varsity totals		98	...	709	...	...	452	665	.680	...	...	1,870	...	...	19.1

NBL and NBA Regular-Season Record

Season	Team	G	Min.	FGM	FGA	Pct.	FTM	FTA	Pct.	Reb.	Ast.	PF	Dq.	Pts.	Averages RPG	APG	PPG
'46–'47	Chi. (NBL)	25	...	147	...	...	119	164	.726	...	...	90	...	413	...	...	*16.5
'47–'48	Minn. (NBL)	56	...	*406	...	...	*383	*509	.752	...	...	210	...	*1,195	...	...	*21.3
'48–'49	Minn. (BAA)	60	...	*583	1,403	.416	*532	*689	.772	...	218	260	...	*1,698	...	3.6	*28.3
'49–'50	Minneapolis	68	...	*649	*1,595	.407	*567	*728	.779	...	197	*297	...	*1,865	...	2.9	*27.4
'50–'51	Minneapolis	68	...	*678	*1,584	.428	*576	*717	.803	958	208	*308	14	*1,932	14.1	3.1	*28.4
'51–'52	Minneapolis	64	2,572	545	*1,414	.385	433	555	.780	866	194	*286	14	*1,523	*13.5	3.0	*23.8
'52–'53	Minneapolis	70	2,651	500	1,252	.399	442	567	.780	*1007	201	290	12	1,442	*14.4	2.9	20.6
'53–'54	Minneapolis	72	2,362	441	1,160	.380	424	546	.777	1,028	174	268	4	1,306	14.3	2.4	18.1
'54–'55							Did not play—retired										
'55–'56	Minneapolis	37	765	148	375	.395	94	122	.771	308	53	153	6	390	8.3	1.4	10.5
Totals		520	...	4,097	...	...	3,570	4,597	.777	...	...	2,162	...	11,764	...	...	22.6

NBL and NBA Playoff Record

Season	Team	G	Min.	FGM	FGA	Pct.	FTM	FTA	Pct.	Reb.	Ast.	PF	Dq.	Pts.	Averages RPG	APG	PPG.
'46–'47	Chi. (NBL)	11	...	72	...	...	73	104	.702	...	...	48	...	217	...	...	19.7
'47–'48	Minn. (NBL)	10	...	88	...	...	68	97	.701	...	...	37	...	244	...	...	24.4
'48–'49	Minn. (BAA)	10	...	103	227	.454	97	121	.802	...	21	44	...	303	...	2.1	30.3
'49–'50	Minneapolis	12	...	121	316	.383	134	170	.788	...	36	47	...	376	...	3.0	31.3
'50–'51	Minneapolis	7	...	62	152	.408	44	55	.800	74	9	25	1	168	10.6	1.3	24.0
'51–'52	Minneapolis	13	553	99	261	.379	109	138	.790	207	36	63	3	307	15.9	2.8	23.6
'52–'53	Minneapolis	12	463	78	213	.366	82	112	.732	185	23	56	5	238	15.4	1.9	19.8
'53–'54	Minneapolis	13	424	87	190	.458	78	96	.813	171	25	56	1	252	13.2	1.9	19.4
'55–'56	Minneapolis	3	60	13	35	.371	10	13	.769	28	5	14	0	36	9.3	1.7	12.0
Totals		91	...	723	...	...	695	906	.767	...	...	390	...	2,141	...	...	23.5

NBA All-Star Game Record

	G	Min.	FGM	FGA	Pct.	FTM	FTA	Pct.	Reb.	Ast.	PF	Dq.	Pts.
Totals	4	...	28	80	.350	22	27	.815	51	7	14	0	78

NBA Coaching Record

Season	Team	W	L	Pct.	Regular Season Finish	Playoffs W	L	Pct.
'57–'58	Minneapolis	9	30	.231		—	—	—

"AS SOON AS GEORGE STOPPED FEELING SORRY FOR HIMSELF AND REALIZED HIS HEIGHT WAS SOMETHING TO BE ADMIRED . . . HE WAS ON HIS WAY TO BEING GREAT."

—RAY MEYER

the marquee at New York's old Madison Square Garden advertised:

**TONITE
GEORGE MIKAN
VS
KNICKS**

"My teammates taught me a little lesson," Mikan said later. "We got into the locker room, and I was the only guy dressing. They all looked at me and said, 'OK, wise guy, you're going to play the Knickerbockers, go play them.' They were really razzing me. We had a great team, a lot of great guys."

In Mikan's five full NBA seasons with the Lakers, they won four titles. He retired at age 31. Not even scorers made that much in those days, and he wanted to start his law practice. He tried a comeback two years later, but it was short-lived.

In later years, when young seven-footers got multimillion-dollar contracts if they seemed 1 percent as dominating as he was, Mikan might have looked awkward in comparison. But they owe him, big-time. In the line of the NBA's greatest big men, he came first. ∎

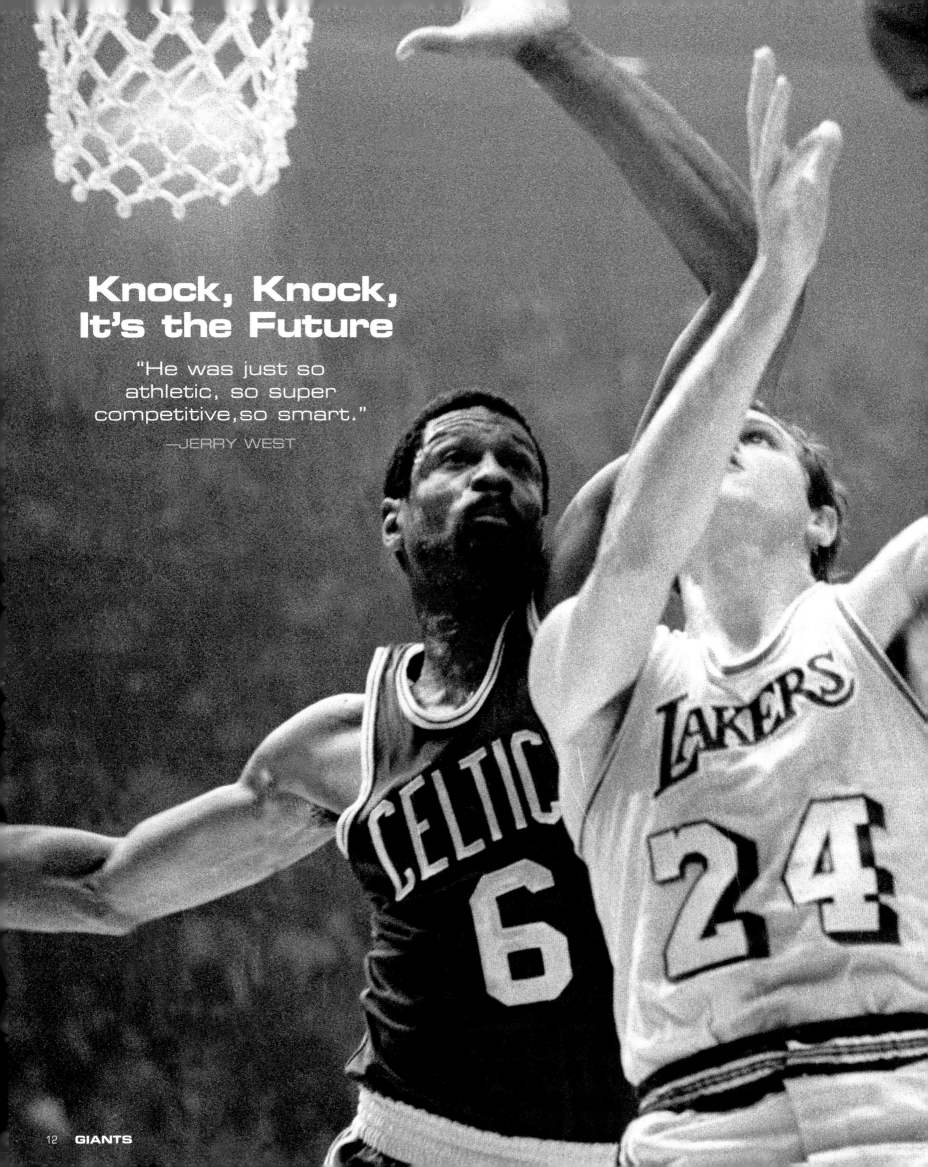

Knock, Knock, It's the Future

"He was just so athletic, so super competitive, so smart."

—JERRY WEST

Bill Russell is widely recognized as the best shot-blocker the game has ever known.

BILL RUSSELL

The NBA dates its early history from the 1946 season opener between the New York Knicks and the Toronto Huskies. This is arguable, since this was the start of the Basketball Association of America season. The entity known as the NBA, formed by a merger of the BAA and the National Basketball League, didn't start play until 1949. The start of the modern era is clear, though: the game between the St. Louis Hawks and the Boston Celtics on December 22, 1956, when Russell made his pro debut. He played only 21 minutes, scored only six points, and took 16 rebounds, but teammate Bob Cousy remembers walking away thinking, "School's out."

Bill Russell had been a star at the University of San Francisco, where he played on back-to-back NCAA championship teams in 1955 and 1956. Russell started his pro career late, arriving in Boston fresh from the Melbourne Olympics. He was the most celebrated rookie to join the young league, but until the day he got there, his projected impact was a matter of debate.

Russell hadn't been the first pick in the 1956 draft, nor the second. Rochester Royals owner Les Harrison, who worried that the kid wanted megabucks (say, $20,000), had seen him once in a college All-Star game and had come away unimpressed, especially by Russell's klutzy offense. When the Celtics offered the Royals a bonus for choosing someone else—an appearance by Celtics owner Walter Brown's Ice Capades—Harrison opted for Duquesne guard Sihugo Green.

The Hawks, choosing second, were just as hard-pressed financially. Newly arrived in St. Louis, a Midwestern city with a Southern sensibility, they may not have been too eager to bring in their first black player. When Red Auerbach offered them Ed Macauley—a 6´8´´ center, an All-Star five years running, and a St. Louis native to boot—along with Cliff Hagan, a promising rookie from the University of Kentucky, Hawks owner Ben Kerner bit.

It would be the most storied trade in NBA history. Everyone in it made the Hall of Fame. Everyone lived up to expectations. It was just that Auerbach's expectations had been a little higher.

"Auerbach wasn't the most beloved coach who ever was around, so people tend not to give him credit for a lot of things," says Cousy. "But in Russell's case, he deserves full credit.

"I remember six months or eight months before, his coming to me. Our talents were evident and our limitations were evident. We ran as good a transition as any team in the league, and we could shoot it like hell and play reasonably good defense. But we needed the anchor, the big guy who could control the defensive board for us and make that transition game work just about every time. And Macauley, while he had certain skills, didn't provide that for us. He weighed, like, 185 pounds soaking wet.

"I remember Auerbach coming to me and saying, 'We're going to get somebody next year that's going to solve all our problems.' I mean, he was in on Russell for whatever reason, well in advance.

"We didn't know what to expect. Russell joined us late. Would we have won it? I don't know, although [rookies Tom] Heinsohn and [Jim] Loscutoff were both rebounding extremely well for us. We were solidly in first. [They were 16–8 when Russell arrived, a better pace than they'd have with him.]

"I guess I had briefly seen Russell in college. I don't know if it was on television. I might have seen him in Madison Square Garden when they played Holy Cross and beat up on them in the NIT. I don't remember forming a strong opinion on him, one way or the other.

"I do remember it was a nationally televised game against St. Louis. I don't remember that he played overwhelming

- Born: February 12, 1934, in Monroe, Louisiana
- College: San Francisco
- 6´10´´/220 pounds
- Named College Player of the Year in 1956
- Averaged 20.7 points and 20.3 rebounds per game in college
- Member of NCAA championship teams in 1955 and 1956
- Named NCAA Tournament Most Outstanding Player in 1955
- Played on the gold medal–winning U.S. Olympic team in 1956
- Averaged 15.1 points and 22.5 rebounds per game during his NBA career
- Ranks second in NBA history with 21,620 rebounds
- Totaled 51 rebounds against Syracuse on February 5, 1960
- Holds NBA single-game record for rebounds in one half with 32 (November 16, 1957, vs. Philadelphia)
- Named NBA Most Valuable Player in 1958, 1961, 1962, 1963, and 1965
- Member of three All-NBA First Teams (1959, 1963, 1965), eight All-NBA Second Teams (1958, 1960, 1961, 1962, 1964, 1966, 1967, 1968), and one NBA All-Defensive First Team (1969)
- Played in 12 All-Star Games, earning Most Valuable Player honors in 1963
- Member of 11 Boston Celtics NBA championship teams (1957, 1959, 1960, 1961, 1962, 1963, 1964, 1965, 1966, 1968, 1969)
- Named The Sporting News Athlete of the Decade for the sixties
- Named Sports Illustrated Sportsman of the Year in 1968
- Served as head coach/player for the Boston Celtics, 1966–67, 1968–69
- Served as head coach and general manager for the Seattle Supersonics, 1973–74, 1976–77
- Member of the NBA 25th Anniversary All-Time Team (1970) and the NBA 35th Anniversary All-Time Team (1980)
- Declared Greatest Player in the History of the NBA by the Professional Basketball Writers Association of America in 1980
- Voted One of the 50 Greatest Players in NBA History in 1996
- Inducted into the Naismith Memorial Basketball Hall of Fame in 1975

" WE'VE NEVER HAD IN THE GAME AS EFFECTIVE A SHOT-BLOCKER AS HE WAS."

—PETE NEWELL

Russell, Red Auerbach, and John Havlicek had plenty to celebrate in their time spent together upholding the Celtics dynasty.

minutes, but I remember walking away from that game and watching the things he came to the table with and saying, 'School's out.'

"Boy, once I saw Russell and the things he could do—and this was before he refined them. . . . I mean, he couldn't hit a bull in the ass there for a while, but by the end of his career, he could give you 20 whenever you needed it."

For years the Celtics were talented little people who won during the season but bowed in the playoffs to talented bigger people. And Russell's will to win was as fearsome as the most driven of the Celtics—Cousy and Bill Sharman.

Russell was the game's first athletic big man and its first dominator. If it was dimly understood before him—and after him—that the position was primarily about defense and rebounding as opposed to scoring, he was 6´9´´, 220 pounds of revelation.

Nowadays, with every team boasting four players his size or larger, Russell's impact can barely be imagined. It didn't occur to the league to chart blocked shots until 1973, when Russell was already gone. The "record" for a game is Elmore Smith's 17, and for a season Mark Eaton's 5.6 average. Russell may have averaged twice that.

Jack Ramsay, a Hall of Fame coach turned TV analyst, once phoned the Celtics hoping to find old game film so he could count Russell's blocks. Told there was none, he asked the 76ers' "Superstat," Harvey Pollack, if there was any data for Wilt Chamberlain.

"Harvey said he used to tell one of his statisticians to keep track of Wilt's blocks in big games," Ramsay says. "One night, they got up to 25. And Russell was the best at it!"

It's hard to imagine Russell having as much impact now, in an era when point guards are nearly his size, but his contemporaries insist to a man that he would still be a mighty force.

"We haven't had in the game as effective a shot-blocker as he was," says Pete Newell. "The problem wasn't just blocking, it was the intimidation he gave you. He had a great skill of not ever being faked into the air. If you ever see a picture of him, you'd always see a flexed knee.

"And he had such a quick jump, you'd shoot the shot and he could get it. Now most guys didn't have that quick a jump; you could get over 'em. Jerry West had it on offense; he'd go right up to you and explode in your face. It's a great innate skill for a player to have.

Collegiate Record

Season	Team	G	Min.	FGM	FGA	Pct.	FTM	FTA	Pct.	Reb.	Ast.	Pts.	Averages RPG	APG	PPG
'52–'53	San Francisco	23	...	...	...	...	...	...	...	...	...	461	...	...	20.0
'53–'54	San Francisco	21	...	150	309	.485	117	212	.552	403	...	417	19.2	...	19.9
'54–'55	San Francisco	29	...	229	423	.541	164	278	.590	594	...	622	20.5	...	21.4
'55–'56	San Francisco	29	...	246	480	.513	105	212	.495	609	...	597	21.0	...	20.6
Varsity totals		79	...	625	1,212	.516	386	702	.550	1,606	...	1,636	20.3	...	20.7

NBA Regular-Season Record

Season	Team	G	Min.	FGM	FGA	Pct.	FTM	FTA	Pct.	Reb.	Ast.	PF	Dq.	Pts.	Averages RPG	APG	PPG
'56–'57	Boston	48	1,695	277	649	.427	152	309	.492	943	88	143	2	706	*19.6	1.8	14.7
'57–'58	Boston	69	2,640	456	1,032	.442	230	443	.519	*1,564	202	181	2	1,142	*22.7	2.9	16.6
'58–'59	Boston	70	*2,979	456	997	.457	256	428	.598	*1,612	222	161	3	1,168	*23.0	3.2	16.7
'59–'60	Boston	74	3,146	555	1,189	.467	240	392	.612	1,778	277	210	0	1,350	24.0	3.7	18.2
'60–'61	Boston	78	3,458	532	1,250	.426	258	469	.550	1,868	268	155	0	1,322	23.9	3.4	16.9
'61–'62	Boston	76	3,433	575	1,258	.457	286	481	.595	1,790	341	207	3	1,436	23.6	4.5	18.9
'62–'63	Boston	78	3,500	511	1,182	.432	287	517	.555	1,843	348	189	1	1,309	23.6	4.5	16.8
'63–'64	Boston	78	3,482	466	1,077	.433	236	429	.550	*1,930	370	190	0	1,168	*24.7	4.7	15.0
'64–'65	Boston	78	*3,466	429	980	.438	244	426	.573	*1,878	410	204	1	1,102	*24.1	5.3	14.1
'65–'66	Boston	78	3,386	391	943	.415	223	405	.551	1,779	371	221	4	1,005	22.8	4.8	12.9
'66–'67	Boston	81	3,297	395	870	.454	285	467	.610	1,700	472	258	4	1,075	21.0	5.8	13.3
'67–'68	Boston	78	2,953	365	858	.425	247	460	.537	1,451	357	242	2	977	18.6	4.6	12.5
'68–'69	Boston	77	3,291	279	645	.433	204	388	.526	1,484	374	231	2	762	19.3	4.9	9.9
Totals		963	40,726	5,687	12,930	.440	3,148	5,614	.561	21,620	4,100	2,592	24	14,522	22.5	4.3	15.1

NBA Playoff Record

Season	Team	G	Min.	FGM	FGA	Pct.	FTM	FTA	Pct.	Reb.	Ast.	PF	Dq.	Pts.	Averages RPG	APG	PPG
'56–'57	Boston	10	409	54	148	.365	31	61	.508	244	32	41	1	139	24.4	3.2	13.9
'57–'58	Boston	9	355	48	133	.361	40	66	.606	221	24	24	0	136	24.6	2.7	15.1
'58–'59	Boston	11	496	65	159	.409	41	67	.612	305	40	28	1	171	27.7	3.6	15.5
'59–'60	Boston	13	572	94	206	.456	53	75	.707	336	38	38	1	241	25.8	2.9	18.6
'60–'61	Boston	10	462	73	171	.427	43	86	.523	229	48	24	0	191	29.9	4.8	19.1
'61–'62	Boston	14	672	116	253	.459	82	113	.726	370	70	49	0	314	26.4	5.0	22.4
'62–'63	Boston	13	617	96	212	.453	72	109	.661	326	66	36	0	264	25.1	5.1	20.3
'63–'64	Boston	10	451	47	132	.356	37	67	.552	272	44	33	0	131	27.2	4.4	13.1
'64–'65	Boston	12	561	79	150	.527	40	76	.526	302	76	43	2	198	25.2	6.3	16.5
'65–'66	Boston	17	814	124	261	.475	76	123	.618	428	85	60	0	324	25.2	5.0	19.1
'66–'67	Boston	9	390	31	86	.360	33	52	.635	198	50	32	1	95	22.0	5.6	10.6
'67–'68	Boston	19	869	99	242	.409	76	130	.585	434	99	73	1	274	22.8	5.2	14.4
'68–'69	Boston	18	829	77	182	.423	41	81	.506	369	98	65	1	195	20.5	5.4	10.8
Totals		165	7,497	1,003	2,335	.430	667	1,106	.603	4,104	770	546	8	2,673	24.9	4.7	16.2

NBA All-Star Game Record

	G	Min.	FGM	FGA	Pct.	FTM	FTA	Pct.	Reb.	Ast.	PF	Dq.	Pts.
Totals	12	343	51	111	.459	18	34	.529	139	39	37	1	120

NBA Coaching Record

Season	Team	Regular Season W	L	Pct.	Finish	Playoffs W	L	Pct.
'66–'67	Boston	60	21	.741	2nd/Eastern Division	4	5	.444
'67–'68	Boston	54	28	.659	2nd/Eastern Division	12	7	.632
'68–'69	Boston	48	34	.585	4th/Eastern Division	12	6	.667
'73–'74	Seattle	36	46	.439	3rd/Pacific Division	—	—	—
'74–'75	Seattle	43	39	.524	2nd/Pacific Division	4	5	.444
'75–'76	Seattle	43	39	.524	2nd/Pacific Division	2	4	.333
'76–'77	Seattle	40	42	.488	4th/Pacific Division	—	—	—
'87–'88	Sacramento	17	41	.293		—	—	—
Totals (8 years)		341	290	.540	Totals (5 years)	34	27	.557

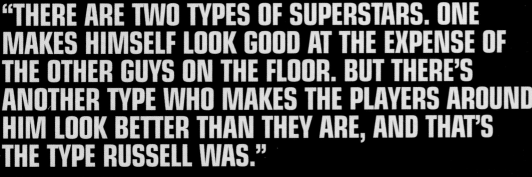

"THERE ARE TWO TYPES OF SUPERSTARS. ONE MAKES HIMSELF LOOK GOOD AT THE EXPENSE OF THE OTHER GUYS ON THE FLOOR. BUT THERE'S ANOTHER TYPE WHO MAKES THE PLAYERS AROUND HIM LOOK BETTER THAN THEY ARE, AND THAT'S THE TYPE RUSSELL WAS."

—DON NELSON

"I don't think I ever saw a guy pump-fake him in the air and shoot over Russell. I'm sure it happened but I never saw it."

Nor is there any comparison to the modern prima donna. Russell was considered aloof and, indeed, teammates say he was clearly ill at ease with outsiders. However, he was polite to the press, if not a quote machine.

"Russ always had a chip on his shoulder," Cousy says. "Russ within the unit, to this day when we're together, he goes through a Jekyll and Hyde personality transformation. Within the unit, he's comfortable with people of all colors, as opposed to stepping out and now he becomes very noncommunicative. You don't recognize the guy."

NBA observers didn't recognize the game when Russell left it in 1969, having won his 11th and most improbable title in 13 seasons, leading his fourth-place team past the Wilt-West-Baylor Lakers in a Game 7 at the Los Angeles Forum. People who played and coached with him and against him say the same thing.

Jerry West, who won a title playing alongside Chamberlain but lost many to Russell, said if he had to take one man for one game, it would have been Russell. Ramsay, who won a title with Bill Walton and considers him "across the board, the best legitimate center the game has known," was once asked who he'd take for one game. Said Ramsay: "It would be hard for me to pass up Bill Russell." ∎

The First Superstar

"Wilt was so dominant that it was almost a joke to watch other players play against him."

—JERRY WEST

Wilt Chamberlain was head and shoulders above the rest of the league throughout his remarkable career.

WILT CHAMBERLAIN

IN THE PAST, MEN LIKE WILT CHAMBERLAIN WEREN'T REAL. THEY WERE LEGENDS, FIGURES IN TALL TALES, POEMS, AND SONGS. THEY WERE OF SUPERHUMAN SIZE, THEY PERFORMED HERCULEAN FEATS, AND THEIR LIVES OFTEN ENDED TRAGICALLY.

But Wilt Chamberlain was real.

To refer to Wilt Chamberlain as the first superstar isn't just overheated sixties hyperbole. In the sixties a new class of celebrity athletes—Wilt Chamberlain, Joe Willie Namath, Muhammad Ali— transcended their sports. As a player, Wilt was a quantum leap into the future.

If Bill Russell was 20 years ahead of his time, Chamberlain may have been 20 years ahead of Russell. Wilt was huge, powerful, agile, athletic enough to be a high jumper in college, fast enough to outrun the guards he played with, and skilled, to boot. He had a remarkable personality. He will inevitably be remembered as much for his eccentricities and failures as for his heroic deeds. He was the first basketball player to get the Big Treatment, a dizzying experience that didn't make it any easier to keep his balance.

Russell entered the NBA as a player, if a celebrated one, but Chamberlain entered as a savior. As a junior at Philadelphia's Overbrook High School, Chamberlain was taken to Kutsher's, a resort in the Catskills in upstate New York, by NBA publicist Haskell Cohen, where he dominated the collegians. He was given a soft job, was coached by Red Auerbach, and came home with a wad of cash, driving a used Oldsmobile. When Wilt was a college senior, Philadelphia Warriors owner Eddie Gottlieb had the territorial draft rules changed to make sure he got Chamberlain. So if Wilt seemed to carry himself as if he were bigger than the league, let's face it: he was.

Everything about him was larger than life. His size was just the beginning. When he entered the league, there were only four players over 6´9´´. He was listed at 7´1´´, 275 pounds as a rookie in 1959, but everyone insisted he was bigger. Everything he did was on a giant scale, and every tale he told was tall.

"He was a guy who dominated every arena he was in," says legendary Philadelphia sportswriter George Kiseda. "By arena, I mean room, restaurant, conversation, dressing room, hall lobby."

If Wilt said something that seemed outrageous, it may not have been exactly true but there was probably something to it. His claim of having slept with 20,000 women kept comedians busy for years, but 76ers publicist Harvey Pollack remembers the night they won the 1967 title in San Francisco and women queued up outside Chamberlain's room in the Jack Tar Hotel.

"There was a bevy of women, of all sizes, shapes, and ages lined up in the hallway," says Pollack. "I happened to be in the room next to Wilt, and they took turns going into the room. The line lasted all night long, far as I know, 'til I went to sleep—and that was deep in the morning."

The NBA record book reads like Chamberlain's bio. Of the NBA's 75 top-scoring games, he has 49. Of its top 46 rebounding games, he has 26. One of his dunks broke the toe of the Syracuse Nats' Johnny Kerr. Half the league, it seemed, went for a ride on his massive shoulders, trying to keep him from going up for a shot.

"He was unbelievably strong," says Elgin Baylor. "I remember one time, Wilt went up to dunk the ball and Dick Barnett [a Knicks guard] jumped on him and grabbed him by the neck. And he took him from the floor, up in the air—you ask Barnett about it— and dunked the basketball.

"And he did it with a couple of our centers, same thing. They were holding him around the shoulders; he just went up and dunked the basketball."

Chamberlain played on two of the game's most dominating teams, the 1967 76ers and the 1972 Lakers, but he is generally remembered as a foil for Russell, whose teams won titles in nine of the 10 seasons in which their careers overlapped.

While Russell was a perfect fit for the Celtics, Wilt was too dominating to fit anywhere. Teammates tended to turn the game over to him and then watch, slack-jawed.

"When I look back on the Wilt-Russell games," says Kiseda, "I divide them into three parts. A third of the time, Wilt outplayed

- Born: August 21, 1936, in Philadelphia; died October 12, 1999
- College: Kansas
- 7´1´´/275 pounds
- Named first-team All-American by *The Sporting News* in 1958
- Averaged 30.1 points per game as a senior in college (1957–58)
- Played with the Harlem Globetrotters in 1958–59
- Became the first player to win the NBA Most Valuable Player Award, Rookie of the Year Award, and All-Star Game Most Valuable Player Award in the same year (1960)
- Named NBA Most Valuable Player in 1960, 1966, 1967, and 1968
- Averaged 30.1 points and 22.9 rebounds per game during his NBA career
- Holds NBA record for career rebounds with 23,924
- Scored 31,419 points in the NBA, third on the career list
- Holds NBA records for single-season points with 4,029 and scoring average at 50.4 (1961–62)
- Holds NBA record for rebounding average in a season at 27.2 (1960–61)
- Led the NBA in scoring for seven straight years (1958–59 to 1964–65) and was the top rebounder for 11 seasons
- Holds NBA record for points in a single game with 100 (March 2, 1962, vs. Knicks); also holds second, third, and fourth place on single-game points list
- Holds NBA record for games with 50 or more points with 118
- Holds NBA record for consecutive field goals made with 35 (February 17 to 28, 1967)
- Holds All-Star Game records for career rebounds (197) and points in a single game (42)
- Member of seven All-NBA First Teams (1960, 1961, 1962, 1964, 1966, 1967, 1968), three All-NBA Second Teams (1963, 1965, 1972), and two NBA All-Defensive Teams (1972, 1973)
- Member of Philadelphia 76ers NBA championship team in 1968
- Member of Los Angeles Lakers NBA championship team in 1972
- Named NBA Finals Most Valuable Player in 1972
- Holds the Golden State Warriors franchise record with 17,783 points (1959–60 through 1964–65)
- Member of the NBA 35th Anniversary All-Time Team (1980)
- Voted One of the 50 Greatest Players in NBA History in 1996
- Inducted into the Naismith Memorial Basketball Hall of Fame in 1978

Chamberlain's 100-point game against the Knicks in 1962 remains one of the most memorable achievements in sports.

"HE WAS UNBELIEVABLY STRONG. OUR CENTERS WOULD HOLD HIM AROUND THE SHOULDERS, AND HE'D JUST GO UP AND DUNK THE BASKETBALL."
—ELGIN BAYLOR

Russell. A third of the time, Russell outplayed Wilt. And there was the other third of the time, when Wilt dominated Russell."

Late in Wilt's career, Lakers coach Bill Sharman convinced him he could accomplish more by doing less, concentrating on defense and shot-blocking and turning his teammates loose on offense. They won a record 33 games in a row and captured a title that way. It was a choice Russell never had to make.

Russell was driven by a need to win. Wilt was ambivalent about it. Kiseda remembers an airplane conversation during the 1967–68 season, when the 76ers were defending champions, in which Wilt argued with coach Alex Hannum, asserting that winning wasn't all-important. That spring the Celtics, down 3–1, forced a seventh game in Philadelphia. In Game 7, Chamberlain shot only two tip-ins in the second half and the Sixers lost.

The next season Chamberlain forced a trade to the Lakers, joining Baylor and Jerry West in the game's first supergroup, but bowed again. The Celtics, so creaky that they finished fourth in the East, made the NBA Finals, forced a seventh game in Los Angeles, and won after Wilt took himself out with an injury and coach Butch van Breda Kolff refused to put him back in.

That summer Russell, just retired, said that Wilt shouldn't have left the game, even if his leg had fallen off. The two had been friends, resisting their gladiator roles, picking each other up at airports, and going out to dinner throughout their careers, but they didn't talk again for more than 20 years.

In 1996 the NBA brought them together again at a press conference. Beforehand, Wilt, Russell, and a few old hands including Pollack wound up in an anteroom.

"The stories that came out of that room. . . ." says Pollack. "I never saw Russell with his hair down. He

Collegiate Record

Season	Team	G	Min.	FGM	FGA	Pct.	FTM	FTA	Pct.	Reb.	Ast.	Pts.	Averages RPG	APG	PPG
'55–'56	Kansas	Freshman team did not play intercollegiate schedule													
'56–'57	Kansas	27	...	275	588	.468	250	399	.627	510	...	800	18.9	...	29.6
'57–'58	Kansas	21	...	228	482	.473	177	291	.608	367	...	633	17.5	...	30.1
Varsity Totals		48	...	503	1,070	.470	427	690	.619	877	...	1,433	18.3	...	29.9

NBA Regular-Season Record

Season	Team	G	Min.	FGM	FGA	Pct.	FTM	FTA	Pct.	Reb.	Ast.	PF	Dq.	Pts.	Averages RPG	APG	PPG
'59–'60	Philadelphia	72	3,338	1,065	2,311	.461	577	991	.582	1,941	168	150	0	2,707	27.0	2.3	37.6
'60–'61	Philadelphia	79	3,773	1,251	2,457	.509	531	1,054	.504	2,149	148	130	0	3,033	27.2	1.9	38.4
'61–'62	Philadelphia	80	3,882	1,597	3,159	.506	835	1,363	.613	2,052	192	123	0	4,029	25.7	2.4	50.4
'62–'63	San Fran.	80	3,806	1,463	2,770	.528	660	1,113	.593	1,946	275	136	0	3,586	24.3	3.4	44.8
'63–'64	San Fran.	80	3,689	1,204	2,298	.524	540	1,016	.532	1,787	403	182	0	298	22.3	5.0	36.9
'64–'65	S.F.-Phil.	73	3,301	1,063	2,083	.510	408	880	.464	1,673	250	146	0	2,534	22.9	3.4	34.7
'65–'66	Philadelphia	79	3,737	1,074	1,990	.540	501	976	.513	1,943	414	171	0	2,649	24.6	5.2	33.5
'66–'67	Philadelphia	81	3,682	785	1,150	.683	386	875	.441	1,957	630	143	0	1,956	24.2	7.8	24.1
'67–'68	Philadelphia	82	3,836	819	1,377	.595	354	932	.380	1,952	702	160	0	1,992	23.8	8.6	24.3
'68–'69	Los Angeles	81	3,669	641	1,099	.583	382	857	.446	1,712	366	142	0	1,664	21.1	4.5	20.5
'69–'70	Los Angeles	12	505	129	227	.568	70	157	.446	221	49	31	0	328	18.4	4.1	27.3
'70–'71	Los Angeles	82	3,630	668	1,226	.545	360	669	.538	1,493	352	174	0	1,696	18.2	.43	20.7
'71–'72	Los Angeles	82	3,469	496	764	.649	221	524	.422	1,572	329	196	0	1,213	19.2	4.0	14.8
'72–'73	Los Angeles	82	3,542	426	586	.727	232	455	.510	1,526	365	191	0	1,084	18.6	4.5	13.2
Totals		1,045	47,859	12,681	23,497	.540	6,057	11,862	.511	23,924	4,643	2,075	0	31,419	22.9	4.4	30.1

NBA Playoff Record

Season	Team	G	Min.	FGM	FGA	Pct.	FTM	FTA	Pct.	Reb.	Ast.	PF	Dq.	Pts.	Averages RPG	APG	PPG
'59–'60	Philadelphia	9	415	125	252	.496	49	110	.445	232	19	17	0	299	25.8	2.1	33.2
'60–'61	Philadelphia	3	144	45	96	.469	21	38	.553	69	6	10	0	111	23.0	2.0	37.0
'61–'62	Philadelphia	12	576	162	347	.467	96	151	.636	319	37	27	0	420	26.6	3.1	35.0
'63–'64	San Fran.	12	558	175	322	.543	66	139	.475	302	39	27	0	416	25.2	3.3	34.7
'64–'65	Philadelphia	11	536	123	232	.530	76	136	.559	299	48	29	0	322	27.2	4.4	29.3
'65–'66	Philadelphia	5	240	56	110	.509	28	68	.412	151	15	10	0	140	30.2	3.0	28.0
'66–'67	Philadelphia	15	718	132	228	.579	62	160	.388	437	135	37	0	326	29.1	9.0	21.7
'67–'68	Philadelphia	13	631	124	232	.534	60	158	.380	321	85	29	0	308	24.7	6.5	23.7
'68–'69	Los Angeles	18	832	96	176	.545	58	148	.392	444	46	56	0	250	24.7	2.6	13.9
'69–'70	Los Angeles	18	851	158	288	.549	82	202	.406	399	81	42	0	398	22.2	4.5	22.1
'70–'71	Los Angeles	12	554	85	187	.455	50	97	.515	242	53	33	0	220	20.2	4.4	18.3
'71–'72	Los Angeles	15	703	80	142	.563	60	122	.492	315	49	47	0	220	21.0	3.3	14.7
'72–'73	Los Angeles	17	801	64	116	.552	49	98	.500	383	60	48	0	177	22.5	3.5	10.4
Totals		160	7,559	1,425	2,728	.522	757	1,627	.465	3,913	673	412	0	3,607	24.5	4.2	22.5

NBA All-Star Game Record

	G	Min.	FGM	FGA	Pct.	FTM	FTA	Pct.	Reb.	Ast.	PF	Dq.	Pts.
Totals	13	388	72	122	.590	47	94	.500	197	36	23	0	191

> ## "HE WAS SUCH AN AWESOME PHYSICAL SPECIMEN. TO BE DOWN THERE AND TO LOOK UP AT HIM WHEN HE'S TOWERING OVER YOU WAITING TO DUNK, THAT'S A TERRIFYING PICTURE."
> —ELVIN HAYES

and Wilt became buddies. They really changed. When they first came into the league, they used to eat over at each other's houses. Then something happened where they drifted apart."

Wilt retired in 1974 at age 36, although he certainly could have played longer. No one wanted to believe he was gone. NBA teams tried to lure him back—the Knicks (team president Mike Burke flew to Los Angeles to meet with him, only to find Wilt had flown to Hawaii), the 76ers, the Nets, and the Clippers (in the late eighties when he was approaching 50).

In 1982, when he was 45 and the Sixers were courting him, the *Houston Chronicle*'s George White asked Elvin Hayes how Wilt would do.

"Some things about Wilt, you never forgot," said Hayes. "He was such an awesome physical specimen. To be down there and to look up at him when he's towering up way over you waiting to dunk, that was a terrifying picture. . . .

"I think Russell realized there was no way he could have stopped Wilt if he had been fully intent on making it a two-man game. No one who ever put on a uniform could have done it. When I played him, I kept this foremost in my mind: above all, don't make him mad."

Wilt Chamberlain died on October 12, 1999. ∎

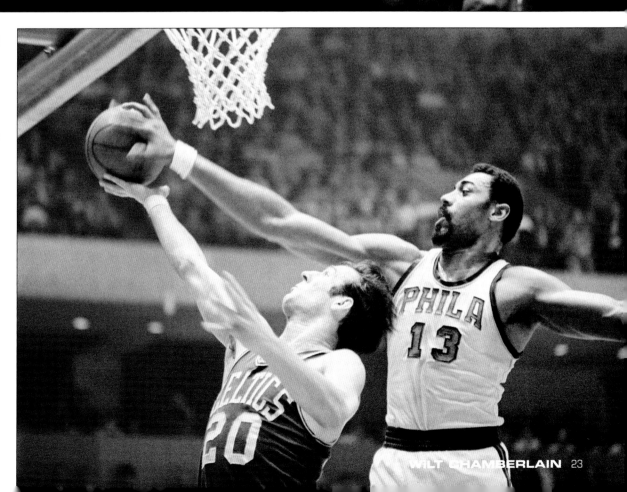

THE | SIXTIES

Nate Thurmond

Willis Reed

Elvin Hayes

Wes Unseld

Kareem Abdul-Jabbar

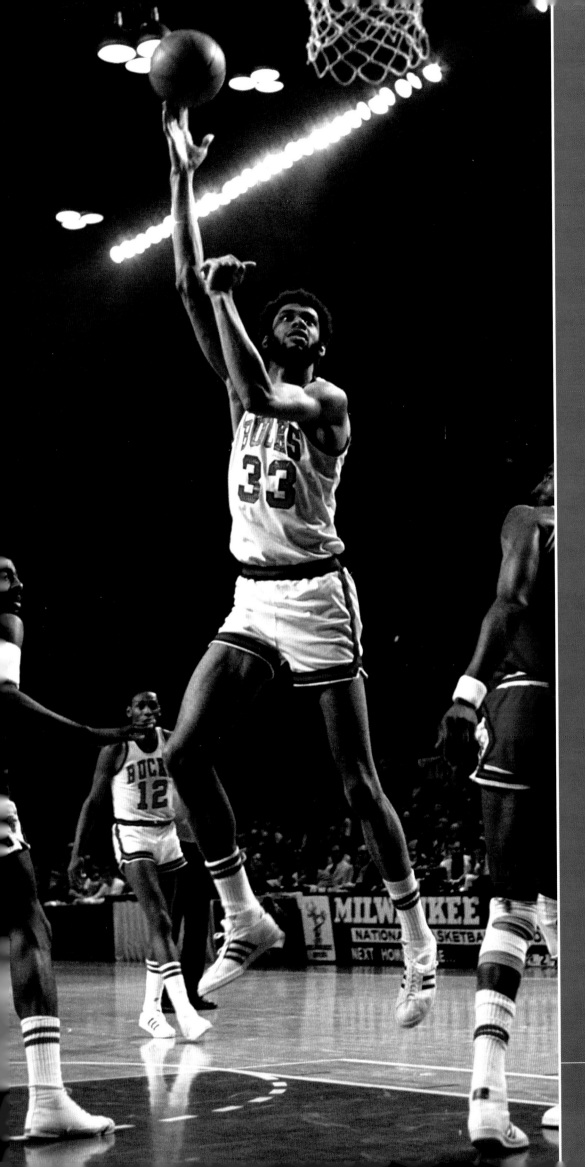

Things were changing fast. John Kennedy became president. The Baby Boomers entered high school. Cars assumed tail fins and eight-cylinder engines.

The NBA was changing fast, too, which was good news because it had a long way to go. The little burgs, Rochester, New York, and Fort Wayne, Indiana, had disappeared in the fifties, but Syracuse and its infamous spitting fans held out until 1963.

George Mikan's name on the marquee notwithstanding, the NBA had its first real matchup, Russell vs. Chamberlain, known in the standings as the Boston Celtics against the Philadelphia Warriors. The only problem was that the Celtics almost always won when it counted.

Instead of starting his own dynasty, Wilt started on his travels, moving with the Warriors to San Francisco and then returning to Philadelphia with the 76ers, whom he turned into one of the great powerhouses. A year after their 1967 title—the only one the Celtics didn't win in the decade—Chamberlain forced a trade to the Lakers.

If the NBA was growing, it was by fits and starts. Chamberlain, a willing and no-holds-barred talker, did a piece for *Sports Illustrated* titled "My Life in a Bush League," for which he caught major flak. He responded that he hadn't written the title, whereupon someone counted up the number of times he'd called something "bush" in the piece (30-something).

Truth must not have counted as a defense because the NBA sixties-style was slick only in comparison to its hand-to-mouth existence in the forties and fifties. At the beginning of the sixties, there were still only eight teams—none west of St. Louis—which spent the season eliminating two (usually the Knicks and one other) from playoff berths.

By the end of the sixties, the NBA included five teams west of the Mississippi. The Lakers, a hit in Los Angeles with Jerry West and Elgin Baylor, had acquired Wilt and were becoming one of the most celebrated teams in history.

Good, young centers arrived, too, although no one who compared to Russell and Chamberlain. That's how far ahead of their time they were. Nate Thurmond broke in in 1963, followed by Willis Reed in 1964 and Elvin Hayes and Wes Unseld in 1968, continuing the trend that Russell and Chamberlain had started toward big, talented athletes. Thurmond could defend up and down the front line. Reed and Hayes could play out on the floor, shoot as well as smaller men, go under the basket, and kick butt.

Then, in 1969, the next generation arrived in the person of Kareem Abdul-Jabbar, who would dominate through the seventies and play on five championship teams in the eighties. As far as giants went, things were developing nicely.

60s

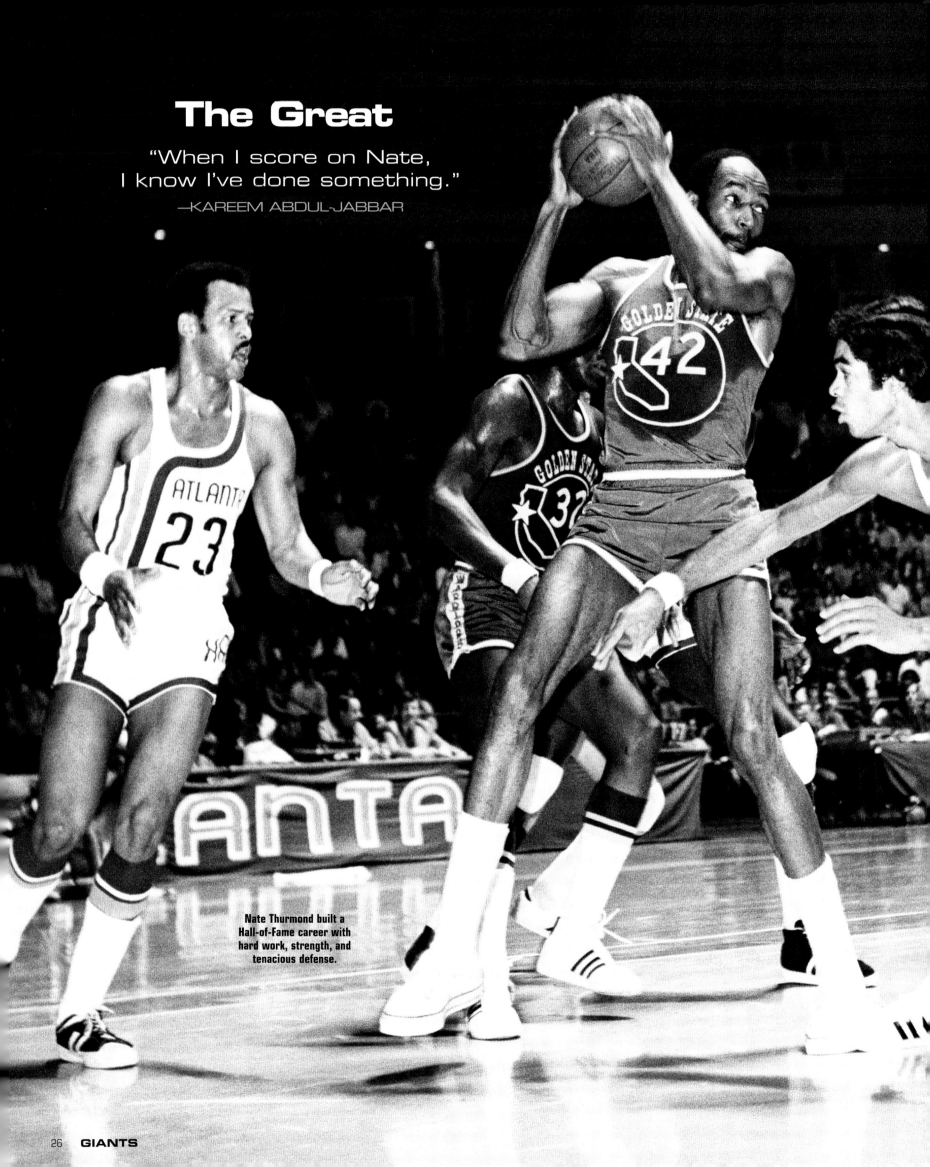

The Great

"When I score on Nate,
I know I've done something."
—KAREEM ABDUL-JABBAR

Nate Thurmond built a
Hall-of-Fame career with
hard work, strength, and
tenacious defense.

OF THE BEST CENTERS, NATE THURMOND LEFT THE LEAST TRACE, INSPIRED THE FEWEST STORIES IN NEWSPAPERS AND MAGAZINES, AND SURVIVES ONLY BRIEFLY IN PHOTOS AND ON FILM.

In the memories of his peers, however, he's still Nate the Great.

Such opponents as Kareem Abdul-Jabbar called him the best defender they'd faced and respected him for approaching defense as basketball, rather than wrestling.

"I still rate him with all the centers. I've had great centers and I rate him right there as a winner," says Bill Fitch, his last coach. "He didn't have the explosion and the points of [Hakeem] Olajuwon. He didn't have the athleticism, but he had the strength. He was the only guy I ever saw who could go out and play Chamberlain one night and play Abdul-Jabbar the next night and hold 'em down and keep 'em below their average."

"Nate was one of those guys who happened to come along when they always had a great center up there who always got all the recognition," says Rick Barry, his San Francisco/Golden State Warriors teammate. "I mean, he came into the league, you had Russell, you had Chamberlain. And then they had Kareem come into the league. Nate never really was the guy who got the recognition as the center. But if you were to ask any one of those guys who were the great players they had to go up against, from a defensive standpoint, Nate's name would always come up.

"Nate didn't have the great, incredible gifts of a Kareem or a Wilt. He was a hard worker who probably got as much out of his ability as anyone who's ever played the game. I loved him because he set good screens and got mc open. The only thing I didn't like about him, and he knows it, Nate didn't want to dunk the ball. On the pick-and-roll, he would lay the ball in the basket. Only when he got mad would he dunk the ball. He had this thing about not wanting to dunk, having people think he was some big freak or something."

Kareem was a prodigy and Wilt was Wilt. Thurmond was a late bloomer from Akron, Ohio, who eased into the NBA.

"I was very late," Thurmond says. "When I graduated from high school, I was all-city and all of that, but I was 6′7½″ and growing. The guy who was the best guy on my team was a guy named Elijah Chapman. He was the plum, he was a guard, 6′3″. . . .

"But once I got there [Bowling Green], then I went to work. It was a game I really liked to play and I just stayed in the gym, stayed in the gym. And finally my coordination caught up with my height and then it was downhill."

He was listed at 6′11″ but, he told friends, he was closer to 6′9″, Russell's size. But he wasn't as athletic as Russell, or as lucky.

When Thurmond joined the San Francisco Warriors in 1963, Wilt was already there, forcing him to play forward for his first season and a half if he wanted to get off the bench. As a rookie, he averaged only 26 minutes and seven points a game, but the Warriors made the NBA Finals.

A year later they went into the dumper, and Chamberlain was traded back to Philadelphia, making Thurmond a center. Rick Barry arrived the season after that, launching a two-year revival that

- Born: July 25, 1941, in Akron, Ohio
- College: Bowling Green State
- 6´11´´/235 pounds
- Named first-team All-American by *The Sporting News* in 1963
- Averaged 17.8 points and 17.0 rebounds per game in college
- Ranks fifth in NBA history in career rebounding average at 15.0
- Scored 14,437 points and grabbed 14,464 rebounds during his NBA career
- Holds NBA record for rebounds in one quarter with 18 (February 28, 1965, vs. Baltimore)
- Became the first NBA player to record a quadruple-double, posting 22 points, 14 rebounds, 13 assists, and 12 blocked shots vs. Atlanta on October 18, 1974
- Member of two NBA All-Defensive First Teams (1969, 1971), three NBA All-Defensive Second Teams (1972, 1973, 1974), and NBA All-Rookie Team (1964)
- Selected to play in seven NBA All-Star Games
- Holds Warriors franchise career record with 12,771 rebounds (1963–64 to 1973–74)
- Voted One of the 50 Greatest Players in NBA History in 1996
- Inducted into the Naismith Memorial Basketball Hall of Fame in 1984

"HE WAS THE ONLY GUY I EVER SAW WHO COULD GO OUT AND PLAY CHAMBERLAIN ONE NIGHT AND PLAY ABDUL-JABBAR THE NEXT NIGHT AND HOLD 'EM DOWN AND KEEP 'EM BELOW THEIR AVERAGE."
—BILL FITCH

culminated with an appearance in the 1967 Finals and ended the following summer when Rick left for the ABA.

After that, Thurmond anchored Warriors teams that were merely respectable, although he was better than that. By his fifth season, his scoring average exceeded 20 and stayed there until the early seventies.

Soft-spoken and gentlemanly, Nate was popular with teammates and fans, a favorite of owner Franklin Mieuli and coach Al Attles. Urbane and debonair, Thurmond opened a restaurant in San Francisco and sometimes acted as maître 'd.

Ironically, the Warriors broke through to win a championship in 1974–75 after trading Nate. He was 33, and his scoring average had dropped from 21 to 17 to 13 in the two preceding seasons. They packed him off to Chicago for a young center named Clifford Ray, intending to get younger and rebuild, only to

catch fire in the playoffs. They beat Thurmond's Bulls in a seven-game Western finals en route to their surprise NBA Finals sweep of the Washington Bullets, but it was a barely recognizable Nate who played those games. He averaged less than 20 minutes and 3.5 points per game in the playoffs.

The next season, the Bulls dispatched him home to Cleveland in return for two nobodies, Eric Fernsten and Steve Patterson. The Cavs were 5–11 when he arrived. It was an unlikely setting for a fairy-tale ending, but they almost made it.

"The guys all loved him," says Fitch, then the Cavs' coach. "He was great around the young guys. He played 18 minutes—Nate the Great.

"Jim Chones [the starting center] became a better player. Chones got hurt before we went into the Eastern Conference finals against Boston. We ended

Collegiate Record

Season	Team	G	Min.	FGM	FGA	Pct.	FTM	FTA	Pct.	Reb.	Ast.	Pts.	RPG	APG	PPG
													Averages		
'59–'60	Bowling Green	17	...	...	...	...	...	...	...	208	...	225	12.2	...	13.2
'60–'61	Bowling Green	24	...	170	427	.398	87	129	.674	449	...	427	18.7	...	17.8
'61–'62	Bowling Green	25	...	163	358	.455	67	113	.593	394	...	393	15.8	...	15.7
'62–'63	Bowling Green	27	...	206	466	.442	124	197	.629	452	...	536	16.7	...	19.9
Varsity totals		76	...	539	1,251	.431	278	439	.633	1,295	...	1,356	17.0	...	17.8

NBA Regular-Season Record

Season	Team	G	Min.	FGM	FGA	Pct.	FTM	FTA	Pct.	Reb.	Ast.	PF	Dq.	Pts.	RPG	APG	PPG
															Averages		
'63–'64	San Fran.	76	1,966	219	554	.395	95	173	.549	790	86	184	2	533	10.4	1.1	7.0
'64–'65	San Fran.	77	3,173	519	1,240	.419	235	357	.658	1,395	157	232	3	1,273	18.1	2.0	16.5
'65–'66	San Fran.	73	2,891	454	1,119	.406	280	428	.654	1,312	111	223	3	1,188	18.0	1.5	16.3
'66–'67	San Fran.	65	2,755	467	1,068	.437	280	445	.629	1,382	166	183	3	1,214	21.3	2.6	18.7
'67–'68	San Fran.	51	2,222	382	929	.411	282	438	.644	1,121	215	137	1	1,046	22.0	4.2	20.5
'68–'69	San Fran.	71	3,208	571	1,394	.410	382	621	.615	1,402	253	171	0	1,524	19.7	3.6	21.5
'69–'70	San Fran.	43	1,919	341	824	.414	261	346	.754	762	150	110	1	943	17.7	3.5	21.9
'70–'71	San Fran.	82	3,351	623	1,401	.445	395	541	.730	1,128	257	192	1	1,641	13.8	3.1	20.0
'71–'72	Golden State	78	3,362	628	1,454	.432	417	561	.743	1,252	230	214	1	1,673	16.1	2.9	21.4
'72–'73	Golden State	79	3,419	517	1,159	.446	315	439	.718	1,349	280	240	2	1,349	17.1	3.5	17.1

Season	Team	G	Min.	FGM	FGA	Pct.	FTM	FTA	Pct.	Rebounds			Ast.	St.	Blk.	TO	Pts.	Averages		
										Off.	Def.	Tot.						RPG	APG	PPG
'73–'74	Golden State	62	2,463	308	694	.444	191	287	.666	249	629	878	165	41		179	807	14.2	2.7	13.0
'74–'75	Chicago	80	2756	250	686	.364	132	224	.589	259	645	904	328	46		195	632	11.3	4.1	7.9
'75–'76	Chi.-Clev.	78	1,393	142	337	.421	62	123	.504	115	300	415	94	22		98	346	5.3	1.2	4.4
'76–'77	Cleveland	49	997	100	246	.407	68	106	.642	121	253	374	83	16		81	268	7.6	1.7	5.5
Totals		964	35,875	5,521	13,105	.421	3,395	5,089	.667	...	...	14,464	2,575	125		553	14,437	15.0	2.7	15.0

Personal fouls/disqualifications: 1973–74, 179/4. 1974–75, 271/6. 1975–76, 160/1. 1976–77, 128/2. Totals, 2,624/34.

NBA Playoff Record

Season	Team	G	Min.	FGM	FGA	Pct.	FTM	FTA	Pct.	Reb.	Ast.	PF	Dq.	Pts.	RPG	APG	PPG
															Averages		
'63–'64	San Fran.	12	410	42	98	.429	36	53	.679	148	12	46	0	120	12.3	1.0	10.0
'66–'67	San Fran.	15	690	93	215	.433	52	91	.571	346	47	52	1	238	23.2	3.1	15.9
'68–'69	San Fran.	6	263	40	102	.392	20	34	.588	117	28	18	0	100	19.5	4.7	16.7
'70–'71	San Fran.	5	192	36	97	.371	16	20	.800	51	15	20	0	88	10.2	3.0	17.6
'71–'72	Golden State	5	230	53	122	.434	21	28	.750	89	26	12	0	127	17.8	5.2	25.4
'72–'73	Golden State	11	460	64	161	.398	32	40	.800	145	40	30	1	160	13.2	3.6	14.5

Season	Team	G	Min.	FGM	FGA	Pct.	FTM	FTA	Pct.	Rebounds			Ast.	St.	Blk.	TO	Pts.	Averages		
										Off.	Def.	Tot.						RPG	APG	PPG
'74–'75	Chicago	13	254	14	38	.368	18	37	.486	24	63	87	31	5		21	46	6.7	2.4	3.5
'75–'76	Cleveland	13	375	37	79	.468	13	32	.406	38	79	117	28	6		29	87	9.0	2.2	6.7
'76–'77	Cleveland	1	1	0	0	...	0	0	...	0	1	1	0	0		1	0	1.0	0.0	0.0
Totals		81	2,875	379	912	.416	208	335	.621	...	...	1,101	227	11		51	966	13.6	2.8	11.9

NBA All-Star Game Record

	G	Min.	FGM	FGA	Pct.	FTM	FTA	Pct.	Reb.	Ast.	PF	Dq.	Pts.
Totals	5	104	14	43	.326	3	8	.375	44	2	5	0	31

> "HE WAS A HARD WORKER WHO PROBABLY GOT AS MUCH OUT OF HIS ABILITY AS ANYONE WHO'S EVER PLAYED THE GAME."
>
> —RICK BARRY

A relatively late bloomer, Thurmond's greatness didn't begin to emerge until he worked on his game at Bowling Green State University.

up because of Nate having the best team in basketball in 1976, but when Chones went down, he had to play the six games against Dave Cowens and he had to play 48 minutes. He just didn't have that much left in the tank.

"I always said he had the bad knee and the ugliest feet in basketball, but other than that he was beautiful."

Cleveland took the title-bound Celtics through a loud, bruising six-game Eastern finals in 1976. Afterward Cowens said that getting past the Cavs was like "having a wall knocked down."

Thurmond retired a year later and returned to the Bay Area, where for the next 16 years he was one of the area's most eligible bachelors.

"I enjoyed being a bachelor in the league," he said. "I got married when I was 50. I look at it as, you can only be a bachelor once and the most advantageous time is when you're young." ■

Starry, Starry Night

"When Willis came out onto the court, it was like the place exploded. Chills were going up and down everyone's spines."

—BILL BRADLEY

WILLIS REED

Willis Reed gets the upper hand on Wilt Chamberlain in this 1973 game.

11

IT ENDED TOO SOON FOR WILLIS REED, WHO PLAYED TEN SEASONS, THE LAST THREE WHILE WRACKED WITH PAIN. HIS CAREER WAS MORE THAN ONE NIGHT, BUT IT WAS *SOME* NIGHT, A MOMENT IN TIME SO PERFECT THAT IT SEEMED TO TRANSCEND EVERYTHING THAT HAD GONE BEFORE OR WOULD COME AFTER.

It certainly transcended the rest of Reed's career. He was 27 years old on that magical night in 1970, but he would play only four more seasons and 162 more games after it.

"I'm sure it hindered his career playing that game," says teammate Walt Frazier, "because most guys would not have suited up for that game. Only Willis Reed probably would have suited up for that final game because he was hell-bent. He had a tenacious work ethic and he always wanted to be out there, so I think, unequivocally, the injuries and playing hurt shortened his career."

It was May 8, 1970, the night of the seventh game of the NBA Finals. The Knicks, once the dregs of the NBA, suddenly became the darlings of New York. They were on the ropes—about to play the game of their lives against the Lakers and Wilt Chamberlain—with only a crippled Reed to contest him. That was, if Willis played at all.

Reed had pulled a muscle in his right hip early in Game 5, but the Knicks had staged a miracle rally, coming from 13 points behind to win in a game so dramatic, Knicks forward Dave DeBusschere called it "one of the greatest ever played."

Two days later in Los Angeles, with Reed on the bench wearing a suit and a somber expression, his right leg extended stiffly before him, Chamberlain netted 45 points in a 135–113 rout to tie the series.

Only two days remained before Game 7, and sophisticated Gotham spent them in turmoil, like one of those burgs that inspired "those little town blues." United in anxiety, the city was obsessed by the plight of a quiet man from a Louisiana village who now eclipsed all the capitalists on Wall Street, the stars on the Great White Way, and Mayor John Lindsay.

Beneath this anxiety lay years of pent-up yearning. In Madison Square Garden, where the stars came to prove their stardom, where the NIT popularized the college game, the Knicks had long been a civic embarrassment—an amusement fit only for gamblers who sat on the baseline, puffing on their cigars and rooting for the action only insofar as it affected the point spread.

When Reed arrived in 1964, the Knicks hadn't made the playoffs in six seasons, an ignominious feat since six of the league's eight teams qualified. They hadn't won a playoff game in 10 years. They were famous for their flops: Darrall Imhoff, Tom Stith, Paul Hogue, and Art Heyman, the four No. 1 draft picks before Reed arrived. As Barry Clemens, who broke in with the Knicks, said of Heyman, chosen ahead of Nate Thurmond in 1963: "typical Knicks choice—a guy with a big name in college, a *Sports Illustrated* cover boy who was really overrated and then didn't do much in the pros."

Reed, a No. 2 pick selected after the more celebrated Bad News Barnes, was different all around. He topped out at 6´9´´ but was barrel-chested and powerfully built, an imposing 240-pounder whom teammates listened to and opponents respected. He had grown up preferring football and switched to basketball reluctantly when he started growing. He reconciled his dilemma by playing basketball with a linebacker's ferocity.

Although from tiny Bernice, Louisiana (as he used to say, a two-stoplight town), and Grambling College, he was determined and unintimidated. At his first Knicks training camp, he asked GM Eddie Donovan for a rule book so he could study up. He became Rookie of the Year ahead of such college stars as Barnes, Luke Jackson, Jeff Mullins, and Barry Kramer. After that camp, nothing he did surprised the Knicks.

Reed was a top-10 rebounder from his rookie season, a 20-point scorer by his third.

- Born: June 25, 1942, in Hico, Louisiana
- College: Grambling State
- 6´9´´/240 pounds
- Was a two-time All-American in college
- Member of NAIA championship team in 1961
- Named NBA Rookie of the Year in 1965 after averaging 19.5 points and 14.7 rebounds per game
- Named NBA Most Valuable Player in 1970
- Voted NBA All-Star Game Most Valuable Player in 1970
- Named NBA Finals Most Valuable Player in 1970 and 1973
- Became the first player named MVP of the All-Star Game, regular season, and playoffs in the same season (1970)
- Selected for the NBA All-Star Game in his first seven years in the league (1965–71)
- Member of one All-NBA First Team (1970), four All-NBA Second Teams (1967, 1968, 1969, 1971), one NBA All-Defensive First Team (1970), and NBA All-Rookie Team (1965)
- Member of New York Knicks NBA championship teams in 1970 and 1973
- Averaged 18.7 points and 12.9 rebounds per game in the NBA with career totals of 12,183 points and 8,414 rebounds
- Had his No. 19 jersey retired by the Knicks on October 21, 1976
- Served as head coach of the New York Knicks, 1977–78, 1978–79
- Served as head coach of the New Jersey Nets, 1987–88, 1988–89
- Voted One of the 50 Greatest Players in NBA History in 1996
- Elected to the NAIA Basketball Hall of Fame in 1970
- Inducted into the Naismith Memorial Basketball Hall of Fame in 1981

"HE'S A MAN'S MAN. HE'S THAT TYPE OF GUY. WE AFFECTIONATELY STILL CALL HIM 'THE CAPTAIN.'"
—WALT FRAZIER

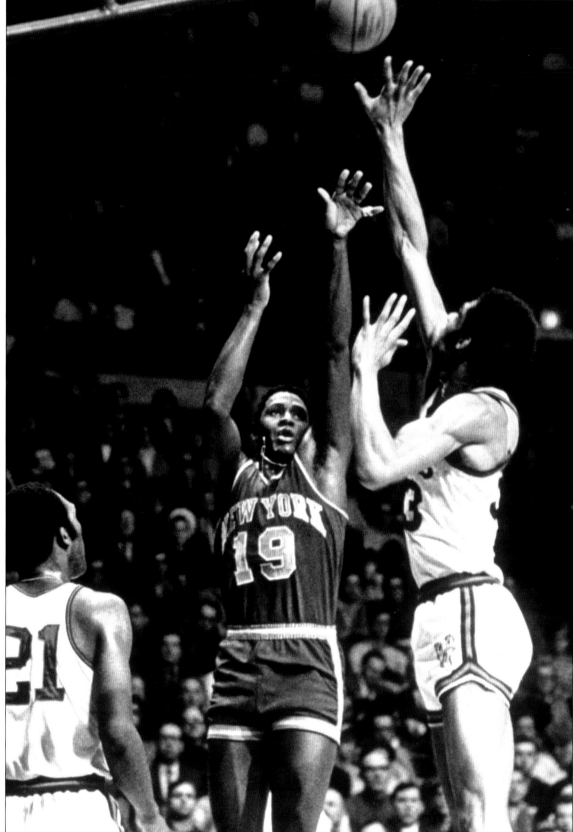

During his 10 years in the league Reed consistently went up against—and over—many of the greatest centers of all time.

In his second, he participated in a memorable rumble, remembered in New York as the night Willis cleaned out the entire Lakers team.

Amazingly enough, it's almost true.

"No, Willis didn't take on the entire Lakers team," says Elgin Baylor. "Willis and Rudy LaRusso got into some hassle under the basket. There was some pushing and shoving and Rudy threw a punch, hit Willis, and before Willis could retaliate, they broke it up.

"And when Willis went to the bench, he was wiping his face with a towel. And he looked at the towel and saw some blood from his mouth. And so right away, he threw the towel down and started toward our bench.

"I was the first guy there, so he said, 'Excuse me Elgin.' I didn't know where he was going, I thought he was going to the locker room.

"He walked right by me. He was looking for Rudy. It so happened, Rudy was down at the far end and we had John Block and Darrall Imhoff. . . . I don't know if he hit John Block, but I know he hit Darrall Imhoff. He swung, hit Darrall Imhoff, knocked him over backwards. Soon as that happened, everybody grabbed Willis and that was the extent of it."

That was enough of an extent.

Collegiate Record

Season	Team	G	Min.	FGM	FGA	Pct.	FTM	FTA	Pct.	Reb.	Ast.	Pts.	RPG	APG	PPG
'60–'61	Grambling State	35	...	146	239	.611	86	122	.705	312	...	378	8.9	...	10.8
'61–'62	Grambling State	26	...	189	323	.585	80	102	.784	380	...	458	14.6	...	17.6
'62–'63	Grambling State	33	...	282	489	.577	135	177	.763	563	...	699	17.1	...	21.2
'63–'64	Grambling State	28	...	301	486	.619	143	199	.719	596	...	745	21.3	...	26.6
Totals		122	...	918	1,537	.597	444	600	.740	1,851	...	2,280	15.2	...	18.7

NBA Regular-Season Record

Season	Team	G	Min.	FGM	FGA	Pct.	FTM	FTA	Pct.	Reb.	Ast.	PF	Dq.	Pts.	RPG	APG	PPG
'64–'65	New York	80	3,042	629	1,457	.432	302	407	.742	1,175	133	339	14	1,560	14.7	1.7	19.5
'65–'66	New York	76	2,537	438	1,009	.434	302	399	.757	883	91	323	13	1,178	11.6	1.2	15.5
'66–'67	New York	78	2,824	635	1,298	.489	358	487	.735	1,136	126	293	16	1,628	14.6	1.6	20.9
'67–'68	New York	81	2,879	659	1,346	.490	367	509	.721	1,073	159	343	12	1,685	13.2	2.0	20.8
'68–'69	New York	82	3,108	704	1,351	.521	325	435	.747	1,191	190	314	7	1,733	14.5	2.3	21.1
'69–'70	New York	81	3,089	702	1,385	.507	351	464	.756	1,126	161	287	2	1,755	13.9	2.0	21.7
'70–'71	New York	73	2,855	614	1,330	.462	299	381	.785	1,003	148	228	1	1,527	13.7	2.0	20.9
'71–'72	New York	11	363	60	137	.438	27	39	.692	96	22	30	0	147	8.7	2.0	13.4
'72–'73	New York	69	1,876	334	705	.474	92	124	.742	590	126	205	0	760	8.6	1.8	11.0

Season	Team	G	Min.	FGM	FGA	Pct.	FTM	FTA	Pct.	Off.	Def.	Tot.	Ast.	St.	Blk.	TO	Pts.	RPG	APG	PPG
'73–'74	New York	19	500	84	184	.457	42	53	.792	47	94	141	30	12	21	...	210	7.4	1.6	11.1
Totals		650	23,073	4,859	10,202	.476	2,465	3,298	.747	...	...	8,414	1,186	12	21	...	12,183	12.9	1.8	18.7

Personal fouls/disqualifications: 1973–74, 49/0.

NBA Playoff Record

Season	Team	G	Min.	FGM	FGA	Pct.	FTM	FTA	Pct.	Reb.	Ast.	PF	Dq.	Pts.	RPG	APG	PPG
'66–'67	New York	4	148	43	80	.530	24	25	.960	66	7	19	1	110	13.8	1.0	27.5
'67–'68	New York	6	210	53	98	.541	22	30	.733	62	11	24	1	128	10.3	1.8	21.3
'68–'69	New York	10	429	101	198	.510	55	70	.786	141	19	40	1	257	14.1	1.9	25.7
'69–'70	New York	18	732	178	378	.471	70	95	.737	248	51	60	0	426	13.8	2.8	23.7
'70–'71	New York	12	504	81	196	.413	26	39	.667	144	27	41	0	188	12.0	2.3	15.7
'72–'73	New York	17	486	97	208	.466	18	21	.857	129	30	65	1	212	7.6	1.8	12.5

Season	Team	G	Min.	FGM	FGA	Pct.	FTM	FTA	Pct.	Off.	Def.	Tot.	Ast.	St.	Blk.	TO	Pts.	RPG	APG	PPG
'73–'74	New York	11	132	17	45	.378	3	5	.600	4	18	22	4	2	0	...	37	2.0	0.4	3.4
Totals		78	2,641	570	1,203	.474	218	285	.765	...	...	801	149	2	0	...	1,358	10.3	1.9	17.4

Personal fouls/disqualifications: 1973–74, 26/0.

NBA All-Star Game Record

		G	Min.	FGM	FGA	Pct.	FTM	FTA	Pct.	Reb.	Ast.	PF	Dq.	Pts.
Totals		7	161	38	84	.452	12	16	.750	58	7	20	1	88

NBA Coaching Record

Season	Team	W	L	Pct.	Finish	W	L	Pct.
'77–'78	New York	43	39	.524	2nd/Atlantic Division	2	4	.333
'78–'79	New York	6	8	.429		—	—	—
'87–'88	New Jersey	7	21	.250	5th/Atlantic Division	—	—	—
'88–'89	New Jersey	26	56	.317	5th/Atlantic Division	—	—	—
Totals (4 years)		82	124	.398	Totals (1 year)	2	4	.333

"WE KNEW HE WAS GOING TO BE GOOD, BUT I NEVER KNEW HE WAS GOING TO BE AS GOOD AS HE TURNED OUT TO BE."

—DICK MCGUIRE,
FORMER COACH OF THE NEW YORK KNICKS

In Reed's sixth season, the Knicks put together their greatest campaign, starting 23–1 including a then-record 18 wins in a row. Reed was the All-Star and regular-season MVP, and—when he scored 37, 29, and 38 points in the first three games of the Finals—was on his way to the hat trick.

Then he went down in Game 5 and sat out Game 6. All of New York held its breath, waiting to see if he'd show up for Game 7.

The Knicks came out to warm up. Reed wasn't with them. Suddenly, a familiar figure walked out between the stands. Fans in the cheap seats let out a whoop—only to find out it was Cazzie Russell.

Moments later, Reed walked out, stolidly, slowly, without limping too much, having just gotten an injection with a needle so large, he said later, his response was, "Holy shit."

Reed didn't even jump for the opening tip, but when the Knicks got the ball back he hit a 16-foot tiptoe jumper for their first points. Dragging his leg, he hit his second shot, too, a 17-footer from the other side, his last points of the game.

Mostly, Willis concentrated on walling off Wilt. The crowd and the Knicks were so psyched that they barely remembered that another team was out there. The Lakers sank without a ripple in the emotional tidal wave. The Knicks raced to leads of 15–6, 30–17, and, when Reed left for good, 61–37.

After that, it was all over except for the presentation ceremonies, when a polished brass trophy seemed inadequate to thank Reed for what he had done. Said ABC's Howard Cosell, in a bit of valedictory that still appears in highlight films, "You have offered, I think, the best that the human spirit can offer."

The Knicks won another title in 1973, with Reed once again winning the NBA Finals MVP award.

"He's a man's man," says Frazier. "He's that type of guy. We affectionately still call him 'the Captain.' Retrospectively, I think if Willis were never injured, we would have won more championships."

Retrospectively, they could have won 100 and they'd still be talking about the first one. ∎

Long May
E Run

"The Big E was among the best of any generation."

—*HOUSTON CHRONICLE*

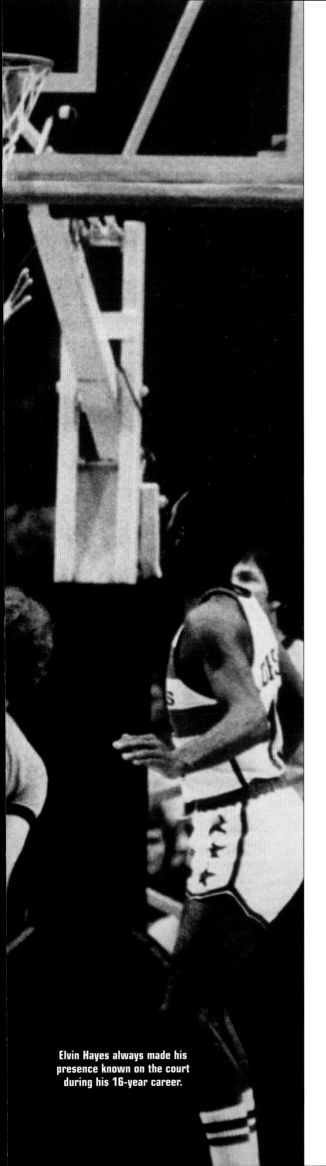

Elvin Hayes always made his presence known on the court during his 16-year career.

ELVIN HAYES

15

AS A CHILD IN TINY RAYVILLE, LOUISIANA, ELVIN HAYES AWOKE IN THE EARLY HOURS OF THE MORNING, CHOPPED COTTON UNTIL MIDDAY, AND THEN WENT TO SCHOOL. HE WAS A SHY YOUNGSTER WITH A SPEECH IMPEDIMENT WHO BECAME A STAR ALMOST BEFORE HE KNEW IT AND SPENT HIS ENTIRE CAREER LEARNING HOW TO HANDLE IT.

Playing was the easy part for him. He missed nine games in 16 seasons and played 50,000 minutes, third only to Kareem Abdul-Jabbar and Karl Malone.

Hayes was like a big cat, 6´9´´ and 235 pounds of desire and shooting ability. Whatever his shortcomings—and they were legendary—whatever standoffs he'd have with teammates, coaches, and management, he was always a force.

"He was as agile as these kids now," says Bill Fitch, his last coach. "He could shoot outside, face up. Great hands.

"The thing he could do and do right to the end was rebound. He was one of those guys with Dennis Rodman tendencies. I mean, when that ball went up, when he got his hands on it, he hung onto it. It was fun to watch him and Wes Unseld play together, and if they got the ball at the same time, see who was going to break it."

Unlike Willis Reed, another rural Louisiana prodigy, Hayes didn't go to a small, black school. He went to the University of Houston, on a tip from the Texas Southern University coach who couldn't land him and then wanted to place Hayes in someone else's conference.

Hayes was a sensation at Houston, averaging 38.6 points as a senior, including the 39 he laid on UCLA and Lew Alcindor in their ballyhooed meeting in the Astrodome on January 20, 1968— a game given credit for putting college basketball on the map. Two seasons before, when UCLA had won its second title, the championship game wasn't televised in many parts of the country. For this game between the number one– and number two–rated teams, a syndicated network of 150 stations was

hastily put together. The University of Houston had moved it into the new Astrodome, then billed as the "eighth wonder of the world," and sold 52,693 tickets.

Hayes was the top pick in the 1968 draft, by the fledgling San Diego Clippers. He led the NBA in scoring as a rookie, in rebounding in his second season. However, even in a business in which big egos roamed freely, teammates complained he was off-the-scale selfish, blaming them for anything that went wrong. The business aspects of his career were similarly beyond him.

Elvin's first contract was a five-year, $500,000 deal. But the following season, when Alcindor got $1 million for five years, Hayes told Rockets owner Bob Breitbard he wanted $1 million, too.

"Breitbard says, 'You're right Elvin, you should get $1 million, we'll extend your contract another five years,'" says Pete Newell, then the Rockets' GM. "Couple

- Born: November 17, 1945, in Rayville, Louisiana
- College: Houston
- 6´9´´/235 pounds
- Led Eula D. Britton High School to 54 consecutive wins while averaging 35 points per game
- Named *The Sporting News* College Player of the Year in 1968
- Named first-team All-American by *The Sporting News* in 1967 and 1968 and second-team in 1966
- Totaled 2,884 points (31.0 per game) and 1,602 rebounds (17.2 per game) during his college career
- Selected with the first overall pick in the 1968 NBA Draft by the San Diego Rockets
- Led the NBA with 28.4 points per game as a rookie
- Holds NBA record for minutes played by a rookie with 3,695 in 1969
- Ranks third in NBA history in minutes (50,000), eighth in games (1,303), sixth in points (27,313), and fourth in rebounds (16.279)
- Averaged 21.0 points and 12.5 rebounds per game in his NBA career
- Member of three All-NBA First Teams (1975, 1977, 1979), three All-NBA Second Teams (1973, 1974, 1976), two NBA All-Defensive Second Teams (1974, 1975), and NBA All-Rookie Team (1969)
- Played in 12 consecutive NBA All-Star Games from 1969 to 1980
- Member of Washington Bullets NBA championship team in 1978
- Shares NBA Finals single-game record for offensive rebounds with 11 (May 27, 1979, vs. Seattle)
- Owns Bullets/Wizards franchise records for points (15,551) and blocked shots (1,558)
- Voted One of the 50 Greatest Players in NBA History in 1996
- Inducted into the Naismith Memorial Basketball Hall of Fame in 1990

"YOU NEVER HAD TO WORRY ABOUT HIM PLAYING HARD."

—GENE SHUE

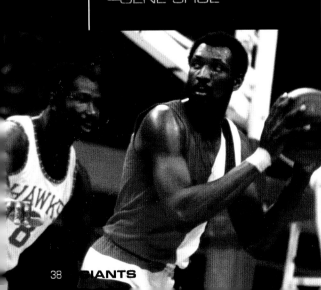

Hayes was a college superstar at Houston (far right) before he later returned to play for the Rockets.

years later, Elvin gets an agent and comes back mad as hell. He found out he was making the same money, and he was tied up five more years."

Hayes' first coaches—Jack McMahon, Alex Hannum, and Tex Winter—wanted to choke him. His game was powerful but limited. He shot the same shots from the same spots. His favorite was the turnaround 15-footer from the left block, on which he always turned the same way. He took coaching suggestions as insults.

"I was always trying to trade for Elvin," says Gene Shue, then the Bullets' coach. "I tried to get him when he was in San Diego. Jack didn't like him, but they couldn't pull the trigger on a player they had drafted.

"Alex didn't like him, but they still couldn't pull the trigger. Finally, after they moved to Houston, when Tex was the coach and Ray Patterson was the GM, they did it.

"My belief has always been that combinations mean everything in basketball. There are a lot of players who aren't the easiest people to handle, and Elvin was not the easiest player in the world to handle.

"But the thing about Elvin, first, he was an extremely talented player, more talented than a lot of the players you see today. And he loved to play basketball and he played hard. He was one of those players, you never had to worry about him playing hard."

The Bullets, sagging as Gus Johnson aged, got Hayes for nothing more than small forward Jack Marin in 1972. They returned to the top of the Eastern Conference for the rest of the decade.

In 1978 Hayes won a title under coach Dick Motta, although they weren't close. Motta used to tell friends he had a recurring nightmare: he was jogging in Central Park and everything was peaceful

Collegiate Record

Season	Team	G	Min.	FGM	FGA	Pct.	FTM	FTA	Pct.	Reb.	Ast.	Pts.	Averages RPG	APG	PPG
'64–'65	Houston	21	...	217	478	.454	93	176	.528	500	43	527	23.8	2.0	25.1
'65–'66	Houston	29	946	323	570	.567	143	257	.556	490	6	789	16.9	0.2	27.2
'66–'67	Houston	31	1,119	373	750	.497	135	227	.595	488	33	881	15.7	1.1	28.4
'67–'68	Houston	33	1,270	519	945	.549	176	285	.618	624	59	1,214	18.9	1.8	36.8
Varsity totals		93	3,335	1,215	2,265	.536	454	769	.590	1,602	98	2,884	17.2	1.1	31.1

NBA Regular-Season Record

Season	Team	G	Min.	FGM	FGA	Pct.	FTM	FTA	Pct.	Reb.	Ast.	PF	Dq.	Pts.	Averages RPG	APG	PPG
'68–'69	San Diego	82	*3,695	*930	*2,082	.447	467	746	.626	1,406	113	266	2	2,327	17.1	1.4	*28.4
'69–'70	San Diego	82	*3,665	914	*2,020	.452	428	622	.688	*1,386	162	270	5	2,256	16.9	2.0	27.5
'70–'71	San Diego	82	3,633	948	*2,215	.428	454	678	.672	1,302	180	225	1	2,350	16.0	2.3	28.7
'71–'72	Houston	82	3,461	832	1,918	.434	399	615	.649	1,197	270	233	1	2,063	14.6	3.3	25.2
'72–'73	Baltimore	81	3,347	713	1,607	.444	291	434	.671	1,177	127	232	3	1,717	14.5	1.6	21.2

Season	Team	G	Min.	FGM	FGA	Pct.	FTM	FTA	Pct.	Rebounds Off.	Def.	Tot.	Ast.	St.	Blk.	TO	Pts.	Averages RPG	APG	PPG
'73–'74	Capital	81	*3,602	689	1,627	.423	357	495	.721	*354	*1,109	*1,463	163	86	240	...	1,735	18.1	2.0	21.4
'74–'75	Wash.	82	3,465	739	1,668	.443	409	534	.766	221	783	1,004	206	158	187	...	1,887	12.2	2.5	23.0
'75–'76	Wash.	80	2,975	649	1,381	.470	287	457	.628	210	668	878	121	104	202	...	1,585	11.0	1.5	19.8
'76–'77	Wash.	82	*3,364	760	1,516	.501	422	614	.687	289	740	1,029	158	87	220	...	1,942	12.5	1.9	23.7
'77–'78	Wash.	81	3,246	636	1,409	.451	326	514	.634	335	740	1,075	149	96	159	229	1,598	13.3	1.8	19.7
'78–'79	Wash.	82	3,105	720	1,477	.487	349	534	.654	312	682	994	143	75	190	235	1,789	12.1	1.7	21.8
'79–'80	Wash.	81	3,183	761	1,677	.454	334	478	.699	269	627	896	129	62	189	215	1,859	11.1	1.6	23.0
'80–'81	Wash.	81	2,931	584	1,296	.451	271	439	.617	235	554	789	98	68	171	189	1,439	9.7	1.2	17.8
'81–'82	Houston	82	3,032	519	1,100	.472	280	422	.664	267	480	747	144	62	104	208	1,318	9.1	1.8	16.1
'82–'83	Houston	81	2,302	424	890	.476	196	287	.683	199	417	616	158	50	81	200	1,046	7.6	2.0	12.9
'83–'84	Houston	81	994	158	389	.406	86	132	.652	87	173	260	71	16	28	82	402	3.2	0.9	5.0
Totals		1,303	50,000	10,976	24,272	.452	5,356	7,999	690	...	...	16,279	2,398	864	1,771	1,358	27,313	12.5	1.8	21.0

Personal fouls/disqualifications: 1973–74, 252/1. 1974–75, 238/0. 1975–76, 293/5. 1976–77, 312/1. 1977–78, 313/7. 1978–79, 308/5. 1979–80, 309/9. 1980–81, 300/6. 1981–82, 287/4. 1982–83, 232/2. 1983–84, 123/1. Totals, 4,193/53.

NBA Playoff Record

Season	Team	G	Min.	FGM	FGA	Pct.	FTM	FTA	Pct.	Reb.	Ast.	PF	Dq.	Pts.	Averages RPG	APG	PPG
'68–'69	San Diego	6	278	60	114	.526	35	53	.660	83	5	21	0	155	13.8	0.8	25.8
'72–'73	Baltimore	5	225	53	105	.505	23	33	.697	57	5	16	0	129	11.4	1.0	25.8

Season	Team	G	Min.	FGM	FGA	Pct.	FTM	FTA	Pct.	Rebounds Off.	Def.	Tot.	Ast.	St.	Blk.	TO	Pts.	Averages RPG	APG	PPG
'73–'74	Capital	7	323	76	143	.531	29	41	.707	31	80	111	21	5	15	...	181	15.9	3.0	25.9
'74–'75	Washington	17	751	174	372	.468	86	127	.677	46	140	186	37	26	39	...	434	10.9	2.2	25.5
'75–'76	Washington	7	305	54	122	.443	32	55	.582	16	72	88	10	5	28	...	140	12.6	1.4	20.0
'76–'77	Washington	9	405	74	173	.428	41	59	.695	29	93	122	17	10	22	...	189	13.6	1.9	21.0
'77–'78	Washington	21	868	189	385	.491	79	133	.594	103	176	279	43	32	52	58	457	13.3	2.0	21.8
'78–'79	Washington	19	786	170	396	.429	87	130	.669	94	172	266	38	17	52	56	427	14.0	2.0	22.5
'79–'80	Washington	2	92	16	41	.390	8	10	.800	10	12	22	6	0	4	4	40	11.0	3.0	20.0
'81–'82	Houston	3	124	17	50	.340	8	15	.533	7	23	30	3	2	10	6	42	10.0	1.0	14.0
Totals		96	4,160	883	1,901	.464	428	656	.652	...	...	1,244	185	77	222	124	2,194	13.0	1.9	22.9

Personal fouls/disqualifications: 1973–74, 23/0. 1974–75, 70/3. 1975–76, 24/0. 1976–77, 39.0. 1977–78, 86/2. 1978–79, 79/3. 1979–80, 8/0. 1981–82, 12/0. Totals, 378/8.

NBA All-Star Game Record

	G	Min.	FGM	FGA	Pct.	FTM	FTA	Pct.	Reb.	Ast.	PF	Dq.	Pts.
Totals	12	264	52	129	.403	22	34	.647	92	17	37	0	126

"THE THING HE COULD DO AND DO RIGHT TO THE END WAS REBOUND. . . . WHEN THAT BALL WENT UP, WHEN HE GOT HIS HANDS ON IT, HE HUNG ONTO IT."
—BILL FITCH

when all of a sudden, who should jump out from behind a tree but Elvin Hayes!

Easy or not, Hayes was always a producer. Through the 1979–80 season, at age 34, he remained a 20-point scorer and a top-10 rebounder and shot-blocker. He tailed off after that and was traded back to the Rockets, who were in the process of bottoming out.

In his second season back in Houston, the Rockets went 14–68 and Fitch replaced Del Harris as coach.

"Elvin was told we've got a young club, we're starting over, we've got no time for past history or anything else," Fitch says. "In other words, here you are at the end of your career but the future for all these kids is down the line.

"That was when everyone was accusing me of throwing games because I was playing Elvin more minutes than I was Ralph Sampson. But Elvin was having a heck of a year. He was blocking shots and playing like a youngster. He wanted to go out in style. He knew it was going to be his last year.

"He was great with the kids. It wasn't any I, I, I. It was we.

"He stood up our last game in Kansas City. He said, 'Coach, can I say something to the team?' He said, 'If I'd have played with guys who were this enthusiastic, this much together, if I'd enjoyed other teams the way I've enjoyed being with you guys, I'd play more. I just want to thank all of you for making my last year as good as it's been.'

"I had to step back. Here's Elvin, who wasn't always known for making speeches and thanking other people. That wasn't the reputation he had."

So after 16 seasons, peace came at last to Elvin Hayes, more or less. Better late than never. ∎

Beloved Fireplug

"He's the classic winning player."
—GENE SHUE

Wes Unseld was one of the greatest passers to ever play the center position.

WES UNSELD

OF ALL THE GREAT CENTERS, WES UNSELD MAY HAVE BEEN THE MOST IMPROBABLE. IN 13 SEASONS, HIS SCORING AVERAGE REACHED DOUBLE FIGURES ONLY SIX TIMES. HE GOT OVER 15 ONCE, AND HE NEVER HIT 17

At his listed height of 6´7´´, he'd have been not only the shortest of the top centers, but the shortest to start at the position in the sixties or ever after. Of course, he may not even have been 6´7´´. After his career, he once confided he wasn't even really 6´6´´.

Not that anyone could get within a gluteus maximus flex of him to measure him. Unseld supposedly weighed 245 when he entered the league in 1968, although he looked more like 265. He might have been 280 when he retired in 1981. After Wilt Chamberlain, Wes was one of the answers, along with Willis Reed and Artis Gilmore, given when people asked who was the strongest man in the game.

Unseld had the body of a sumo wrestler, the disposition of a grizzly bear, and, though he saved it for after games and tried to hide it, a notoriously warm heart. In a business in which players made hospital appearances trailed by camera crews for the sake of public relations, Unseld quietly made widespread, gargantuan charitable efforts, wincing if asked about them.

On a basketball court, he was all business, scowling and growling until his appointed rounds had been covered. After the game, he'd scowl at the reporters, too, or, if cornered, say something bland to discourage further probing. At other times, if a reporter just wanted to chat, he was actually friendly. Unseld's indifference to publicity was truly genuine.

"Wes was a remarkable player," says Bill Walton, "because he was able to get it done while being so short. I mean, this guy gave up huge size. He gave up size and speed. Usually you make up for lack of size with speed, and he gave up both of them.

"But the strength in his hands—and the thought process and the preparation and concept, that it was truly about positioning and timing and teamwork and leadership. He couldn't get it done against the really tall

centers. Abdul-Jabbar and Wilt, they had their way with him, but they had their way with everybody.

"It's too bad that his contribution to outlet passing is not carried into this current generation of players, who refuse to outlet the ball. Players just do not get it out anymore. The only ones who do get it out are the ones who dribble it out themselves. . . . No one just grabs it and snaps an outlet pass like Wes Unseld, and it's very sad. It's one of the reasons the scores are so much lower today."

Other factors contributed to the death of the outlet. New zone defense rules persuaded offenses to space themselves wider, putting more defenders back against the break and cutting off the old outlet lanes. But it was true, no one ever got the ball out faster and threw it farther than Unseld. Walton was great at it, but Wes was the master of the art form. It was actually breathtaking, like seeing

- Born: March 14, 1946, in Louisville, Kentucky
- College: Louisville
- 6′7′′/245 pounds
- Named second-team All-American by *The Sporting News* in 1967 and 1968
- Averaged 20.6 points and 18.9 rebounds per game in college
- Totaled 1,491 rebounds in 1968–69, third most ever by an NBA rookie
- Voted NBA Most Valuable Player and NBA Rookie of the Year in 1969 (one of only two players, along with Wilt Chamberlain, to achieve both awards in the same year)
- Named to the All-NBA Team and NBA All-Rookie Team in 1969
- Ranks 11th in NBA history with 13,679 rebounds, an average of 14.0 per game
- Named to five NBA All-Star teams
- Member of Washington Bullets NBA championship team in 1978
- Voted NBA Finals Most Valuable Player in 1978
- Holds NBA records for offensive rebounds during a seven-game playoff series with 45 (1979, Washington vs. San Antonio) and defensive rebounds during a two-game playoff series with 23 (1978, Washington vs. Atlanta)
- Holds Bullets/Wizards franchise records for minutes (35,832), rebounds (13,769), and assists (3,822)
- Received the NBA's J. Walter Kennedy Citizenship Award for community service in 1975
- Served as head coach of the Washington Bullets from 1987–88 to 1993–94
- Voted One of the 50 Greatest Players in NBA History in 1996
- Inducted into the Naismith Memorial Basketball Hall of Fame in 1987

> ## "WES WAS A REMARKABLE PLAYER BECAUSE HE WAS ABLE TO GET IT DONE WHILE BEING SO SHORT. HE GAVE UP SIZE AND SPEED. USUALLY YOU MAKE UP FOR LACK OF SIZE WITH SPEED, AND HE GAVE UP BOTH."
>
> —BILL WALTON

Despite his relative lack of height, Unseld's career contributions to the Bullets franchise were gargantuan.

Willie Mays catch one over his shoulder or Michael Jordan soaring to the hoop.

Despite his short trunk, Unseld had long, powerful arms and great hands. Bullets guards always congratulated themselves on their luck at playing with him. He set definitive picks, had such great hands that it was impossible to throw him a bad pass, launched lobs on fast break after fast break, and, best of all, never wanted to shoot! He would tear the ball down, turn, and without further ado, without as much as another step, rifle a two-handed pass that would arrive, trailing sparks, to someone like Kevin Porter, who'd be waiting on the sideline at halfcourt—or even farther.

Few players would ever do so much dirty work so gladly. Unseld was a throwback to the game before

celebrity entered in, whenever that was. His first coach, Gene Shue, called him "the classic winning player."

In his rookie season in 1968–69, Unseld averaged a modest 13.8 points, but he snatched 18.2 rebounds per game and was voted MVP, a distinction attained by only one other rookie, Chamberlain, who averaged 37.6 points as a rookie.

Unseld's value was measured in wins. When he arrived, the Bullets, who had never finished over .500, were starting a rookie, a second-year man (Earl Monroe), and a third-year man (Jack Marin). The team went from 36–46 to 57–25 in 1968–69.

In Wes' 13-year career, they made the NBA Finals three times, won a title in 1978, and failed to qualify for the playoffs once—in his final season, when he was 35.

Collegiate Record

Season	Team	G	Min.	FGM	FGA	Pct.	FTM	FTA	Pct.	Reb.	Ast.	Pts.	RPG	APG	PPG
'64–'65	Louisville	14	...	214	312	.686	73	124	.589	331	...	501	23.6	...	35.8
'65–'66	Louisville	26	...	195	374	.521	128	202	.634	505	...	518	19.4	...	19.9
'66–'67	Louisville	28	...	201	374	.537	121	177	.684	533	...	523	19.0	...	18.7
'67–'68	Louisville	28	...	234	382	.613	177	275	.644	513	...	645	18.3	...	23.0
Varsity totals		82	...	630	1,130	.558	426	654	.651	1,551	...	1,686	18.9	...	20.6

NBA Regular-Season Record

Season	Team	G	Min.	FGM	FGA	Pct.	FTM	FTA	Pct.	Reb.	Ast.	PF	Dq.	Pts.	RPG	APG	PPG
'68–'69	Baltimore	82	2,970	427	897	.476	277	458	.605	1,491	213	276	4	1,131	18.2	2.6	13.8
'69–'70	Baltimore	82	3,234	526	1,015	.518	273	428	.638	1,370	291	250	2	1,325	16.7	3.5	16.2
'70–'71	Baltimore	74	2,904	424	040	.501	100	303	.667	1,253	203	235	2	1,047	16.9	4.0	14.1
'71–'72	Baltimore	76	3,171	409	822	.498	171	272	.629	1,336	278	218	1	989	17.6	3.7	13.0
'72–'73	Baltimore	79	3,085	421	854	.493	149	212	.703	1,260	347	168	0	991	15.9	4.4	12.5

Season	Team	G	Min.	FGM	FGA	Pct.	FTM	FTA	Pct.	Off.	Def.	Tot.	Ast.	St.	Blk.	TO	Pts.	RPG	APG	PPG
'73–'74	Capital	56	1,727	146	333	.438	36	55	.655	152	365	517	159	56	16	...	328	9.2	2.8	5.9
'74–'75	Wash.	73	2,904	273	544	.502	126	184	.685	318	759	1,077	297	115	68	...	672	*14.8	4.1	9.2
'75–'76	Wash.	78	2,922	318	567	*.561	114	195	.585	271	765	1,036	404	84	59	...	750	13.3	5.2	9.6
'76–'77	Wash.	82	2,860	270	551	.490	100	166	.602	243	634	877	363	87	45	...	640	10.7	4.4	7.8
'77–'78	Wash.	80	2,644	257	491	.523	93	173	.538	286	669	955	326	98	45	173	607	11.9	4.1	7.6
'78–'79	Wash.	77	2,406	346	600	.577	151	235	.643	274	556	830	315	71	37	156	843	10.8	4.1	10.9
'79–'80	Wash.	82	2,973	327	637	.513	139	209	.665	334	760	1,094	366	65	61	153	794	13.3	4.5	9.7
'80–'81	Wash.	63	2,032	225	429	.524	55	86	.640	207	466	673	170	52	36	97	507	10.7	2.7	8.0
Totals		984	35,832	4,369	8,586	.509	1,883	2,976	.633	...	...	13,769	2,822	628	367	579	10,624	14.0	3.9	10.8

Personal fouls/disqualifications: 1973–74, 121/1. 1974–75, 180/1. 1975–76, 203/3. 1976–77, 253/5. 1977–78, 234/2. 1978–79, 204/2. 1979–80, 249/5. 1980–81, 171/1. Totals, 2,762/29.

NBA Playoff Record

Season	Team	G	Min.	FGM	FGA	Pct.	FTM	FTA	Pct.	Reb.	Ast.	PF	Dq.	Pts.	RPG	APG	PPG
'68–'69	Baltimore	4	165	30	57	.526	15	19	.789	74	5	14	0	75	18.5	1.3	18.8
'69–'70	Baltimore	7	289	29	70	.414	15	19	.789	165	24	25	1	73	23.6	3.4	10.4
'70–'71	Baltimore	18	759	96	208	.462	46	81	.568	339	69	60	0	238	18.8	3.8	13.2
'71–'72	Baltimore	6	266	32	65	.492	10	19	.526	75	25	22	0	74	12.5	4.2	12.3
'72–'73	Baltimore	5	201	20	48	.417	9	19	.474	76	17	12	0	49	15.2	3.4	9.8

Season	Team	G	Min.	FGM	FGA	Pct.	FTM	FTA	Pct.	Off.	Def.	Tot.	Ast.	St.	Blk.	TO	Pts.	RPG	APG	PPG
'73–'74	Capital	7	297	31	63	.492	9	15	.600	22	63	85	27	4	1	...	71	12.1	3.9	10.1
'74–'75	Wash.	17	734	71	130	.546	40	61	.656	65	211	2	...	...	...	...	...	...	...	...
'75–'76	Wash.	7	310	18	39	.462	13	24	.542	26	59	85	28	6	4	...	49	12.1	4.0	7.0
'76–'77	Wash.	9	368	30	54	.556	7	12	.583	24	81	105	44	8	6	...	67	11.7	4.9	7.4
'77–'78	Wash.	18	677	71	134	.530	27	46	.587	72	144	216	79	14	7	36	169	12.0	4.4	9.4
'78–'79	Wash.	19	736	78	158	.494	39	64	.609	90	163	253	64	17	14	30	195	13.3	3.4	10.3
'79–'80	Wash.	2	87	7	14	.500	4	6	.667	7	21	28	7	0	3	3	18	14.0	3.5	9.0
Totals		119	4,889	513	1,040	.493	234	385	.608	...	...	1,777	453	67	55	69	1,260	14.9	3.8	10.6

Personal fouls/disqualifications: 1973–74, 15/0. 1974–75, 39/0. 1975–76, 19/0. 1976–77, 32/0. 1977–78,62/2. 1978–79, 66/2. 1979–80, 5/0. Totals, 371/5.

NBA All-Star Game Record

	G	Min.	FGM	FGA	Pct.	FTM	FTA	Pct.	Reb.	Ast.	PF	Dq.	Pts.
Totals	5	77	14	28	.500	3	5	.600	36	6	10	0	31

NBA Coaching Record

Season	Team	W	L	Pct.	Finish	W	L	Pct.
'87–'88	Washington	30	25	.545	2nd/Atlantic Division	2	3	.400
'88–'89	Washington	40	42	.488	4th/Atlantic Division	—	—	—
'89–'90	Washington	31	51	.378	4th/Atlantic Division	—	—	—
'90–'91	Washington	30	52	.366	4th/Atlantic Division	—	—	—
'91–'92	Washington	25	57	.305	6th/Atlantic Division	—	—	—
'92–'93	Washington	22	60	.268	7th/Atlantic Division	—	—	—
'93–'94	Washington	24	58	.293	7th/Atlantic Division	—	—	—
Totals		202	345	.369	Totals (1 year)	2	3	.400

"HE HAS GREAT ANTICIPATION AND IMAGINATION. HE CAN SEE SOMETHING DEVELOP, AND HE GETS THE PASS THERE AT THE RIGHT TIME."
—FORMER BULLETS GENERAL MANAGER BOB FERRY

"On the teams I've played on as a pro, nobody has paid to see me play," Unseld told Bob Rubin for his book *Great Centers of Pro Basketball*. "They paid to see Earl Monroe and Gus Johnson when they were on the team, and now they pay to see [Phil] Chenier and Elvin Hayes. My style simply isn't flashy, on or off the court. Lack of publicity doesn't bother me. In fact, publicity annoys me. It's embarrassing to talk about yourself, and it's embarrassing to think that somebody would want to read about me. This hero worship stuff is wrong."

For Unseld, every night was a mismatch. Some of them were ridiculous. Picture a 6´7´´ man (or a 6´6´´ man, or 6´5´´) trying to stop the magnificent release high above the head of the 7´2´´ Kareem Abdul-Jabbar.

That was the matchup in the 1971 NBA Finals, which the Milwaukee Bucks won 4–0. Not that you couldn't see it coming. The Bullets were injured, and after Game 1 Unseld confided, "I'm looking into Kareem's belly button." Of course, Unseld fought the inevitable with all he had for all four games.

He may be right, this hero thing is wrong. But if you had to have one, Wes Unseld was a wise choice. In an increasingly fake business, he was a worthwhile and an unfailingly real person who was, coincidentally, a great player, too. ∎

The Superstar in the Bubble

"Kareem, in my mind, kind of combined skill-wise what Russell and Chamberlain specialized in."

—BOB COUSY

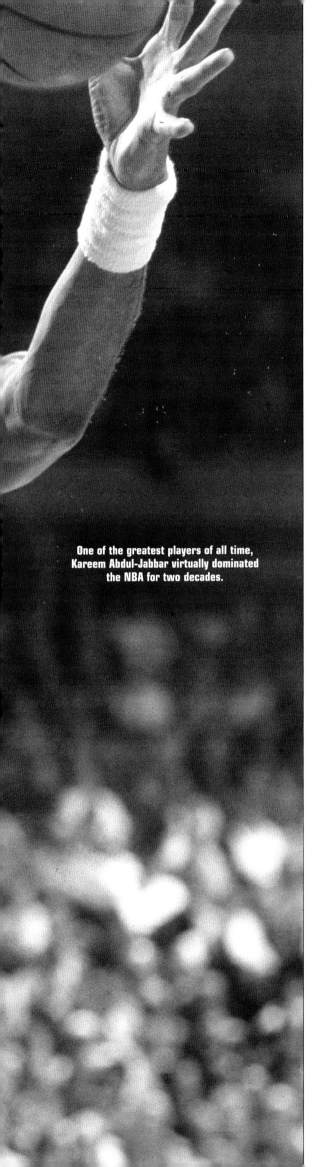

One of the greatest players of all time, Kareem Abdul-Jabbar virtually dominated the NBA for two decades.

KAREEM ABDUL-JABBAR

EVERYTHING ABOUT KAREEM ABDUL-JABBAR WAS SINGULAR, WITHOUT A TRUE PEER IN HIS PRIME. WILT CHAMBERLAIN WAS TOO OLD, BILL WALTON TOO BRITTLE... HE ENTERED THE NBA AT THE END OF THE SIXTIES, TOWERED OVER THE SEVENTIES, AND LASTED ALMOST ALL THE WAY THROUGH THE EIGHTIES.

He was there and yet he wasn't, impossible to guard during games, well guarded after them. He piled up 38,387 points, more than any player in NBA history. He played on six championship teams. He lasted so long, people forgot his religious conversion and his unapologetic militancy and accorded him the respect he had long since gotten from his fellow athletes.

"Kareem was by far the best player I ever played against," says Walton. "Not just the best center. He was the best player. Better than Michael Jordan. Better than Magic Johnson and Larry Bird. Better than Hakeem Olajuwon.

"What separated Kareem, he had the magnificent coaching, the magnificent body. He had everything. All the skills, the conditioning, it was all there. His mental dominance, his pride, his sense of responsibility—he carried the NBA for 20 years.

"His offense was virtually unstoppable. You worked your tail off to get him to take the worst shot in the world, an 18-foot fadeaway hook shot, and he'd swish it every time. Much like Hakeem, you get him behind the backboard, he's falling backward, he threw it up, swishes in.

"I had to play my absolute best against him. He was always the guy, every operation, every physical therapy, every training session, I'm just telling myself, 'Jabbar! Jabbar! I'm going to get that guy.'

"And I knew I had to play my best every time I went downcourt. And I did play my best against him. And he just killed me every time.

"He would throw 50 on me. He would throw 50 on anybody's face at any time he wanted to, particularly the new guys. Whenever a new guy would come up, he would never say a thing about them. Just walk out there and get 50 and walk out of there and say, 'Yep, OK. Welcome to my league.'"

Abdul-Jabbar was as singular a man as a player. He was a superstar from puberty when his name was Lew Alcindor, but he was never comfortable in the role, not as a young firebrand or a wizened veteran. He loosened up with teammates, but they said he was hard to know. Magic Johnson says they coexisted for five years before actually becoming friends.

Abdul-Jabbar was 15 when fame hit. (He kept a *New York Journal-American* clipping with the headline "High School Goliath Powers to the Top.") His success, however, soon turned from neat to hassle.

His UCLA career was a three-year tour de force (three national titles, three NCAA Tournament Most Outstanding Player trophies), but he said the expectations took the fun out of it. He boycotted the 1968 Olympics and told Joe Garagiola on the *Today Show*, "It's really not my country."

Said UCLA coach John Wooden after Kareem's last game: "It was not as easy an era as it might have seemed to outsiders."

Nor was the NBA any playground in the sky. Abdul-Jabbar didn't like Milwaukee ("cold beyond belief," he wrote in his book *Giant Steps*) or the beatings he took in the paint or from the press ("little guys who derived great pleasure from tweaking the tiger's whiskers . . . the striped-shirt-and-checked-pants set").

"Basketball had ceased to be fun," he wrote. "It was work and with every game, my abilities might have been growing but the people who ran the game were taking chunks out of me, the way the white man had devoured the Indian."

In his own little space, he was unapproachable but something to behold. If it was a job, it was one he took seriously.

His hook became the famous "skyhook," so christened by Bucks announcer Eddie Doucette, trying to describe the majestic, sweeping shot that seemed to drop from the heavens—the NBA's ultimate sword of doom.

- Born: April 16, 1947, in New York City
- College: UCLA
- 7´2´´/267 pounds
- Named College Player of the Year by *The Sporting News* in 1967 and 1969
- Won the Naismith Award in 1969
- Named first-team All-American by *The Sporting News* in 1967, 1968, and 1969
- Led UCLA to the NCAA championship in 1967, 1968, and 1969, and was named NCAA Tournament Most Outstanding Player each year
- Led NCAA Division I in field-goal percentage in 1967 (66.7) and 1969 (63.5)
- Voted NBA Rookie of the Year in 1970
- Won NBA Most Valuable Player Award in 1971, 1972, 1974, 1976, 1977, and 1980
- Member of 10 All-NBA First Teams (1971, 1972, 1973, 1974, 1976, 1977, 1980, 1981, 1984, 1986), five All-NBA Second Teams (1970, 1978, 1979, 1983, 1985), five NBA All-Defensive First Teams (1974, 1975, 1979, 1980, 1981), six NBA All-Defensive Second Teams (1970, 1971, 1976, 1977, 1978, 1984), and NBA All-Rookie Team (1970)
- Holds NBA career records for minutes (57,446), points (38,387), field goals made (15,837), and field goals attempted (28,307)
- Holds NBA records for defensive rebounds in a season with 1,111 (1976) and defensive rebounds in a game with 29 (December 14, 1975, vs. Detroit)
- Ranks second in NBA history in games (1,560), blocked shots (3,189), and seasons (20)
- Averaged 24.6 points and 11.2 rebounds per game during his NBA career
- Holds NBA playoff records for seasons (18, tied with John Stockton), games (237), minutes (8,851), field goals made (2,356), and blocked shots (476)
- Holds NBA All-Star Game career records for games (18), minutes (449), and blocked shots (31)
- Holds Milwaukee Bucks career records for points with 14,211 and rebounds with 7,161 (1969–70 through 1974–75)
- Holds Lakers franchise record for blocked shots with 2,694 (1975–76 through 1988–89)
- Member of Milwaukee Bucks NBA championship team in 1971
- Member of Los Angeles Lakers NBA championship teams in 1980, 1982, 1985, 1987, and 1988
- Earned NBA Finals Most Valuable Player Award in 1971 and 1985
- Member of the NBA 35th Anniversary All-Time Team in 1980
- Voted One of the 50 Greatest Players in NBA History in 1996
- Inducted into the Naismith Memorial Basketball Hall of Fame in 1995

Then known as Lew Alcindor, Abdul-Jabbar first entered the spotlight as a high school phenom for Power Memorial in New York City.

"KAREEM WAS BY FAR THE BEST PLAYER I EVER PLAYED AGAINST. NOT JUST THE BEST CENTER. HE WAS THE BEST PLAYER. BETTER THAN MICHAEL JORDAN."
—BILL WALTON

Kareem developed other moves, such as a feint toward the right baseline and a reverse back across the middle from his preferred right block for a jumper, a lefty hook, or a dunk.

Mostly, though, he'd go right to the baseline for the hook. It was like Jerry West's right hand; opponents couldn't take it away, even though they knew it was coming. If you cut Kareem off, he'd pull back, make you stop with him, and then go right again to drop that hammer on you.

He grew to a solid 7´2´´, 250, but he didn't see the game as wrestling. He liked being roughed up even less, but you couldn't run him off. He took his beatings (or swung back or broke his hand punching a basket support) and stayed in there hooking.

Abdul-Jabbar wasn't a great rebounder or defender, and he paced himself to a fault. However, no one else in the history of the game ever had a shot as devastating—not Jordan's midair repertoire, or Bird's three-pointer, or Wilt's fadeaway.

Kareem got it whenever he wanted. He was absolutely cold-blooded. In the waning moments of double overtime of Game 6 in the 1974 Finals, the Celtics needed just one win to nail down the championship. They led 101–100. Then, with the Boston fans on their feet, getting set to run onto the parquet, Kareem dropped a 17-foot skyhook on them. The Bucks won 102–101, but Boston took Game 7 for the title.

Despair caught up with Kareem in Milwaukee, and he demanded a trade to the Lakers. He won MVPs in

Collegiate Record

Season	Team	G	Min.	FGM	FGA	Pct.	FTM	FTA	Pct.	Reb.	Ast.	Pts.	RPG	APG	PPG
'65–'66	UCLA	21	...	295	432	.683	106	179	.592	452	...	696	21.5	...	33.1
'66–'67	UCLA	30	...	346	519	.667	178	274	.650	466	...	870	15.5	...	29.0
'67–'68	UCLA	28	...	294	480	.613	146	237	.616	461	...	734	16.5	...	26.2
'68–'69	UCLA	30	...	303	477	.635	115	188	.612	440	...	721	14.7	...	24.0
Varsity totals		88		943	1,476	.639	439	699	.628	1,367	...	2,325	15.5	...	26.4

NBA Regular-Season Record

Season	Team	G	Min.	FGM	FGA	Pct.	FTM	FTA	Pct.	Reb.	Ast.	PF	Dq.	Pts.	RPG	APG	PPG
'69–'70	Milwaukee	82	3,534	*938	1,810	.518	485	743	.653	1,190	337	283	8	*2,361	14.5	4.1	28.8
'70–'71	Milwaukee	82	3,288	*1,063	1,843	.577	470	681	.690	1,311	272	264	4	*2,596	16.0	3.3	*31.7
'71–'72	Milwaukee	81	3,583	*1,159	2,019	.574	504	732	.680	1,346	370	235	1	*2,822	16.6	4.6	*34.8
'72–'73	Milwaukee	76	3,254	982	1,772	.554	328	460	.713	1,224	379	208	0	2,292	16.1	5.0	30.2

Season	Team	G	Min.	FGM	FGA	Pct.	FTM	FTA	Pct.	Off.	Def.	Tot.	Ast.	St.	Blk.	TO	Pts.	RPG	APG	PPG
'73–'74	Milwaukee	81	3,548	*948	1,759	.539	295	420	.702	287	891	1,178	386	112	283	...	2,191	14.5	4.8	27.0
'74–'75	Milwaukee	65	2,747	812	1,584	.513	325	426	.763	194	718	912	264	65	212	...	1,949	14.0	4.1	30.0
'75–'76	Los Angeles	82	*3,379	914	1,728	.529	447	636	.7032	272	*1,111	*1,383	413	119	*338	...	2,275	*16.9	5.0	27.7
'76–'77	Los Angeles	82	3,016	*888	1,533	*.579	376	536	.703	266	*824	*1,090	319	101	*261	...	2,152	13.3	3.9	26.2
'77–'78	Los Angeles	62	2,265	663	1,205	.550	274	350	.783	186	615	801	269	103	185	208	1,600	12.9	4.3	25.8
'78–'79	Los Angeles	80	3,157	777	1,347	.577	349	474	.736	207	818	1,025	431	76	*316	282	1,903	12.8	5.4	23.8
'79–'80	Los Angeles	82	3,143	835	1,383	.604	364	476	.765	190	696	886	371	81	*280	297	2,034	10.8	4.5	24.8
'80–'81	Los Angeles	80	2,976	836	1,457	.574	423	552	.766	197	624	821	272	59	228	249	2,095	10.3	3.4	26.2
'81–'82	Los Angeles	76	2,677	753	1,301	.579	312	442	.706	172	487	659	225	63	207	230	1,818	8.7	3.0	23.9
'82–'83	Los Angeles	79	2,554	722	1,228	.588	278	371	.749	167	425	592	200	61	170	200	1,722	7.5	2.5	21.8
'83–'84	Los Angeles	80	2,622	716	1,238	.578	285	394	.723	169	418	587	211	55	143	221	1,717	7.3	2.6	21.5
'84–'85	L.A. Lakers	79	2,630	723	1,207	.599	289	395	.732	162	460	622	249	63	162	197	1,735	7.9	3.2	22.0
'85–'86	L.A. Lakers	79	2,629	755	1,338	.564	336	439	.765	133	345	478	280	67	130	203	1,846	6.1	3.5	23.4
'86–'87	L.A. Lakers	78	2,441	560	993	.564	245	343	.714	152	371	523	203	49	97	186	1,355	6.7	2.6	17.5
'87–'88	L.A. Lakers	80	2,308	480	903	.532	205	269	.762	118	360	478	135	48	92	159	1,165	6.0	1.7	14.6
'88–'89	L.A. Lakers	74	1,695	313	659	.475	122	165	.739	103	231	334	74	38	85	95	748	4.5	1.0	10.1
Totals		1,560	57,446	15,837	28,307	.559	6,712	9,304	.721	...	...	17,440	5,660	1,160	3,189	2,527	38,387	11.2	3.6	24.6

Personal fouls/disqualifications: 1973–74, 238/2. 1974–75, 205/2. 1975–76, 292/6. 1976–77, 262/4. 1977–78, 182/1. 1978–79, 230/3. 1979–80, 216/2. 1980–81, 244/4. 1981–82, 224/0. 1982–83, 220/1. 1983–84, 211/1. 1984–85, 238/3. 1985–86, 248/2. 1986–87, 245/2. 1987–88, 216/1. 1988–89, 196/1. Totals, 4,657/48.

NBA Playoff Record

Season	Team	G	Min.	FGM	FGA	Pct.	FTM	FTA	Pct.	Reb.	Ast.	PF	Dq.	Pts.	RPG	APG	PPG
'69–'70	Milwaukee	10	435	139	245	.567	74	101	.733	168	41	25	1	352	16.8	4.1	35.2
'70–'71	Milwaukee	14	577	152	295	.515	68	101	.673	238	35	45	0	372	17.0	2.5	26.6
'71–'72	Milwaukee	11	510	139	318	.437	38	54	.704	200	56	35	0	316	18.2	5.1	28.7
'72–'73	Milwaukee	6	276	59	138	.428	19	35	.543	97	17	26	0	137	16.2	2.8	22.8

Season	Team	G	Min.	FGM	FGA	Pct.	FTM	FTA	Pct.	Off.	Def.	Tot.	Ast.	St.	Blk.	TO	Pts.	RPG	APG	PPG
'73–'74	Milwaukee	16	758	224	402	.557	67	91	.736	67	186	253	78	20	39	...	515	15.8	4.9	32.2
'76–'77	Los Angeles	11	467	147	242	.607	87	120	.725	51	144	195	45	19	38	...	381	17.7	4.1	34.6
'77–'78	Los Angeles	3	134	38	73	.521	5	9	.556	14	27	41	11	2	12	14	81	13.7	3.7	27.0
'78–'79	Los Angeles	8	367	88	152	.579	52	62	.839	18	83	101	38	8	33	29	228	12.6	4.8	28.5
'79–'80	Los Angeles	15	618	198	346	.572	83	105	.790	51	130	181	46	17	58	55	479	12.1	3.1	31.9
'80–'81	Los Angeles	3	134	30	65	.462	20	28	.714	13	37	50	12	3	8	11	80	16.7	4.0	26.7
'81–'82	Los Angeles	14	493	115	221	.520	55	87	.632	33	86	119	51	14	45	41	285	8.5	3.6	20.4
'82–'83	Los Angeles	15	588	163	287	.568	80	106	.755	25	90	115	42	17	55	50	406	7.7	2.8	27.1
'83–'84	Los Angeles	21	767	206	371	.555	90	120	.750	56	117	173	79	23	45	45	502	8.2	3.8	23.9
'84–'85	L.A. Lakers	19	610	168	300	.560	80	103	.777	50	104	154	76	23	36	52	416	8.1	4.0	21.9
'85–'86	L.A. Lakers	14	489	157	282	.557	48	61	.787	26	57	83	49	15	24	42	362	5.9	3.5	25.9
'86–'87	L.A. Lakers	18	559	127	234	.530	97	122	.795	39	84	123	36	8	35	40	345	6.8	2.0	19.2
'87–'88	L.A. Lakers	24	718	141	304	.464	56	71	.789	49	82	131	36	15	37	46	338	5.5	1.5	14.1
'88–'89	L.A. Lakers	15	351	68	147	.463	31	43	.721	13	46	59	19	5	11	22	167	3.9	1.3	11.1
Totals		237	8,851	2,356	4,422	.533	1,050	1,419	.740	...	...	2,481	767	189	476	447	5,762	10.5	3.2	24.3

Personal fouls/disqualifications: 1973–74, 41/0. 1976–77, 42/0. 1977–78, 14/1. 1978–79, 26/0. 1979–80, 51/0. 1980–81, 14/0. 1981–82, 45/0. 1982–83, 61/1. 1983–84, 71/2. 1984–85, 67/1. 1985–86, 54/0. 1986–87, 56/0. 1987–88, 81/1. 1988–89, 43/0. Totals, 797/7.

NBA All-Star Game Record

	G	Min.	FGM	FGA	Pct.	FTM	FTA	Pct.	Reb.	Ast.	PF	Dq.	Pts.
Totals	18	449	105	213	.493	41	50	.820	149	51	57	1	251

"WHY JUDGE ANYMORE? WHEN A MAN HAS BROKEN RECORDS, WON CHAMPIONSHIPS, ENDURED TREMENDOUS CRITICISM AND RESPONSIBILITY, WHY JUDGE? LET'S TOAST HIM AS THE GREATEST PLAYER EVER."

—PAT RILEY

three of his first five seasons in Los Angeles, and, when Johnson arrived in his fifth, started the glory run of the eighties.

Along the way, Abdul-Jabbar mellowed. He wasn't always smiling, like Magic, but he wasn't always scowling, as he had been. Angry or mellow, as long as he had a uniform on, he was the man. In the 1988 Finals, at 41, with his scoring average having dropped below 15 for the first time in his career, with other weapons such as Magic and James Worthy, the Lakers were still going to him in crunch time.

Trailing the Pistons 3–2 in the Finals and 102–101 with 27 seconds left in Game 6, Pat Riley designed the last play to Abdul-Jabbar, who had missed 11 of 14 shots that day. "Hey," said Riley later, pausing for effect, "we'll always . . . go . . . to . . . him . . . always, as long as he's on the floor."

It worked that time, too. Bill Laimbeer was called for a foul, and Abdul-Jabbar made two free throws. Two days later, the Lakers won their fifth title in the eighties—the sixth of Kareem's career.

He retired a year later. His last season featured ceremonies in each NBA city. He was showered with gifts and given ovations that probably surprised the guest of honor as much as the people who found themselves applauding.

"Kareem, in my mind, kind of combined skill-wise what Russell and Chamberlain specialized in," says Bob Cousy. "He was the prototype complete center. Had all the skills. Could put it to the floor. Facing up. Do whatever he had to do. But if he had played with near the intensity of Russell, I think he'd have been even far greater than he became."

It was enough as it was. ∎

THE SEVENTIES

Bob Lanier

Dave Cowens

Dan Issel

Artis Gilmore

Bob McAdoo

Bill Walton

Moses Malone

Robert Parish

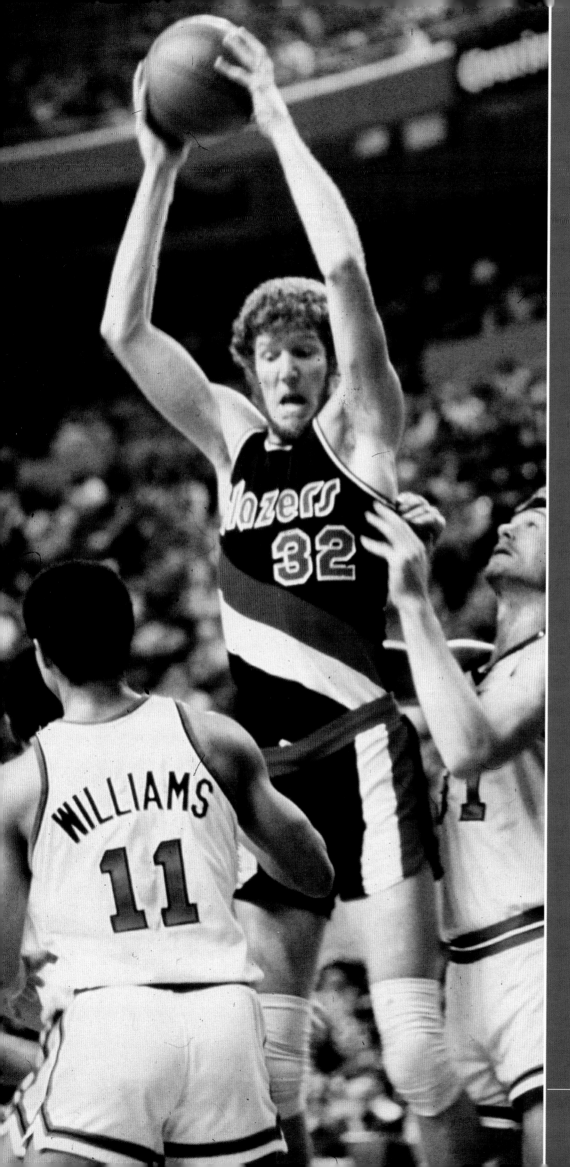

Richard Nixon was president. The Beatles were gone, and psychedelia was ebbing. Disco was coming. It wasn't going to be an easy decade.

The NBA got a lift when the Knicks won championships in 1970 and 1973. The old marquee matchup, Chamberlain and Russell, had never involved New York, the nation's media capital, but the Knicks' rise captivated Gotham, Madison Avenue, and publishers' row, giving the NBA a new hot look.

Basketball was proclaimed "The Sport of the Seventies," which made it even more dramatic when injuries to Willis Reed ended the Knicks' run and the league flopped at the decade's end.

In point of fact, the game was overextended. The American Basketball Association, formed in the late sixties, had driven salaries up. For all the romance and nostalgia that would come to surround the ABA, it was founded by a Southern California huckster named Gary Davidson, who wasn't in it for love of the game. He and his friends were in the process of launching one rival league after another, in hockey, in football, in tennis, in any field they could attract investors. The ABA was the hoop version of a pyramid scheme.

The 1976 merger of the NBA and the ABA ended years of bidding wars. Several franchises folded, but the NBA absorbed a few, some from small markets such as Indianapolis and San Antonio. With the high entrance fee the established teams would demand, these franchises were soon in jeopardy of folding, too.

The decade featured glamour matchups involving the Knicks and Lakers early, a dramatic seven-game Finals between Kareem Abdul-Jabbar's Bucks and Dave Cowens' Celtics in 1974, and the celebrated meeting of the star-studded Julius Erving–George McGinnis 76ers and Bill Walton's Blazers in 1977. After that, the league hit a black hole.

Having finally proved his brilliance at the pro level, Walton's career was effectively ended by injuries, just when it should have been taking off. The decade ended with two Finals between the Bullets and the Sonics, with few Eastern newspapers bothering to make the trip west. When the Sonics won in 1979, it was like Gabby Hartnett's famous "homer in the gloaming." This was the title in the gloaming.

Even though the business was precarious, the game was nevertheless turning out more good players all the time. Of the twenty-five men profiled in this book, eight turned pro during the seventies—thirteen from 1968 to 1980.

Big men were more multiskilled and came in all shapes and sizes, with varying approaches and games. The seventies produced Bob Lanier, a one-time fat kid with a silky touch and an unstoppable assortment of moves; Bob McAdoo, who at 6´9´´ could handle the ball like a forward and shoot with any guard; Dave Cowens, another undersized guy with a warrior ethic that made him a force far greater than his 6´8´´ height; Moses Malone, an unfinished, boards-crashing terror; and Bill Walton, one of the most refined and highly evolved technicians the center position would ever know. Even though the NBA was in trouble, the game was all right.

70s

An explosive offensive scorer throughout his career, Bob Lanier knew how to play a little defense, too.

Detroit Fats

"He was an unstoppable scorer. He could swing the hook, hit face-up jumpers, get shots in transition."

—BILL WALTON

Lanier—"Bobadob" or "Dobber" to intimates—was big (6´11´´), round, and not too firmly packed (he blew up to 294 as a St. Bonaventure sophomore), but he played with an artistry seldom seen in anyone of any body type.

"Probably had as soft of hands as anyone who ever played the game," says Bill Walton. "Could obviously stroke it. He could pass it, but the beauty of it was the ball just came out of his hands, be it a make or a miss, like a guard's, like somebody who's spent his whole life handling the ball." Of course, it took a while for people to appreciate what they were looking at.

Lanier would deal with girth, expectations, bad jokes, and bad wheels throughout his professional career. On top of everything, he had size 22 feet that were taken to be one of the wonders of the ages. Today, Shaquille O'Neal's 22s are rarely mentioned.

"At 8:40, Bob Lanier's feet began to emerge from the St. Bonaventure locker room," wrote the *Philadelphia Daily News*' Bill Conlin. "At 8:45, Bob Lanier emerged."

"It would be OK if I was a clumsy ox," said Lanier, who had heard it before and would hear it many more times, "but I'm not."

It was a long struggle, though. As a child in Buffalo, New York, Lanier was huge and prone to falling over his soon-to-be-famous feet. By age 11, he was 6´2´´ and wore size 11s. In grade school, the basketball coach thought he was too awkward. However, a friendly coach at the local Boys Club encouraged him and protected him from the taunts of the other kids, letting him work out after hours when no one else was around.

A star at Bennett High School, Bob chose St. Bonaventure in nearby Olean, New York, so his parents could watch him play. He averaged 27 points in his first varsity season and went from there. As a senior, he scored 50 points against Purdue in the finals of the Holiday Festival at Madison Square Garden—making himself the top player in a class that included Pete Maravich, Rudy Tomjanovich, and Dave Cowens.

In the 1970 NCAA Tournament, however, Lanier tripped over the foot of Villanova's Chris Ford and tore up his right knee. He was still in the hospital when the Detroit Pistons made him the first pick in the draft.

No conditioning freak anyway, Lanier was behind in his first training camp and never caught up. He wound up splitting the center position with journeyman Otto Moore and averaging a mere 15.6 points as the fans groused about his $1.3 million (multiyear) contract. The Pistons missed the playoffs.

"Fred Zollner [Pistons owner] said if we made the playoffs, he would send us all to Hawaii," says teammate Steve Mix. "There were big expectations on Bob. We had Jimmy Walker and Dave Bing, and we had a 6´11´´ center.

"Bob was one of those guys who didn't really come to practice and lace up his sneakers all the time. Unfortunately, I think it took him a while. I played with Bob in Milwaukee as well, my last year. He was a lot different."

Fans booed. The press made foot jokes. Once, in a nationally televised game, Lanier, getting ready to jump for the opening tip, saw a CBS reporter holding up one of his shoes for the camera. Laughing, he stuck his tongue out at her and it went out over the air.

"I knew what they were saying about me in the beginning, calling me the Million Dollar Bum," says Lanier. "But you go back and look at the movies. Study them. I had no lateral movement in my legs because of the injury. I couldn't get off my hook shot, and I couldn't move side to side at all. I'm not a good jumper. I've got to move laterally to get into position to shoot. I just couldn't do it. . . . It was a bad situation."

His knee recovered. The Pistons, impressed by Bill Russell's scathing commentary (whatever Lanier's weaknesses were, he was always better on offense than defense), brought him in to work with their center.

- Born: September 10, 1948, in Buffalo, New York
- College: St. Bonaventure
- 6´11´´/265 pounds
- Named first-team All-American by *The Sporting News* in 1970
- Averaged 27.6 points and 15.7 rebounds per game in college
- Selected first overall by the Detroit Pistons in the 1970 NBA Draft
- Named to the NBA-All Rookie Team in 1971
- Averaged 20.1 points and 10.1 rebounds per game during his NBA career
- Posted an NBA career free throw percentage of 76.7
- Ranks 32nd in combined ABA/NBA career scoring with 19,248 points
- Voted Most Valuable Player of the NBA All-Star Game in 1974
- Received the NBA's J. Walter Kennedy Citizenship Award in 1978
- Inducted into the Naismith Memorial Basketball Hall of Fame in 1991

"IF EVERY PLAYER HAD A BOB LANIER ATTITUDE, IT WOULD BE EASY FOR A COACH TO FUNCTION."

—DICK VITALE

After a disappointing rookie year, Lanier rebounded with a huge season in 1971–72.

Collegiate Record

Season	Team	G	Min.	FGM	FGA	Pct.	FTM	FTA	Pct.	Reb.	Ast.	Pts.	Averages		
													RPG	APG	PPG
'66–'67	St. Bonaventure	15	...	...	...	...	...	...	...	...	...	450	...	...	30.0
'67–'68	St. Bonaventure	25	...	272	466	.584	112	175	.640	390	...	656	15.6	...	26.2
'68–'69	St. Bonaventure	24	...	270	460	.587	114	181	.630	374	...	654	15.6	...	27.3
'69–'70	St. Bonaventure	26	...	308	549	.561	141	194	.727	416	...	757	16.0	...	29.1
Varsity totals		75	...	850	1,475	.576	367	550	.667	1,180	...	2,067	15.7	...	27.6

NBA Regular-Season Record

Season	Team	G	Min.	FGM	FGA	Pct.	FTM	FTA	Pct.	Reb.	Ast.	PF	Dq.	Pts.	Averages		
															RPG	APG	PPG
'70–'71	Detroit	82	2,017	504	1,108	.455	273	376	.726	665	146	272	4	1,281	8.1	1.8	15.6
'71–'72	Detroit	80	3,092	834	1,690	.494	388	505	.768	1,132	248	297	6	2,056	14.2	3.1	25.7
'72–'73	Detroit	81	3,150	810	1,654	.490	307	397	.773	1,205	260	278	4	1,927	14.9	3.2	23.8

Season	Team	G	Min.	FGM	FGA	Pct.	FTM	FTA	Pct.	Rebounds			Ast.	St.	Blk.	TO	Pts.	Averages		
										Off.	Def.	Tot.						RPG	APG	PPG
'73–'74	Detroit	81	3,047	748	1,483	.504	326	409	.797	269	805	1,074	343	110	247	...	1,822	13.3	4.2	22.5
'74–'75	Detroit	76	2,907	731	1433	.510	361	450	.802	225	689	914	350	75	172	...	1,823	12.0	4.6	24.0
'75–'76	Detroit	64	2,363	541	1,017	.532	284	370	.768	217	529	746	217	79	86	...	1,366	11.7	3.4	21.3
'76–'77	Detroit	64	2,446	678	1,269	.534	260	318	.818	200	545	745	214	70	126	...	1,616	11.6	3.3	25.3
'77–'78	Detroit	63	2,311	622	1,159	.537	298	386	.772	197	518	715	216	82	93	225	1,542	11.3	3.4	24.5
'78–'79	Detroit	53	1,835	489	950	.515	275	367	.749	164	330	494	140	50	75	175	1,253	9.3	2.6	23.6
'79–'80	Detroit-Mil.	63	2,131	466	867	.537	277	354	.782	152	400	552	184	74	89	162	1,210	8.8	2.9	19.2
'80–'81	Milwaukee	67	1,753	376	716	.525	208	277	.751	128	285	413	179	73	81	139	961	6.2	2.7	14.3
'81–'82	Milwaukee	74	1,986	407	729	.558	182	242	.752	92	296	388	219	72	56	166	996	5.2	3.0	13.5
'82–'83	Milwaukee	39	978	163	332	.491	91	133	.684	58	142	200	105	34	24	82	417	5.1	2.7	10.7
'83–'84	Milwaukee	72	2,007	392	685	.572	194	274	.708	141	314	455	186	58	51	163	978	6.3	2.6	13.6
Totals		959	32,103	7,761	15,092	.514	3,724	4,858	.767	...	...	9,698	3,007	777	1,100	1,112	19,248	10.1	3.1	20.1

Personal fouls/disqualifications: 1973–74, 273/7. 1974–75, 237/1. 1975–76, 203/2. 1976–77, 174/0. 1977–78, 185/2. 1978–79, 181/5. 1979–80, 200/3. 1980–81, 184/0. 1981–82, 211/3. 1982–83, 125/2. 1983–84, 228/8. Totals: 3,048/47.

NBA Playoff Records

Season	Team	G	Min.	FGM	FGA	Pct.	FTM	FTA	Pct.	Rebounds			Ast.	St.	Blk.	TO	Pts.	Averages		
										Off.	Def.	Tot.						RPG	APG	PPG
'73–'74	Detroit	7	303	77	152	.507	30	38	.789	26	81	107	21	4	14	...	184	15.3	3.0	26.3
'74–'75	Detroit	3	128	26	51	.510	9	12	.750	5	27	32	19	4	12	...	61	10.7	6.3	20.3
'75–'76	Detroit	9	359	95	172	.552	45	50	.900	39	75	114	30	8	21	...	235	12.7	3.3	26.1
'76–'77	Detroit	3	118	34	54	.630	16	19	.842	13	37	50	6	3	7	...	84	16.7	2.0	28.0
'79–'80	Milwaukee	7	256	52	101	.515	31	42	.738	17	48	65	31	7	8	17	135	9.3	4.4	19.3
'80–'81	Milwaukee	7	236	50	85	.588	23	32	.719	12	40	52	28	12	8	15	123	7.4	4.0	17.6
'81–'82	Milwaukee	6	212	41	80	.513	14	25	.560	18	27	45	22	8	5	14	96	7.5	3.7	16.0
'82–'83	Milwaukee	9	250	51	89	.573	21	35	.600	17	46	63	23	5	14	21	123	7.0	2.6	13.7
'83–'84	Milwaukee	16	499	82	171	.480	39	44	.886	32	85	117	55	11	10	38	203	7.3	3.4	12.7
Totals		67	2,361	508	955	.532	228	297	.768	179	466	645	235	62	99	105	1,244	9.6	3.5	18.6

Personal fouls, disqualifications: 1973–74, 28/1. 1974–75, 10/0. 1975–76, 34/1. 1976–77, 10/0. 1979–80, 23/0. 1980–81, 18/0. 1981–82, 21/2. 1982–83, 32/2. 1983–84, 57/1. Totals, 233/7.

NBA All-Star Game Record

	G	Min.	FGM	FGA	Pct.	FTM	FTA	Pct.	Reb.	Ast.	PF	Dq.	Pts.
Totals	8	121	32	55	.582	10	12	.833	45	12	15	0	74

"HE COULD PASS IT, BUT THE BEAUTY OF IT WAS THE BALL JUST CAME OUT OF HIS HANDS, BE IT A MAKE OR A MISS, LIKE A GUARD'S, LIKE SOMEBODY WHO'S SPENT HIS WHOLE LIFE HANDLING THE BALL."

—BILL WALTON

"I remember how he greeted me," Lanier said later. "He said, 'You big overweight ox, I'm gonna run that baby fat off you.'" Lanier became an acceptable rebounder and defender, and an exceptional offensive player. From his second season until his eighth, he was never under 21.3 points a game. From his fifth season through his twelfth, he never shot worse than 51 percent from the floor.

"He was an unstoppable scorer," says Walton. "He could swing the hook, hit face-up jumpers, get shots in transition.

"He was a good rebounder. Not a great leaper. Did not have good speed but really understood positioning and timing and movement. But cursed with bad legs. Couldn't move enough to keep up with the shorter, faster guys. Couldn't move enough to get around the really big power guys."

At 31, with his legs aching and his franchise deteriorating around him, Lanier was traded to Milwaukee in 1980 for nothing more than Kent Benson, a college star but already an NBA bust, and a No. 1 pick. Bucks coach Don Nelson had built an exciting little team, but he'd never had a real center. With a rejuvenated Lanier, the Bucks posted a 60–22 record in 1980–81, their most wins since the departure of Kareem Abdul-Jabbar.

Milwaukee won three more Midwest Division titles in Lanier's final three seasons. He retired in 1984 at age 36 with seven All-Star appearances and a career 20.1 scoring average, 752 points short of the 20,000 mark. In 1991 he entered the Hall of Fame in his size 22s. ■

The Wild One

"I thought he was a wild man. I'd never seen anybody with that much talent play that aggressively."

—PAUL SILAS

Dave Cowens' spirit and leadership injected new life into the post–Bill Russell Celtics.

13 DAVE COWENS

He was Dave Cowens, the greatest middle linebacker ever to go out for a center jump in the NBA, a free spirit whose tenure was as unforgettable as it was brief.

Cowens played ten seasons in Boston, although only the first eight could be called great ones. In that time, however, the Celtics won two titles, coming back from the post-Russell team that had finished 26 games out of first place before he arrived.

At 6´8´´, he was too small to be a center. And the Celtics, who had 6´7´´ Paul Silas and 6´5´´ John Havlicek on the front line with him, were a little short to be winning titles. But Cowens refused to concede anything, so they didn't have to.

He took big centers outside, shot over them, zipped by them, outran them on the break, fired jump hooks in their faces, stood and fought when he had to. His Celtics once won 10 games in a row over Kareem Abdul-Jabbar teams.

"I loved Dave Cowens' game because he played with so much heart," says Bill Walton. "Cowens was the only guy I ever saw who could outplay Wilt and Kareem. Not all the time, but could outplay them at times. And to do that at 6´8´´ and 6´9´´, whatever size he was, considering the size of Abdul-Jabbar and Chamberlain. . . .

"He had the complete package, played with a real passion and a sense of what he was trying to do, a Celtic-like sense. I'm a huge Celtics fan, and it's three guys, really. It's Russell and the guys around him, Cowens and the guys around him, and Bird and the guys around him. Without those three guys, it would have been good teams, yes, but it wouldn't have been 16 championships.

"You loved to play against him because he never, ever complained about how hard you hit him. I mean, you could smack him, just crack him in the back of the head. He'd say, 'Oh, jeez!' but he'd never say anything to the ref and he'd never say anything to you.

"He'd just say, 'Well, that's part of it, keep coming right back.'"

Off the court, Cowens was even more unconventional. He wasn't a hippie like Walton or a yuppie like the other guys; he was just . . . Dave. He seemed indifferent to the material world. He dressed in knock-around plaids and corduroys. Once, he left the team and drove a cab.

"How do you sum it up?" says the *Boston Globe*'s Bob Ryan. "The rookie year he decides he's got too much time on his hands in this new life of professional basketball—hey, what do you do? You go to practice for a couple of hours and you're free the rest of the day. He was bored, so he enrolled in a course of auto repair.

"He lived in this guest cottage. He answered an ad from this attorney in Weston, and he spent two or three years there. The guy became his lawyer, Richard Gold.

"Dave was just a different kind of guy, just naturally and totally intellectually curious. He was an interesting guy to have conversations with. He's one of the two or three athletes who ever asked about my job, the logistics, the thought process."

A native of Newport, Kentucky, Cowens was a late bloomer in high school and, because his Florida State team was on probation, little known in college. The pros found him anyway. He went No. 4 in the 1970 draft, after Bob Lanier, Rudy Tomjanovich, and Pete Maravich. Boston GM Red Auerbach said he liked him, and asked Bill Russell to take a look at him. Russell gave an enthusiastic endorsement. However, Don Nelson, then a Celtic, claimed Red wanted Sam Lacey. Bob Cousy, then the coach of the Cincinnati Royals, who were at No. 5, said Auerbach told him he'd take Lacey. But, contended Cousy, Red was talked into Cowens at the last moment by scout Mal Graham.

Everyone got to know Cowens fast enough. In the Maurice Stokes benefit game at the Kutsher's resort in the Catskills, he scored 32 points, took 22 rebounds, and was the MVP. He ran around so frantically during exhibition games, Auerbach told him to save some for the season.

As a rookie, Cowens averaged 17 points, 15 rebounds, and three assists. The Celtics improved from 34 victories to 44. In 1972 Auerbach hornswoggled the Suns out of Silas (for Charlie Scott, a guard Red got with a seventh-round pick after he signed with the ABA).

In 1974 the Celtics won their first post-Russell title, as Cowens scored 28 points and grabbed 14 rebounds in a Game 7 victory over Abdul-Jabbar's Bucks in Milwaukee. In 1976 they beat the Suns in six.

- Born: October 25, 1948, in Newport, Kentucky
- College: Florida State
- 6´8´´/230 pounds
- Named second-team All-American by *The Sporting News* in 1970
- Averaged 19.0 points and 17.2 rebounds per game in college while shooting 52 percent from the field
- Voted NBA co-Rookie of the Year in 1971 after averaging 17.0 points and 15.0 rebounds per game
- Averaged 17.6 points and 13.6 rebounds per game during NBA career
- Voted NBA Most Valuable Player in 1973
- Member of three All-NBA Second Teams (1973, 1975, 1976), one NBA All-Defensive First Team (1976), two NBA All-Defensive Second Teams (1975, 1980), and NBA All-Rookie Team (1971)
- Shares NBA record for defensive rebounds in a single playoff game with 20 (April 22, 1975, vs. Houston and May 1, 1977, vs. Philadelphia)
- Member of Boston Celtics NBA championship teams in 1974 and 1976
- Selected for seven NBA All-Star Games
- Voted NBA All-Star Game Most Valuable Player in 1973
- Served as player-coach of the Boston Celtics in 1978–79
- Served as head coach of the Charlotte Hornets from 1996 to 1999
- Served as head coach of the Golden State Warriors from 2000 to 2002
- Voted One of the 50 Greatest Players in NBA History in 1996
- Inducted into the Naismith Memorial Basketball Hall of Fame in 1990

> **"A DEDICATED KID ISN'T UNHEARD OF, BUT THERE AREN'T AS MANY AROUND AS WE WOULD LIKE. BUT OUR PROBLEM WITH COWENS IS TELLING HIM WHEN TO LAY OFF. HE DOES TOO MUCH."**
> —RED AUERBACH

Cowens led the Celtics to two titles during his 10 seasons in Boston.

That summer, however, contract negotiations between the proud Silas and the stubborn Auerbach reached an impasse. Silas was thus dealt away for Curtis Rowe. Silas was Cowens' spiritual twin, and when he left Cowens was heartbroken.

For Cowens, an ache in the heart was worse than one in the knee. He took a sabbatical for two months, drove a cab, returned, and played three more seasons. But he never found the old fire.

"It was Dave," says Ryan. "He was in this thing where he decided basketball wasn't important. He said he realized winning and losing didn't matter to him enough, that it wasn't right to be playing, so he took this two-month sabbatical. Then he came back, and he was in and out that year and the rest of his career."

Cowens retired unexpectedly during the 1980 exhibition season. The Celtics, who now had Bird, were on an Indiana exhibition tour. They had played the night before in Terre Haute and were sitting on a bus for that night's game in Evansville when Cowens got on and broke the news.

He was out for two years before trying a comeback with coach Don Nelson in Milwaukee. The attempt lasted 40 games.

Today, Cowens is remembered for his spirit as much as anything. His highlights live forever, like his famous belly flop in the NBA Finals against Milwaukee, in which he slid halfway across the parquet on his No. 18 for a loose ball.

Then there was his demonstration of a charging foul.

"Dave's number one pet peeve was guys drawing offensive fouls," Ryan says. "Johnny Most [Celtics radio broadcaster] called it the phony flop, the ACC flop. Dave hated this. It's well known, on the record, he despises this."

Collegiate Record

Season	Team	G	Min.	FGM	FGA	Pct.	FTM	FTA	Pct.	Reb.	Ast.	Averages Pts.	RPG	APG	PPG
'66–'67	Florida State	18	...	105	208	.515	49	90	.544	357	...	259	19.8	...	14.4
'67–'68	Florida State	27	...	206	383	.538	96	131	.733	456	...	508	16.9	...	18.8
'68–'69	Florida State	25	...	202	384	.526	104	164	.634	437	...	508	17.5	...	20.3
'69–'70	Florida State	26	...	172	355	.490	115	169	.680	447	...	463	17.2	...	17.8
Varsity totals		78	...	582	1122	.519	315	464	.679	1340	...	1479	17.2	...	19.0

NBA Regular-Season Record

Season	Team	G	Min.	FGM	FGA	Pct.	FTM	FTA	Pct.	Reb.	Ast.	PF	Dq.	Pts.	Averages RPG	APG	PPG
'70–'71	Boston	81	3,076	550	1,302	.422	273	373	.732	1,216	225	*350	15	1,373	15.0	2.8	17.0
'71–'72	Boston	79	3,186	657	1,357	.484	175	243	.720	1,203	245	*314	10	1,489	15.2	3.1	18.8
'72–'73	Boston	82	3,425	740	1,637	.452	204	262	.779	1,329	333	311	7	1,684	16.2	4.1	20.5

Season	Team	G	Min.	FGM	FGA	Pct.	FTM	FTA	Pct.	Rebounds Off.	Def.	Tot.	Ast.	St.	Blk.	TO	Pts.	Averages RPG	APG	PPG
'73–'74	Boston	80	3,352	645	1,475	.439	228	274	.832	264	993	1,257	354	95	101	...	1,518	15.7	4.4	19.0
'74–'75	Boston	65	2,632	569	1,199	.475	191	244	.783	229	729	958	296	87	73	...	1,329	14.7	4.6	20.4
'75–'76	Boston	78	3,101	611	1,305	.468	257	340	.756	335	911	1,246	325	94	71	...	1,479	16.0	4.2	19.0
'76–'77	Boston	50	1,888	328	756	.434	162	198	.818	147	550	697	248	46	49	...	818	13.9	5.0	16.4
'77–'78	Boston	77	3,215	598	1,220	.490	239	284	.842	248	830	1,078	351	102	67	217	1,435	14.0	4.6	18.6
'78–'79	Boston	68	2,517	488	1,010	.483	151	187	.807	152	500	652	242	76	51	174	1,127	9.6	3.6	16.6
'79–'80	Boston	66	2,159	422	932	.453	95	122	.779	126	408	534	206	69	61	108	940	8.1	3.1	14.2
'80–'81						Did not play—retired														
'81–'82						Did not play—retired														
'82–'83	Milwaukee	40	1,014	136	306	.444	52	63	.825	73	201	274	82	30	15	44	324	6.9	2.1	8.1
Totals		766	29,565	5,744	12,499	.460	2,027	2,590	.783	...	...	10,444	2,910	599	488	543	13,516	13.6	3.8	17.6

Personal fouls/disqualifications: 1973–74, 294/7. 1974–75, 243/7. 1975–76, 314/10. 1976–77, 181/7. 1977–78, 297/5. 1978–79, 263/16. 1979–80, 216/2. 1982–83, 137/4. Totals, 2,920/90.

NBA Playoff Record

Season	Team	G	Min.	FGM	FGA	Pct.	FTM	FTA	Pct.	Reb.	Ast.	PF	Dq.	Pts.	Averages RPG	APG	PPG
'71–'72	Boston	11	441	71	156	.455	28	47	.596	152	33	50	2	170	13.8	3.0	15.5
'72–'73	Boston	13	598	129	273	.473	27	41	.659	216	48	54	2	285	16.6	3.7	21.9

Season	Team	G	Min.	FGM	FGA	Pct.	FTM	FTA	Pct.	Rebounds Off.	Def.	Tot.	Ast.	St.	Blk.	TO	Pts.	Averages RPG	APG	PPG
'73–'74	Boston	18	772	161	370	.435	47	59	.797	60	180	240	66	21	17	...	369	13.3	3.7	20.5
'74–'75	Boston	11	479	101	236	.428	23	26	.885	49	132	181	46	18	6	...	225	16.5	4.2	20.5
'75–'76	Boston	18	798	156	341	.457	66	87	.759	87	209	296	83	22	13	...	378	16.4	4.6	21.0
'76–'77	Boston	9	379	66	148	.446	17	22	.773	29	105	134	36	8	13	...	149	14.9	4.0	16.6
'79–'80	Boston	9	301	49	103	.476	10	11	.909	18	48	66	21	9	7	8	108	7.3	2.3	12.0
Totals		89	3,768	733	1,627	.451	218	293	.744	...	...	1,285	333	78	56	8	1,684	14.4	3.7	18.9

Personal fouls/disqualifications: 1973–74, 85/2. 1974–75, 50/2. 1975–76, 85/4. 1976–77, 37/3. 1979–80, 37/0. Totals, 398/15.

NBA All-Star Game Record

	G	Min.	FGM	FGA	Pct.	FTM	FTA	Pct.	Reb.	Ast.	PF	Dq.	Pts.
Totals	6	154	33	66	.500	10	14	.714	81	12	21	0	76

NBA Coaching Record

Season	Team	W	L	Pct.	Regular Season Finish	Playoffs W	L	Pct.
'78–'79	Boston	27	41	.397	5th/Atlantic Division	—	—	—
'96–'97	Charlotte	54	28	.659	3rd/Central Division	0	3	.000
'97–'98	Charlotte	51	31	.622	3rd/Central Division	4	5	.444
'98–'99	Charlotte	4	11	.267		—	—	—
'00–'01	Golden State	17	65	.207	7th/Pacific Division	—	—	—
'01–'02	Golden State	8	15	.348		—	—	—
Totals (6 years)		161	191	.457	Totals (2 years)	4	8	.333

CBA Coaching Record

Season	Team	W	L	Pct.	Regular Season Finish	Playoffs W	L	Pct.
'84–'85	Bay State	20	28	.417	6th/Atlantic Division	—	—	—

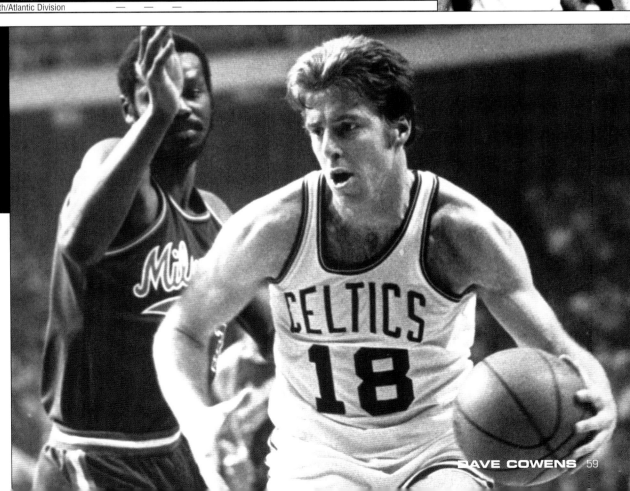

"COWENS WAS THE ONLY GUY I EVER SAW WHO COULD OUTPLAY WILT AND KAREEM."
—BILL WALTON

"They're playing Houston at home. In the first period, Mike Newlin jumps behind Cowens on the high post, Dave turns around, Newlin does a flop and gets the call. So now it's late in the third quarter and Houston is winning the game by roughly a dozen. Same situation, Cowens, high post pass, Newlin draws a foul. So Cowens is incensed.

"Picture Newlin running down the right-hand side of the court. Picture Cowens coming at him from across the court. He arrives and unloads a double forearm shiver. He whacks him, knocks him on his butt and runs over to referee Bill Jones and says, 'Now that's a foul.'"

They don't make them like that any more. As a matter of fact, they only made one. That was Dave. ∎

A Plow Horse
at Churchill Downs

"He's a dinosaur.
He believes in an
honest day's work."

—FORMER NUGGETS
GENERAL MANAGER CARL SHEER

DAN ISSEL WAS A STAR IN THE "OTHER" LEAGUE BEFORE ENTERING THE NBA IN FAR-OFF DENVER. HE WASN'T CENTER-SIZED, OR SLEEK, OR DEFINED. WITH HIS BRIDGE OUT AND A THREE-INCH GAP BETWEEN HIS INCISORS, HE LOOKED MORE LIKE A BOXER THAN A BASKETBALL PLAYER—ONE WHO'D BEEN KO'D IN THE FIRST.

He wasn't quick and he wasn't fast. He was Everyman, grown to 6´9´´ and 240 pounds, a plow horse in a corral with gazelles.

Yet when Issel retired in 1985, he had scored 27,482 points, trailing only Kareem Abdul-Jabbar, Wilt Chamberlain, Julius Erving, and Moses Malone. It's an achievement marked only on a combined NBA/ABA list, and as such is often overlooked. The fifth highest scorer in NBA/ABA basketball history didn't make the list of the NBA's top 50 players.

Not that he was any less successful in the "established" league. In Issel's last ABA season, he averaged 23 points for the Denver Nuggets. In their first season in the NBA, he averaged 22.3.

"As the years went by," says Bill Walton, "he lost something physically, but the skill development was so magnificent, the shooting touch, the positioning, the ability to draw opponents out. . . . He was very much like Jerry Lucas. It was a mental game to him. He could always draw fouls and always get to the line.

"He was cursed in that he never really had the great teammates that he had in the ABA when they were winning the championships."

Issel was a farm boy from Batavia, Illinois, a high school teammate of Kenny Anderson, the future Bengals quarterback. Issel went on to set a University of Kentucky scoring record, averaging 34 points as a senior.

He played on an ABA title–winning Kentucky Colonels team with Artis Gilmore in 1975, even if they weren't all best friends. Coach Hubie Brown says he asked Issel to give up shot attempts for the good of the team, and Issel was so unhappy about it that he asked to be traded after the season. The Colonels sent him to the short-lived Baltimore Claws, who passed him on to the Nuggets three weeks later.

"He didn't enjoy this less-shots routine," says Brown. "He went to Denver, which was perfect for him. He could shoot his ass off and it didn't matter if they won a championship or not."

Who knows, maybe Issel doesn't remember Hubie fondly, either. In any event, Issel's average went back up, from 18 points in his last season in Kentucky to 23 in Denver. And the Nuggets played for the 1976 title, losing in the last ABA Finals to Erving's New York Nets.

The following season, the leagues merged. With 50 wins, the Nuggets showed up everyone by finishing first in the Midwest Division. They may not have been a championship-caliber team, but they were the next best thing. With Issel and David Thompson, they were a hustling, high-scoring, crowd-pleasing team. They might have had a longer run, but coach Larry Brown left and Thompson had substance abuse problems.

By the 1982–83 season, Thompson was gone, too. Denver rebuilt quickly around Issel, Alex English, and Kiki Vandeweghe. The Nuggets averaged 123 points a game, a league best. "My 6´9´´ stiff," coach Doug Moe used to call Issel.

What Issel lacked in grace, he made up for in skill. He was comfortable on the perimeter, where the real centers were loath to venture. If they were slow or late coming out, he shot over them. If they got close, he faked a shot and drove, looking for contact and a trip to the free throw line.

"It's the worst fake in the history of basketball, and it works every time," Issel once told *Sports Illustrated*'s Doug Looney. "I can't believe anyone goes for it."

They went for it and went for it and went for it. In 1982–83, when he was 34 and even slower, Issel averaged 21.6 points and shot 51 percent from the field. The following season, at 35, he was still at 19.8 and 49 percent.

At 36, playing only a little more than 20 minutes a game, he dropped to 12.8, a sign it was time to say good-bye.

Easygoing and pleasant off the floor, Issel was popular in Denver and became a Nuggets announcer. However, after the team posted 20- and 24-win seasons in the early nineties, management asked him to try coaching, and he did.

Not a prototypical center, Dan Issel could take it to the hoop or beat competitors from the perimeter.

- Born: October 25, 1948, in Batavia, Illinois
- College: Kentucky
- 6´9´´/240 pounds
- Named first-team All-American by *The Sporting News* in 1970 and second-team in 1969
- Averaged 25.8 points and 13.0 rebounds per game in college
- Named ABA co-Rookie of the Year in 1971
- Led ABA in scoring in 1970–71 with 29.9 points per game
- Member of one ABA All-Star First Team (1972), four ABA All-Star Second Teams (1971, 1973, 1974, 1976), and ABA All-Rookie Team (1971)
- Named ABA All-Star Game Most Valuable Player in 1972
- Member of Kentucky Colonels ABA championship team in 1975
- Made top-20 list for points in a season six times during his NBA career
- Holds Denver Nuggets NBA career record for rebounds with 6,630 (1976–77 through 1984–85)
- Owns combined ABA/NBA career averages of 22.6 points and 9.1 rebounds per game
- Ranks seventh in combined ABA/NBA scoring with 27,482 points
- Received the NBA's J. Walter Kennedy Citizenship Award in 1985
- Served as head coach of the Denver Nuggets from 1992 to 1995 and 1999 to 2001
- Inducted into the Naismith Memorial Basketball Hall of Fame in 1993

"HE WAS VERY MUCH LIKE JERRY LUCAS. IT WAS A MENTAL GAME TO HIM."

—BILL WALTON

Issel was a superstar at the University of Kentucky prior to his ABA/NBA playing career. He was every bit as fiery when he became a coach (below left) as he was when he played.

Collegiate Record

Season	Team	G	Min.	FGM	FGA	Pct.	FTM	FTA	Pct.	Reb.	Ast.	Pts.	RPG	APG	PPG
'66–'67	Kentucky	20	...	168	332	.506	80	111	.721	.355	...	416	17.8	...	20.8
'67–'68	Kentucky	27	836	171	390	.438	102	154	.662	328	10	444	12.1	0.4	16.4
'68–'69	Kentucky	28	1,063	285	534	.534	176	232	.759	381	49	746	13.6	1.8	26.6
'69–'70	Kentucky	28	1,044	369	667	.553	210	275	.764	369	39	948	13.2	1.4	33.9
Varsity totals		83	2,943	825	1,591	.519	488	661	.738	1,078	98	2,138	13.0	1.2	25.8

ABA Regular-Season Record

Season	Team	G	Min.	FGM (2-Point)	FGA (2-Point)	Pct.	FGM (3-Point)	FGA (3-Point)	Pct.	FTM	FTA	Pct.	Reb.	Ast.	Pts.	RPG	APG	PPG
'70–71	Kentucky	83	3,274	938	1,989	.472	0	5	.000	604	748	.807	1,093	162	*2,480	13.2	2.0	*29.9
'71–72	Kentucky	83	3,570	969	1,990	.487	3	11	.273	591	*753	.785	931	195	*2,538	11.2	2.3	30.6
'72–73	Kentucky	84	*3,531	899	1,742	.516	3	15	.200	485	635	.764	922	220	*2,292	11.0	2.6	27.3
'73–74	Kentucky	83	3,347	826	1,709	.483	3	17	.176	457	581	.787	847	137	2,118	10.2	1.7	25.5
'74–75	Kentucky	83	2,864	614	1,298	.473	0	5	.000	237	321	.738	710	188	1,465	8.6	2.3	17.7
'75–76	Denver	84	2,858	751	1,468	.512	1	4	.250	425	521	.816	923	201	1,930	11.0	2.4	23.0
Totals		500	19,444	4,997	10,196	.490	10	57	.175	2,799	3,559	.786	5,426	1,103	12,823	10.9	2.2	25.6

ABA Playoff Record

Season	Team	G	Min.	FGM (2-Point)	FGA (2-Point)	Pct.	FGM (3-Point)	FGA (3-Point)	Pct.	FTM	FTA	Pct.	Reb.	Ast.	Pts.	RPG	APG	PPG
'70–71	Kentucky	19	670	207	408	.507	0	0	...	123	141	.872	221	28	536	11.6	1.5	28.2
'71–72	Kentucky	6	269	47	113	.416	0	1	.000	38	50	.760	54	5	132	9.0	0.8	22.0
'72–73	Kentucky	19	821	197	392	.503	1	6	.167	124	156	.795	225	28	521	11.8	1.5	27.4
'73–74	Kentucky	8	311	60	135	.444	0	0	...	28	33	.848	87	14	148	10.9	1.8	18.5
'74–75	Kentucky	15	578	122	261	.467	0	0	...	60	74	.811	119	29	304	7.9	1.9	20.3
'75–76	Denver	13	470	111	226	.491	0	1	.000	44	56	.786	156	32	266	12.0	2.5	20.5
Totals		80	3,119	744	1,535	.485	1	8	.125	417	510	.818	862	136	1,907	10.8	1.7	23.8

ABA All-Star Game Record

	G	Min	FGM (2-Point)	FGA (2-Point)	Pct.	FGM (3-Point)	FGA (3-Point)	Pct.	FTM	FTA	Pct.	Reb.	Ast.	Pts.
Totals	6	163	42	79	.532	0	0	...	19	26	.731	47	16	103

NBA Regular-Season Record

Season	Team	G	Min.	FGM	FGA	Pct.	FTM	FTA	Pct.	Off.	Def.	Tot.	Ast.	St.	Blk.	TO	Pts.	RPG	APG	PPG
'76–77	Denver	79	2,507	660	1,282	.515	445	558	.798	211	485	696	177	91	29	...	1,765	8.8	2.2	22.3
'77–78	Denver	82	2,851	659	1,287	.512	428	547	.782	253	577	830	304	100	41	259	1,746	10.1	3.7	21.3
'78–79	Denver	81	2,742	532	1,030	.517	316	419	.754	240	498	738	255	61	46	171	1,380	9.1	3.1	17.0
'79–80	Denver	82	2,938	715	1,416	.505	517	667	.775	236	483	719	198	88	54	163	1,951	8.8	2.4	23.8
'80–81	Denver	80	2,641	614	1,220	.503	519	685	.759	229	447	676	158	83	53	130	1,749	8.5	2.0	21.9
'81–82	Denver	81	2,472	651	1,236	.527	546	655	.834	174	434	608	179	67	55	169	1,852	7.5	2.2	22.9
'82–83	Denver	80	2,431	661	1,296	.510	400	479	.835	151	445	596	223	83	43	174	1,726	7.5	2.8	21.6
'83–84	Denver	76	2,076	569	1,153	.494	364	428	.850	112	401	513	173	60	44	122	1,506	6.8	2.3	19.8
'84–85	Denver	77	1,684	363	791	.459	257	319	.806	80	251	331	137	65	31	93	984	4.3	1.8	12.8
Totals		718	22,342	5,424	10,711	.506	3,792	4,756	.797	1,686	4,021	5,707	1,804	698	396	1,281	14,659	7.9	2.5	20.4

NBA Playoff Record

Season	Team	G	Min.	FGM	FGA	Pct.	FTM	FTA	Pct.	Off.	Def.	Tot.	Ast.	St.	Blk.	TO	Pts.	RPG	APG	PPG
'76–77	Denver	6	222	49	96	.510	34	45	.756	18	40	58	17	5	4	...	132	9.7	2.8	22.0
'77–78	Denver	13	460	103	212	.486	56	65	.862	41	93	134	53	7	3	39	262	10.3	4.1	20.2
'78–79	Denver	3	109	24	45	.533	25	31	.806	7	21	28	10	0	0	9	73	9.3	3.3	24.3
'81–82	Denver	3	103	32	60	.533	12	12	1.000	8	13	21	5	3	1	7	76	7.0	1.7	25.3
'82–83	Denver	8	227	69	136	.507	25	29	.862	13	45	58	25	9	5	10	163	7.3	3.1	20.4
'83–84	Denver	5	153	52	102	.510	32	39	.821	10	30	40	8	6	6	15	137	8.0	1.6	27.4
'84–85	Denver	15	325	73	159	.459	39	48	.813	14	40	54	27	12	5	13	186	3.6	1.8	12.4
Totals		53	1,599	402	810	.496	223	269	.829	111	282	393	145	42	24	93	1,029	7.4	2.7	19.4

NBA All-Star Game Record

	G	Min.	FGM	FGA	Pct.	FTM	FTA	Pct.	Off.	Def.	Tot.	Ast.	PF	Dq.	St.	Blk.	TO	Pts.
	1	10	0	3	.000	0	0	...	1	0	1	0	0	0	0	0	...	0

Combined ABA and NBA Regular-Season Records

	G	Min.	FGM	FGA	Pct.	FTM	FTA	Pct.	Off.	Def.	Tot.	Ast.	St.	Blk.	TO	Pts.	RPG	APG	PPG
	1,218	41,786	10,431	20,964	.498	6,591	8,315	.793	...	...	11,133	2,907	...	...	...	27,482	9.1	2.4	22.6

NBA Coaching Record

Season	Team	W (Regular Season)	L	Pct.	Finish	W (Playoffs)	L	Pct.
'92–'93	Denver	36	46	.439	4th/Midwest Division	—	—	—
'93–'94	Denver	42	40	.512	4th/Midwest Division	6	6	.500
'94–'95	Denver	18	16	.529		—	—	—
'99–'00	Denver	35	47	.427	5th/Midwest Division	—	—	—
'00–'01	Denver	40	42	.488	6th/Midwest Division	—	—	—
'01–'02	Denver	9	17	.346		—	—	—
Totals (6 years)		180	208	.464	Totals (1 year)	6	6	.500

He was just as popular with the players. In their second season together, 1993–94, the Nuggets made the playoffs with such young stars as Dikembe Mutombo and LaPhonso Ellis. In the first round they slew the Sonics, who'd posted the best regular-season record that year, and took the Jazz to seven games in the second round.

The following season, however, Issel resigned abruptly, persuaded that this was no job for an easygoing man. Mutombo would always attribute the subsequent immediate fall of the franchise to Dan's departure. In 1998 he returned to his beloved Nuggets, working first in the front office and then again as head coach in 1999.

Coaching didn't get Issel to the Hall of Fame, but his playing career did.

"He's not a pro-type center," said Pat Williams when he was the 76ers GM, "not defensive-minded, not an intimidator, and you can't win a title with him. But when his career is over, he'll be an immortal." ∎

"HE WAS ONE OF THE TOUGHEST CENTERS TO PLAY THE GAME AND ALSO ONE OF THE BEST CENTERS. THE FAKE AND THE JUMPER, THOSE WERE HIS TRADE-MARKS."
—ALEX ENGLISH

Gentle Giant

In a league of giraffes, Gilmore was more like a Tyrannosaurus Rex.

25 ARTIS GILMORE

MAYBE IT WAS JUST THE WAY EVERYONE SAID IT WAS: HE WAS TOO NICE, TOO SENSITIVE, OR TOO LIMITED. MAYBE EVERYONE JUST EXPECTED TOO MUCH.

Artis Gilmore looked like Kareem Abdul-Jabbar, grown up. Kareem was lithe, but Artis was 7´2´´, 265, with strength that was the stuff of legend. Wes Unseld said he was the strongest player since Wilt Chamberlain.

In a league of giraffes, Gilmore was more like a Tyrannosaurus Rex. He had a 32-inch waist, 27-inch thighs, and an Afro that must have gone four inches, easy. *Sports Illustrated*'s Rick Telander once wrote that Artis, in the platform shoes that guys wore in the seventies, might have measured 7´9´´ from the ground to the top of his haircut.

If it had been a pose-down, as in bodybuilding, Gilmore would have gone home with the title annually.

In 1970 Gilmore's Jacksonville Dolphins reached the NCAA finals, but he wound up playing Goliath to Sidney Wicks' David. The 6´8´´ Bruin rose up to block five of his shots as UCLA won.

Gilmore put up dominating numbers in the ABA, but his Kentucky Colonels won only one title in five seasons. Dave Vance, the GM, once called him "maybe too nice a guy for his own good."

"Now, for me, he was incredible," says Hubie Brown, the Colonels coach when they won the title. "You can go back and check the statistics. He was amazing in the finals. He was averaging 27, 28 rebounds a game. We're talking about 1975. That was against Indiana— George McGinnis, Dan Roundfield, Len Elmore, Darnell Hillman. We're talking about some good guys. The backcourt was Billy Knight and Don Buse, so their guards were 6´7´´, 6´5´´.

"I had been on the Milwaukee Bucks [with Abdul-Jabbar] in '73 and '74 and I had never seen anything like that. The guy [Gilmore] absolutely put it together for one full year. But the next year we didn't have [Dan] Issel and we lost in the playoffs. And then came the merger. . . .

"Yes, he was methodical, but you could hit him with an axe and he'd still take you to the rim. He was as strong as anybody. You talk to the guys who played in the seventies and eighties: next to

Wilt, he was the strongest guy around. And fortunately, he was a good person or he could have hurt guys. Very coachable. I don't think you'll find anybody who'd say anything bad about him."

For all his power and touch, Gilmore was methodical and had bad hands. He used so much stickum that it got on the ball, and teammates complained when it stuck to their hands.

Reggie Theus, a flashy young point guard from UNLV, showed up with that new sensation, the no-look pass, and bounced a couple off Artis' head.

"He would get mad at me and start yelling at me on the court," says Theus, laughing. "He would corner me in the locker room and threaten me with bodily harm. He used to say, 'Reggie, you can't throw the ball when I'm not looking at it. How am I supposed to know you're going to pass the ball?'"

Gilmore struggled with the big city, too. He was from Chipley, Florida, a village of 3,000, one of ten children of an itinerant

- Born: September 21, 1949, in Chipley, Florida
- College: Jacksonville
- 7′2″/265 pounds
- Named first-team All-American by *The Sporting News* in 1971 and second-team in 1970
- Led NCAA Division I with 22.2 rebounds per game in 1970 and 23.2 rebounds per game in 1971
- Holds NCAA career record for rebounds per game with 22.7
- Named ABA Rookie of the Year and Most Valuable Player in 1972
- Member of five ABA All-Star First Teams (1972, 1973, 1974, 1975, 1976), four ABA All-Defensive Teams (1973, 1974, 1975, 1976), one NBA All-Defensive Second Team (1978), and ABA All-Rookie Team (1972)
- Holds ABA single-season record for blocked shots with 422 (1972)
- Holds ABA single-game record for rebounds with 40 (February 3, 1974, vs. New York)
- Voted ABA All-Star Game Most Valuable Player in 1974
- Member of Kentucky Colonels ABA championship team in 1975
- Selected as Most Valuable Player of the ABA playoffs in 1975
- Holds NBA career record for highest field-goal percentage at 59.9
- Holds Chicago Bulls career record for blocked shots with 1,017 (1976–77 through 1981–82 and 1987–88)
- Posted combined ABA/NBA career averages of 18.8 points and 12.3 rebounds per game

"ARTIS HAD SUCH GREAT STRENGTH, HE WOULD FLATTEN THE SPALDING ON YOU."
—BOB MCADOO

Gilmore brought his high-flying game to Chicago, but he wasn't able to turn the lowly Bulls into consistent winners.

fisherman who didn't work, meaning sometimes they didn't eat. Even when Artis began to grow and a world he'd only seen in books began to open up, he hated the thought of leaving Chipley.

After Julius Erving, he was considered the plum of the ABA. When he joined the NBA's Chicago Bulls in 1976, he was touted as their long-sought savior. That illusion died his first month in town, when they started 2–14.

Chicago finished 1976–77 at 44–38, an improvement of 20 wins over the season before, but the operation was strictly Keystone Kops. In Gilmore's six seasons in Chicago, he played for five coaches.

Artis would become a six-time All-Star, averaging 17 points and 10 rebounds in a 12-year NBA career that didn't begin until he was 27. He had nothing against the media, but he was shy, soft-spoken, and bewildered by the expectations people had of him. He'd as soon have been left alone. He hated going before cameras.

Artis was happiest away from basketball, in situations where he was treated like anyone else. He was a scuba enthusiast. "The fish don't see him as anything special," said his wife, Enola, "just part of the landscape, I guess."

Collegiate Record

Season	Team	G	Min.	FGM	FGA	Pct.	FTM	FTA	Pct.	Reb.	Ast.	Pts.	RPG	APG	PPG
'67-'68	Gardner-Webb J.C.	31	...	296	...	...	121	...	...	...	...	713	...	...	23.0
'68-'69	Gardner-Webb J.C.	36	...	326	...	...	140	...	...	...	...	792	...	...	22.0
'69-'70	Jacksonville	28	...	307	529	.580	128	202	.634	621	51	742	22.2	1.8	26.5
'70-'71	Jacksonville	26	...	229	405	.565	112	188	.596	603	42	570	23.2	1.6	21.9
Junior college totals		67	...	622	...	...	261	...	...	...	...	1,505	...	...	22.5
4-year college totals		54	...	536	934	.574	240	390	.615	1,224	93	1,312	22.7	1.7	24.3

ABA Regular-Season Record

Season	Team	G	Min.	FGM	FGA (2-Point)	Pct.	FGM	FGA (3-Point)	Pct.	FTM	FTA	Pct.	Reb.	Ast.	Pts.	RPG	APG	PPG
'71-'72	Kentucky	84	*3,666	806	1,348	*.598	0	0	...	391	605	.646	*1,491	230	2,003	*17.8	2.7	23.8
'72-'73	Kentucky	84	3,502	686	1,226	*.560	1	2	.500	368	572	.643	*1,476	295	1,743	*17.6	3.5	20.8
'73-'74	Kentucky	84	3,502	621	1,257	.494	0	3	.000	326	489	.667	*1,538	329	1,568	*18.3	3.9	18.7
'74-'75	Kentucky	84	*3,493	783	1,349	.580	1	2	.500	412	592	.696	*1,361	208	1,981	16.2	2.5	23.6
'75-'76	Kentucky	84	3,286	773	1,401	.552	0	0	...	521	*764	.682	*1,303	211	2,067	*15.5	2.5	24.6
Totals		420	17,449	3,669	6,581	.558	2	7	.286	2,018	3,022	.668	7,169	1,273	9,362	17.1	3.0	22.3

ABA Playoff Record

Season	Team	G	Min.	FGM	FGA (2-Point)	Pct.	FGM	FGA (3-Point)	Pct.	FTM	FTA	Pct.	Reb.	Ast.	Pts.	RPG	APG	PPG
'71-'72	Kentucky	6	285	52	90	.578	0	1	.000	27	38	.711	106	25	131	17.7	4.2	21.8
'72-'73	Kentucky	19	780	142	261	.544	0	0	...	77	123	.626	260	75	361	13.7	3.9	19.0
'73-'74	Kentucky	8	344	71	127	.559	0	0	...	38	66	.576	149	28	180	18.6	3.5	22.5
'74-'75	Kentucky	15	679	132	245	.539	0	0	...	98	127	.772	264	38	362	17.6	2.5	24.1
'75-'76	Kentucky	10	390	93	153	.608	0	0	...	56	74	.757	152	19	242	15.2	1.9	24.2
Totals		58	2,478	490	876	.559	0	1	.000	296	428	.692	931	185	1276	16.1	3.2	22.0

ABA All-Star Game Record

	G	Min	FGM	FGA (2-Point)	Pct.	FGM	FGA (3-Point)	Pct.	FTM	FTA	Pct.	Reb.	Ast.	Pts.
Totals	5	140	24	40	.600	0	0	...	19	34	.559	59	6	67

NBA Regular-Season Record

Season	Team	G	Min.	FGM	FGA	Pct.	FTM	FTA	Pct.	Off.	Def.	Tot.	Ast.	St.	Blk.	TO	Pts.	RPG	APG	PPG
'76-'77	Chicago	82	2,877	570	1,091	.522	387	586	.660	313	757	1,070	199	44	203	...	1,527	13.0	2.4	18.6
'77-'78	Chicago	82	3,067	704	1,260	.559	471	*669	.704	318	753	1,071	263	42	181	*366	1,879	13.1	3.2	22.9
'78-'79	Chicago	82	3,265	753	1,310	.575	434	587	.739	293	750	1,043	274	50	156	310	1,940	12.7	3.63	23.7
'79-'80	Chicago	48	1,568	305	513	.595	245	344	.712	108	324	432	133	29	59	133	855	9.0	2.8	17.8
'80-'81	Chicago	82	2,832	547	816	*.670	375	532	.705	220	608	828	172	47	198	236	1,469	10.1	2.1	17.9
'81-'82	Chicago	82	2,796	546	837	*.652	424	552	.768	224	611	835	136	49	220	227	1,517	10.2	1.7	18.5
'82-'83	San Ant.	82	2,797	556	888	*.626	367	496	.740	299	685	984	126	40	192	254	1,479	12.0	1.5	18.0
'83-'84	San Ant.	64	2,034	351	556	*.631	280	390	.718	213	449	662	70	36	132	149	982	10.3	1.1	15.3
'84-'85	San Ant.	81	2,756	532	854	.623	484	646	.749	231	615	846	131	40	173	241	1,548	10.4	1.6	19.1
'85-'86	San Ant.	71	2,395	423	684	.618	338	482	.701	166	434	600	102	39	108	186	1184	8.5	1.4	16.7
'86-'87	San Ant.	82	2,405	346	580	.597	242	356	.680	185	394	579	150	39	95	178	934	7.1	1.8	11.4
'87-'88	Chi.-Bos.	71	893	99	181	.547	67	128	.523	69	142	211	21	15	30	67	265	3.0	0.3	3.7
Totals		909	29,685	5,732	9,570	.599	4,114	5,768	.713	2,639	6,522	9,161	1,777	470	1,747	2,347	15,579	10.1	2.0	17.1

NBA Playoff Record

Season	Team	G	Min.	FGM	FGA	Pct.	FTM	FTA	Pct.	Off.	Def.	Tot.	Ast.	St.	Blk.	TO	Pts.	RPG	APG	PPG
'76-'77	Chicago	3	126	19	40	.475	18	23	.783	15	24	39	6	3	8	...	56	13.0	2.0	18.7
'80-'81	Chicago	6	247	35	59	.593	38	55	.691	24	43	67	12	6	17	17	108	11.2	2.0	18.0
'82-'83	San Antonio	11	401	76	132	.576	32	46	.696	37	105	142	18	9	34	27	184	12.9	1.6	16.7
'84-'85	San Antonio	5	185	29	52	.558	31	45	.689	10	40	50	7	2	7	23	89	10.0	1.4	17.8
'85-'86	San Antonio	3	104	16	24	.667	8	14	.571	7	11	18	3	7	1	10	40	6.0	1.0	13.3
'87-'88	Boston	14	86	4	8	.500	7	14	.500	4	16	20	1	0	4	4	15	1.4	0.1	1.1
Totals		42	1,152	179	315	.568	134	197	.680	97	239	336	47	27	71	81	492	8.0	1.1	11.7

NBA All-Star Game Record

	G	Min.	FGM	FGA	Pct.	FTM	FTA	Pct.	Off.	Def.	Tot.	Ast.	PF	Dq.	St.	Blk.	TO	Pts.
Totals	6	95	18	29	.621	15	19	.789	5	14	19	8	18	0	4	4	5	51

Combined ABA and NBA Regular-Season Records

G	Min.	FGM	FGA	Pct.	FTM	FTA	Pct.	Off.	Def.	Tot.	Ast.	St.	Blk.	TO	Pts.	RPG	APG	PPG
1,329	33,356	9,403	16,158	.582	6,132	8,790	.698	...	...	16,330	3,050	...	...	...	24,041	12.3	2.3	18.1

Italian League Record

Season	Team	G	Min.	FGM	FGA	Pct.	FTM	FTA	Pct.	Reb.	Ast.	Pts.	RPG	APG	PPG
'85-'89	Bologna Arimo	35	1,101	166	270	.615	97	147	.660	386	21	429	11.0	0.6	12.3

"YES, HE WAS METHODICAL, BUT YOU COULD HIT HIM WITH AN AXE AND HE'D STILL TAKE YOU TO THE RIM. HE WAS AS STRONG AS ANYBODY."

—HUBIE BROWN

After six seasons in Chicago, in which the Bulls averaged 35 wins, he was traded to San Antonio, a smaller city with a better team, briefly. The Spurs in 1982–83 won 53 games, finished first in the Midwest Division, and took the Lakers to six games in the Western Finals.

But Artis was 34 and slowing down. With George Gervin slipping fast, the Spurs played the rest of the decade under .500. In 1987 Gilmore was traded back to the Bulls (for a No. 2 draft pick), waived, then caught on as a Celtics backup for the rest of the season.

In 17 seasons in two leagues, he scored 24,941 points, 17th best. Had he entered the NBA younger, it might have been different. Had he been different, it might have been different.

As it was, he was unforgettable, and as a person, thank heaven, there was no such thing as being "too nice."

"You're talking about one of the all-time nice guys who ever lived," says Hubie Brown. "He was the best, and he was just as nice to the equipment man and the trainer. Never late for anything. He was a different kind of guy." ■

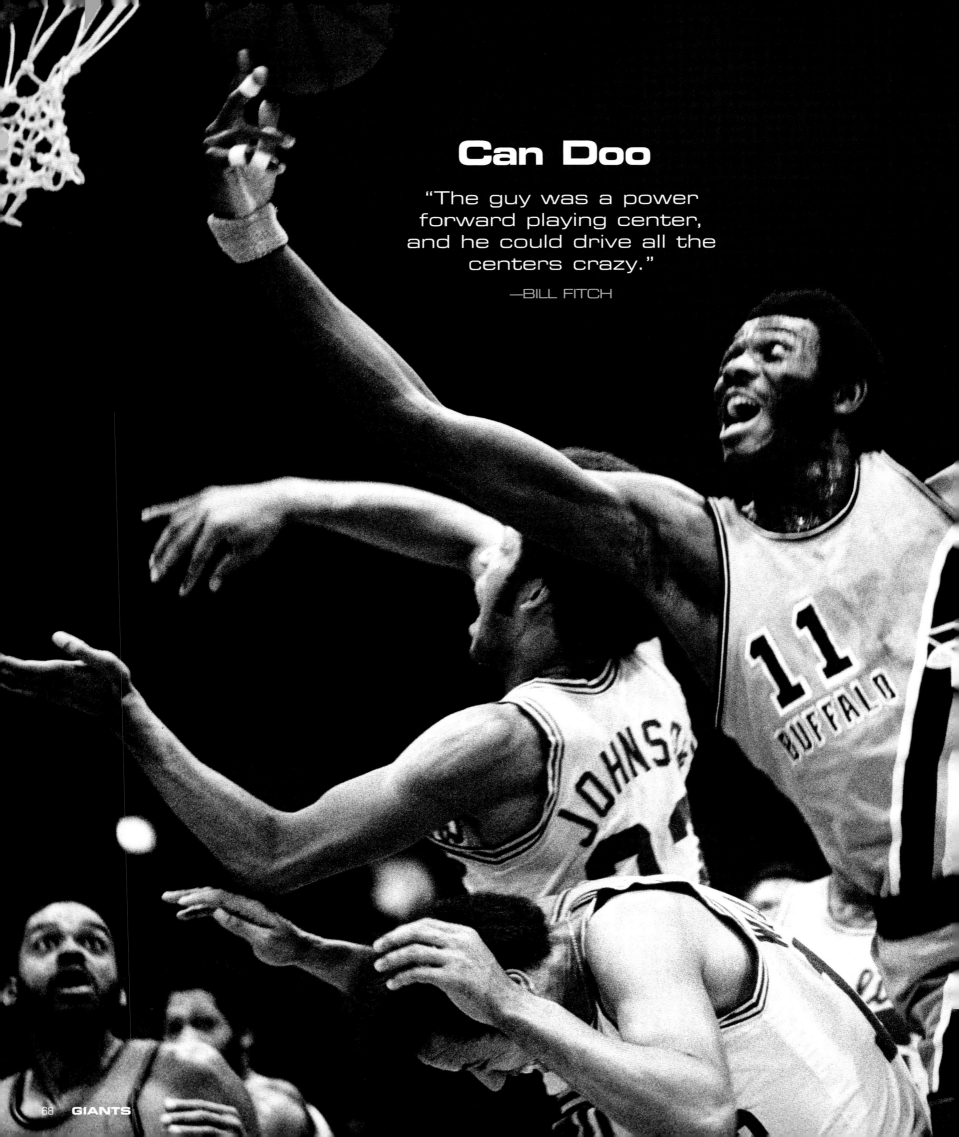

Can Doo

"The guy was a power forward playing center, and he could drive all the centers crazy."

—BILL FITCH

Bob McAdoo was a prolific scorer who averaged more than 30 points per game for three straight years in Buffalo.

23 BOB McADOO

HE HAD LIDDED EYES, A SLEEPY EXPRESSION, AND A JUMP SHOT TO DIE FOR, OR FROM. HIS WILLOWY 6'9" BODY CARRIED LITTLE MORE THAN 220 POUNDS. HIS FIRST COACH, JACK RAMSAY, STARTED HIM AT SMALL FORWARD. HE WAS BOB MCADOO— "DOO" TO FRIENDS—THE FASTEST GUN THE CENTER POSITION EVER SAW, AND ONE OF THE LEAST APPRECIATED.

He had his best seasons out of sight in little Buffalo. He was hyped as a savior for woebegone Knicks and Celtics teams, and when he couldn't strap their franchises to his slender back, he was forwarded to the Pistons and Nets, where his career rolled and tumbled into disrepute. His rep became another fancy gunner, just interested in his points, played when he felt like it. Or as Leon the Barber, the famous Detroit heckler, used to chant: "McAdoo, McAdon't, McAwill, McAwon't."

Yet Bob averaged 22.1 points over his career and shot over 50 percent, remarkable considering where he was shooting from. In his second, third, and fourth seasons, 1973–74 through 1975–76, he averaged 32 points and led the NBA in scoring three times. He was MVP in 1975 after finishing first in scoring, fifth in shooting, fourth in rebounds, and sixth in shot-blocks. He complained ever after that he should have won the year before, too (he finished second behind someone named Kareem Abdul-Jabbar), when he went 1-1-3-3 in the four categories.

"McAdoo, I think, was the best overall shooter among big men that the game has known," says Ramsay, who coached him in Buffalo from 1972 to 1976. "He was just a great scorer and a maker of clutch shots, among the best the game has ever seen.

"I have a lot of regard for Bob McAdoo. He made so many big field goals for us that are almost uncountable, a shot-blocker, a volume rebounder, and a fierce competitor."

"McAdoo was the best shooter that ever played for a big guy, I think," says Bill Walton. "Patrick Ewing has more range than McAdoo had—only because they didn't have a three-point line. If they'd have had a three-point line, McAdoo would have backed up farther. He only backed up as far as he had to because the big guys wouldn't go out and chase him.

"McAdoo's approach to the game was to outscore you. He didn't have the versatility of a Dave Cowens, of an Abdul-Jabbar, of a Wilt. He didn't have the physical strength to bang and knock people around."

During the 1975–76 season, McAdoo got into a dispute with the tempestuous Buffalo owner, Paul Snyder, as did Jack Ramsay, who resigned. The next season, McAdoo was traded to the Knicks for cash and journeyman John Gianelli. Bob averaged 26 points and 13 rebounds in his only full Knicks season, got them into the playoffs (their lone appearance in a five-year span), and in 1979 was sent to Boston, where they would really hate him, for three No. 1 picks.

"Nobody deserved to be thrust into a situation like that," says the *Boston Globe*'s Bob Ryan of McAdoo's season as a Celtic. "He arrives unwanted by everybody. The owner [John Y. Brown, who was about to swap franchises with San Diego] shoved him down everyone's throat.

"Red [Auerbach] didn't want him. Dave Cowens was the coach, and he didn't want him. The fans, of course, detested him because he was an enemy and he had an image of being a player 'we don't like.' No one was giving him the benefit of the doubt in any way."

No one gave him any help, either. Cowens had big plans for the three draft picks John Y. gave to the Knicks. He all but surrendered when McAdoo arrived. The new Celtic first reported to the team in San Antonio, but Cowens—rather than fitting McAdoo in at practice—went scouting. Returning for the next game, without announcement, Cowens, still the team's best player, benched himself and started McAdoo.

Catching their drift, McAdoo turned as sullen as everyone else. After the season, he was sent to Detroit for M. L. Carr, a career reserve, and two No. 1 picks. In 1981 the Pistons waived him. He signed with the Nets, played a few games, and was

- Born: September 25, 1951, in Greensboro, North Carolina
- College: North Carolina
- 6´9´´/225 pounds
- Named first-team All-American by *The Sporting News* in 1972
- Averaged 19.5 points and 10.1 rebounds per game in college
- Was the second overall pick in the 1972 NBA Draft, going to the Buffalo Braves after his junior season
- Named NBA Rookie of the Year in 1973
- Voted NBA Most Valuable Player in 1975
- Led NBA in scoring for three consecutive seasons, averaging 30.6, 34.5, and 31.1 points per game from 1973–74 through 1975–76
- Averaged 22.1 points and 9.4 rebounds per game during his NBA career
- Holds NBA records for points in a two-game playoff series with 68 (New York vs. Cleveland in 1978) and defensive rebounds in a three-game playoff series with 43 (Buffalo vs. Philadelphia in 1978)
- Member of All-NBA First Team in 1975, All-NBA Second Team in 1974, and NBA All-Rookie Team in 1973
- Member of Los Angeles Lakers NBA championship teams in 1982 and 1985
- Holds Braves/Clippers franchise record with 4,229 rebounds (1972–73 through 1976–77)
- Inducted into the Naismith Memorial Basketball Hall of Fame in 2000

> "HE WAS THE MOST COMPETITIVE GUY I'D EVER MET. HE ALWAYS WANTED TO BEAT YOU AND WHEN HE DID, HE WOULDN'T SHUT UP ABOUT IT. . . ."
>
> —MAGIC JOHNSON

Unlike a lot of the great tall players, "Doo" was a lights-out shooter from long range.

traded—the price now down to a single No. 2 pick—to the Lakers, who didn't hire a brass band to meet him, either.

"People said McAdoo was a head case," Magic Johnson wrote in his book *My Life*. "They said he was lazy and a loser. But [Pat] Riley insisted on giving him a chance and Kareem supported the idea.

"I was one of the skeptics but Riley and Kareem were right. I don't know what had happened with McAdoo on some of the other teams but when he came to us, he turned out the opposite of what everybody had said. He was a great character, a good player, and a tremendous amount of fun.

"He was the most competitive guy I'd ever met. He always wanted to beat you and when he did, he wouldn't shut up about it. . . . He loved to crow about how good he was. But his style of bragging was funny and good-natured rather than annoying. . . .

"McAdoo was always looking for respect. There was one year back in the mid-seventies when Kareem won the MVP although McAdoo had scored more points. McAdoo just wouldn't let it go. 'Kareem,' he would say, 'you still keeping my MVP trophy in your house?'

"It got so bad that we had a little saying. 'If you do it, Doo do it. But Doo do it better.'"

Collegiate Record

Season	Team	G	Min.	FGM	FGA	Pct.	FTM	FTA	Pct.	Reb.	Ast.	Pts.	RPG	APG	PPG
'69–70	Vincennes	32	...	258	...	...	101	134	.754	320	...	617	10.0	...	19.3
'70–71	Vincennes	27	...	273	...	...	129	164	.787	297	...	675	11.0	...	25.0
'71–72	North Carolina	31	...	243	471	.516	118	167	.707	312	72	604	10.1	2.3	19.5
Junior college totals		59	...	531	...	...	230	298	.772	617	...	1,292	10.5	...	21.9
4-year college totals		31	...	243	471	.516	118	167	.707	312	72	604	10.1	2.3	19.5

NBA Regular-Season Record

Season	Team	G	Min.	FGM	FGA	Pct.	FTM	FTA	Pct.	Reb.	Ast.	PF	Dq.	Pts.	RPG	APG	PPG
'72–73	Buffalo	80	2,562	585	1,293	.452	271	350	.774	728	139	256	6	1,441	9.1	1.7	18.0

Season	Team	G	Min.	FGM	FGA	Pct.	FTM	FTA	Pct.	Off.	Def.	Tot.	Ast.	St.	Blk.	TO	Pts.	RPG	APG	PPG
'73–74	Buffalo	74	3,185	901	1,647	*.547	459	579	.793	281	836	1,117	170	88	246	...	*2,261	15.1	2.3	*30.6
'74–75	Buffalo	82	*3,539	*1,095	2,138	.5132	641	*796	.805	307	848	*1,155	179	92	174	...	*2,831	14.1	2.2	*34.5
'75–76	Buffalo	78	3,328	*934	*1,918	.487	559	*734	.762	241	724	965	315	93	160	...	*2,427	12.4	4.0	*31.1
'76–77	Buff-Knicks	72	2,798	740	1,445	.512	381	516	.738	199	727	926	205	77	99	...	1,861	12.9	2.8	25.8
'77–78	New York	79	3,182	814	1,564	.520	469	645	.727	236	774	1,010	298	105	126	346	2,097	12.8	3.8	26.5
'78–79	N.Y.-Boston	60	2,231	596	1,127	.529	295	450	.656	130	390	520	168	74	67	217	1,487	8.7	2.8	24.8
'79–80	Detroit	58	2,097	492	1,025	.480	235	322	.730	100	367	467	200	73	65	238	1,222	8.1	3.4	21.1
'80–81	Detroit-N.J.	16	321	68	157	.433	29	41	.707	17	50	67	30	17	13	32	165	4.2	1.9	10.3
'81–82	Los Angeles	41	746	151	330	.458	90	126	.714	45	114	159	32	22	36	51	392	3.9	0.8	9.6
'82–83	Los Angeles	47	1,019	292	562	.520	119	163	.730	76	171	247	39	40	40	68	703	5.3	0.8	15.0
'83–84	Los Angeles	70	1,456	352	748	.471	212	264	.803	82	207	289	74	42	50	127	916	4.1	1.1	13.1
'84–85	L.A. Lakers	66	1,254	284	546	.520	122	162	.753	79	216	295	67	18	53	95	690	4.5	1.0	10.5
'85–86	Philadelphia	29	609	116	251	.462	62	81	.765	25	78	103	35	10	18	49	294	3.6	1.2	10.1
Totals		852	28,327	7,420	14,751	.503	3,944	5,229	.754	...	...	8,048	1,951	751	1,147	1,223	18,787	9.4	2.3	22.1

Personal fouls/disqualifications: 1973–74, 252/3. 1974–75, 278/3. 1975–76, 298/5. 1976–77, 262/3. 1977–78, 297/6. 1978–79, 189/3. 1979–80, 178/3. 1980–81, 38/0. 1981–82, 109/1. 1982–83, 153/2. 1983–84, 182/0. 1984–85, 170/0. 1985–86, 64/0. Totals, 2,726/35.

NBA Playoff Record

Season	Team	G	Min.	FGM	FGA	Pct.	FTM	FTA	Pct.	Off.	Def.	Tot.	Ast.	St.	Blk.	TO	Pts.	RPG	APG	PPG
'73–74	Buffalo	6	271	76	159	.478	38	47	.809	14	68	82	9	6	13	...	190	13.7	1.5	31.7
'74–75	Buffalo	7	327	104	216	.481	54	73	.740	25	69	94	10	6	19	...	262	13.4	1.4	37.4
'75–76	Buffalo	9	406	97	215	.451	58	82	.707	31	97	128	29	7	18	...	252	14.2	3.2	28.0
'77–78	New York	6	238	61	126	.484	21	35	.600	11	47	58	23	7	12	23	143	9.7	3.8	23.8
'81–82	Los Angeles	14	388	101	179	.564	32	47	.681	21	74	95	22	10	21	35	234	6.8	1.6	16.7
'82–83	Los Angeles	8	166	37	84	.440	11	14	.786	15	31	46	5	11	10	14	87	5.8	0.6	10.9
'83–84	Los Angeles	20	447	111	215	.516	57	81	.704	30	78	108	12	12	27	39	279	5.4	0.6	14.0
'84–85	L.A. Lakers	19	398	91	193	.472	35	47	.745	25	61	86	15	9	26	32	217	4.5	0.8	11.4
'85–86	Philadelphia	5	73	20	36	.556	14	16	.875	8	6	14	2	4	5	2	54	2.8	0.4	10.8
Totals		94	2,714	698	1,423	.491	320	442	.724	180	531	711	127	72	151	145	1,718	7.6	1.4	18.3

NBA All-Star Game Record

	G	Min.	FGM	FGA	Pct.	FTM	FTA	Pct.	Off.	Def.	Tot.	Ast.	PF	Dq.	St.	Blk.	TO	Pts.
Totals	5	126	37	64	.578	14	19	.737	13	17	30	6	18	0	4	2	3	88

Italian League Record

Season	Team	G	Min.	FGM	FGA	Pct.	FTM	FTA	Pct.	Reb.	Ast.	Pts.	RPG	APG	PPG
'86–87	Tracer Milan	38	1,320	387	730	.530	205	268	.765	388	54	991	10.2	1.4	26.1
'87–88	Tracer Milan	39	1,398	422	730	.578	236	293	.805	333	71	1,097	8.5	1.8	28.1
'88–89	Philips Milano	38	1,195	334	610	.548	161	200	.805	299	60	861	7.9	1.6	22.7
'89–90	Philips Milano	33	1,014	329	587	.560	178	215	.828	248	41	851	7.5	1.2	25.8
'90–91	Filanto	23	858	278	490	.567	179	225	.796	219	28	759	9.5	1.2	33.0
'91–92	Filanto Forli	20	700	199	399	.499	129	159	.811	188	20	538	9.4	1.0	26.9
'92–93	Teamsystem Fabriano	2	58	14	27	.519	12	17	.706	13	2	44	6.5	1.0	22.0
Totals		193	6,543	1,963	3,573	.549	1,100	1,377	.799	1,688	276	5,141	8.7	1.4	26.6

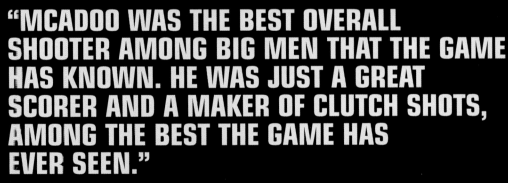

"MCADOO WAS THE BEST OVERALL SHOOTER AMONG BIG MEN THAT THE GAME HAS KNOWN. HE WAS JUST A GREAT SCORER AND A MAKER OF CLUTCH SHOTS, AMONG THE BEST THE GAME HAS EVER SEEN."

—JACK RAMSAY

The merry-go-round stopped. McAdoo played four seasons with the Lakers, accepting a role, coming off the bench to average 12 points in 20 minutes a game, picking up two championship rings. In 1985, when he was 34, the Lakers let him go to the 76ers as a free agent. He played a few games there, then seven seasons in Italy, showing them real American jump shooting. U.S. players were always coming back from Europe, marveling about him. In 1993, at 42, he played his last two games in Italy—scoring 44 points, shooting 52 percent—and retired.

McAdoo was still looking for respect. In a celebrated omission, he was left off the NBA's top-50 list in 1996. His peers are more respectful, though.

"He was good enough to make the top 40, let alone the top 50," says Bill Fitch. "The guy was a power forward playing center, and he could drive all the centers crazy, taking them outside. He could run the floor endlessly. Bob McAdoo was a hell of a player."

The NBA Hall of Fame finally granted him the respect he so long coveted when he was elected to the Hall in 2000. ∎

The Whole Package, on Crutches

"Bill Walton, across the board, I think, was the best legitimate center the game has known."

—JACK RAMSAY

Bill Walton led a young Blazers team to an improbable title in 1977, but injuries saddled him for the next six years.

LONGEVITY WASN'T BILL WALTON'S BEST SUBJECT. ALMOST HALF OF HIS FOURTEEN NBA SEASONS BARELY EXISTED. HE SAT OUT FOUR ENTIRELY, PLAYED 10 GAMES IN A FIFTH, 14 IN A SIXTH.

He didn't play 70 games until his 12th season, when he was a Celtics reserve. Kareem scored 38,387 points, Wilt 31,419. Walton had 6,215. He had only two productive seasons as a starting NBA center, but they were unforgettable.

"Bill Walton, across the board, I think, was the best legitimate center the game has known," says Jack Ramsay, his coach those two seasons in Portland.

"Now, I understand that Bill Russell was a greater intimidator and shot-blocker, Wilt Chamberlain was more powerful, Abdul-Jabbar a better scorer, Nate Thurmond maybe a better overall defender. But Walton did all of those things almost as well as those guys. Plus, he was the best passing center in the halfcourt that the game has known."

Walton was a walking clinic. Everything he did was picture-perfect, like his spread-eagle stance blocking out for rebounds: crouched, legs wide, butt out, arms extended, fingers out as far as he could get them.

He was desire incarnate. He had the size and skills of the masters and the zeal of the possessed, like Dave Cowens and Alonzo Mourning.

His pro career was a decade and a half of frustration. People muttered that he couldn't play hurt, that his vegetarian diet made his bones brittle, that he was cuckoo. Bob Cousy, who coached him on an AAU team that played the Russians in 1973, thought he just went at it too hard.

"He played with complete commitment and abandon, and that probably is why he had the shortened career that he did," Cousy says. "He probably hurt himself a lot more than he normally would. . . .

"I remember, we worked double sessions in L.A. for 10 days prior to that first game. Walton had a year to go [at UCLA]. I remember [UCLA coach] John [Wooden] used to come to our practice and sit there, flanked by two doctors.

"And I remember we spent more time in those two sessions tending to poor Walton, who was on the floor. He inadvertently hurt himself often because he was so active. He played in practice the way he played in the game."

When granted what would be the rare gift of health, Walton's impact rivaled that of any of the immortals. His UCLA teams won three NCAA titles in four years. He was a junior before he lost a college game. He hit 21 of 22 shots in the 1973 finals against Memphis State.

Walton missed almost half the games in his first two NBA seasons, but in his third, in 1976–77, he led Portland, with no starter over 25 on a franchise that had never even been to the playoffs, to an NBA title. In the last game, he amassed 20 points, 23 rebounds, seven assists, and eight blocks.

- Born: November 5, 1952, in La Mesa, California
- College: UCLA
- 6´11´´/235 pounds
- Selected as College Player of the Year by *The Sporting News* in 1972, 1973, and 1974
- Won the Naismith Award in 1972, 1973, and 1974
- Named first-team All-American by *The Sporting News* in 1972, 1973, and 1974
- Averaged 20.3 points and 15.7 rebounds per game in college
- Member of NCAA Division I championship teams in 1972 and 1973
- Voted NCAA Tournament Most Outstanding Player in 1972 and 1973
- Holds NCAA Tournament career record for highest field-goal percentage at 68.6 percent (1972 through 1974)
- Holds NCAA Tournament single-season record for highest field-goal percentage at 76.3 percent (1973)
- Voted NBA Most Valuable Player in 1978
- Won the NBA Sixth Man Award in 1986
- Member of All-NBA First Team in 1978, All-NBA Second Team in 1977, and NBA All-Defensive First Teams in 1977 and 1978
- Member of Portland Trail Blazers NBA championship team in 1977
- Member of Boston Celtics NBA championship team in 1986
- Earned the NBA Finals Most Valuable Player Award in 1977
- Shares NBA Finals single-game record for defensive rebounds with 20 (June 3, 1977, vs. Philadelphia and June 5, 1977, vs. Philadelphia)
- Shares NBA Finals single-game record for blocked shots with eight (June 5, 1977, vs. Philadelphia)
- Received NBA Players Association's Oscar Robertson Leadership Award in 1991
- Inducted into the Naismith Memorial Basketball Hall of Fame in 1993
- Voted One of the 50 Greatest Players in NBA History in 1996

> **"HE PLAYED WITH COMPLETE COMMITMENT AND ABANDON, AND THAT PROBABLY IS WHY HE HAD THE SHORTENED CAREER THAT HE DID."**
>
> —BOB COUSY

Walton came off the bench to help the Celtics win the 1986 championship.

He was as fierce as a lion, wild as the wind. He didn't have interests, he had passions: politics, the outdoors, the Grateful Dead—except for basketball, which went beyond that into obsession.

He was a lot to handle, or too much. He barely deigned to talk to the press, which he considered running dogs of the imperialist power structure. He tested coaches daily, even his beloved Wooden, who sent him out for a haircut at the first UCLA practice each season, turned down his request to smoke marijuana for his aching knees, even if he brought a note from his doctor, but acceded to his request to use his office for meditation.

With Walton, life was a test a day, as when he was arrested for lying down on Wilshire Boulevard to protest the mining of Haiphong harbor. Wooden admonished the young man to work for change within the system.

"He just told me, 'Bill, that's just not the right way to do things. You should write a letter and express your disappointment,'" Walton said later. "So I went in and got some UCLA basketball stationery. You know, it had 'UCLA Basketball, NCAA Champions, '64, '65, '67, John Wooden, *Sports Illustrated* Sportsman of the Year'—the fancy stationery. I typed up this great letter to Nixon, outlining his crimes against humanity. I said, 'We insist on your resignation. Thanks in advance for your cooperation.' Then I signed it, 'Bill Walton, captain, UCLA varsity basketball.'

"Took it to the locker room. Everybody goes, 'Yeah, let me sign it!' Everybody signs it, and I take it in to coach Wooden after practice one day and he's standing there, getting dressed after taking a shower.

"I said, 'Coach, I took your advice and wrote a letter, and I'd like you to sign it.'

"He says, 'Sure, what have you got, Bill?'

"He starts reading it, and you can see him just wanting to crumple it and throw it away. But he didn't. He looked at me with those sad, soft eyes and said, 'Bill, I can't sign this letter—you know I can't sign this. Please don't send this letter.'

"I sent the letter and, sure enough, the president resigned in a couple months."

As defending champions, the Trail Blazers started the 1977–78 season 50–10, a pace that would have translated to 68 wins, then second best all-time, when Walton's foot problems flared up and everything blew asunder. What followed was even more remarkable, a quest through pain and medical practice, his body betraying him every step of the way, his passion inextinguishable.

Walton would undergo some 30 surgeries and procedures. He jumped to the San Diego Clippers in 1979, converted to the mainstream, appeared on a *Sports Illustrated* cover in a three-piece suit, and played 169 games in six years (out of 492) before the gods took pity on him and brought him to the Celtics.

In the 1985–86 season, he backed up Robert Parish, Kevin McHale, and Larry Bird—an entire front line and sixth man destined for the Hall of Fame as well as the 1986 NBA title. The gods, obviously, didn't want to go overboard. The next season, Walton played 10 games.

Collegiate Record

Season	Team	G	Min.	FGM	FGA	Pct.	FTM	FTA	Pct.	Reb.	Ast.	Pts.	Averages RPG	APG	PPG
'70–71	UCLA	20	...	155	266	.583	52	82	.634	321	74	362	16.1	3.7	18.1
'71–72	UCLA	30	...	238	372	.640	157	223	.704	466	...	633	15.5	...	21.1
'72–73	UCLA	30	...	277	426	.650	58	102	.569	506	168	612	16.9	5.6	20.4
'73–74	UCLA	27	...	232	349	.665	58	100	.580	398	148	522	14.7	5.5	19.3
Varsity totals		87	...	747	1,147	.651	273	425	.642	1,370	...	1,767	15.7	...	20.3

NBA Regular-Season Record

Season	Team	G	Min.	FGM	FGA	Pct.	FTM	FTA	Pct.	Off.	Def.	Tot.	Ast.	St.	Blk.	TO	Pts.	RPG	APG	PPG
'74–75	Portland	35	1,153	177	345	.513	94	137	.686	92	349	441	167	29	94	...	448	12.6	4.8	12.8
'75–76	Portland	51	1,687	345	732	.471	133	228	.583	132	549	681	220	49	82	...	823	13.4	4.3	16.1
'76–77	Portland	65	2,264	491	930	.528	228	327	.697	211	723	934	245	66	211	...	1,210	*14.4	3.8	18.6
'77–78	Portland	58	1,929	460	882	.522	177	246	.720	118	648	766	291	60	146	206	1,097	13.2	5.0	18.9
'78–79	Portland								Did not play—injured											
'79–80	San Diego	14	337	81	161	.503	32	54	.593	28	98	126	34	8	38	37	194	9.0	2.4	13.9
'80–81	San Diego								Did not play—injured											
'81–82	San Diego								Did not play—injured											
'82–83	San Diego	33	1,099	200	379	.528	65	117	.556	75	248	323	120	34	119	105	465	9.8	3.6	14.1
'83–84	San Diego	55	1,476	288	518	.556	92	154	.597	132	345	477	183	45	88	177	668	8.7	3.3	12.1
'84–85	L.A. Clip.	67	1,647	269	516	.521	138	203	.680	168	432	600	156	50	140	174	676	9.0	2.3	10.1
'85–86	Boston	80	1,546	231	411	.562	144	202	.713	136	408	544	165	38	106	151	606	6.8	2.1	7.6
'86–87	Boston	10	112	10	26	.385	8	15	.533	11	20	31	9	1	10	15	28	3.1	0.9	2.8
'87–88	Boston								Did not play—injured											
Totals		468	13,250	2,552	4,900	.521	1,111	1,683	.660	1,103	3,820	4,923	1,590	380	1,034	864	6,215	10.5	3.4	13.3

NBA Playoff Record

Season	Team	G	Min.	FGM	FGA	Pct.	FTM	FTA	Pct.	Off.	Def.	Tot.	Ast.	St.	Blk.	TO	Pts.	RPG	APG	PPG
'76–77	Portland	19	755	153	302	.507	39	57	.684	56	232	288	104	20	64	...	345	15.2	5.5	18.2
'77–78	Portland	2	49	11	18	.611	5	7	.714	5	17	22	4	3	3	6	27	11.0	2.0	13.5
'85–86	Boston	16	291	54	93	.581	19	23	.826	25	78	103	27	6	12	22	127	6.4	1.7	7.9
'86–87	Boston	12	102	12	25	.480	5	14	.357	9	22	31	10	3	4	8	29	2.6	0.8	2.4
Totals		49	1,197	230	438	.525	68	101	.673	95	349	444	145	32	83	36	528	9.1	3.0	10.8

Personal fouls/disqualifications: 1976–77, 80/3. 1977–78, 1/0. 1985–86, 45/1. 1986–87, 23/0. Totals, 149/4.

NBA All-Star Game Record

	G	Min.	FGM	FGA	Pct.	FTM	FTA	Pct.	Off.	Def.	Tot.	Ast.	PF	Dq.	St.	Blk.	TO	Pts.
Totals	1	31	6	14	.429	3	3	1.000	2	8	10	2	3	0	3	2	4	15

> # "JULIUS ERVING MADE IT ON SHOWMANSHIP. WALT BELLAMY MADE IT ON NUMBERS. BILL WALTON MADE IT ON LOVE."
> —LOS ANGELES TIMES

In his final one, though he remained on the roster, he played none. Years later, a full page on him remained in the Celtics media guide, asserting, "[He] will forever be identified for his play in the Green and White."

In 1993 Walton was named to the Hall of Fame. He arrived in a suit and sneakers, since dress shoes were too painful.

"I go from chair to chair, and I'm very glad I have a chair right now," he said. "I do pay for it, but it was a price well worth it. I loved the game of basketball.

"It was painful in that I did not accomplish more. My career is one of frustration and disappointment, which makes today even more special because everyone else here has the career numbers, the career statistics, career accomplishments to back up their being here.

"I really don't but again, I'm here, and I'm not going to say no I'm not going to say no thanks. I'm going to say, thank you ever so much."

You're welcome. It's the least we can do.

"Julius Erving made [it] on showmanship," said the Los Angeles Times of the Hall of Fame class of 1993. "Walt Bellamy made it on numbers. Bill Walton made it on love." ∎

Basically, He Went to the Rack

"I always called him James Brown, the hardest-working man in show business. He just worked."
—DOC RIVERS

Moses Malone was the first player to make the leap straight from high school to the pros, averaging 19 points and 15 rebounds per game for the ABA Utah Stars in his rookie season.

MOSES MALONE

By 1974, when Moses Malone finished high school in little Petersburg, Virginia, John Wooden had won nine of his ten championships at UCLA. Programs nationwide were gearing up to try to catch the Bruins, none more determinedly than Maryland, which coach Lefty Driesell proclaimed the UCLA of the East.

Since Wooden prided himself on never contacting a player outside his home state first, someone with one less scruple might gain a lasting advantage by camping on the next phenom's doorstep. Suddenly, there was a new priority in the game—recruiting—and just as suddenly, it became a jungle out there.

This was a rare phenom, indeed, the biblically named, 6´10´´, no-prisoner-taking Malone, who awoke one day to find coaches, assistants, and fat-cat alumni besieging his ramshackle house on St. Matthews Street, courting his coach, his relatives, his friends.

Even in the days before Dick Vitale, the newspapers covered it in detail. Scouting "gurus" (another new class of middlemen) crowed to the press, as if in unison, "Moses will lead [insert your program here] to the Promised Land."

It should not have been surprising that a certain spirit of auction prevailed. Moses' father was absent, his mother bagged groceries at a Safeway for $100 a week, and their suitors were as well heeled as they were desperate. There were assistant coaches who never left town, who booked rooms in the local motels and stayed. Clemson coach Tates Locke came at the head of a delegation, with a conscience so guilty, he wrote later, he thought NCAA investigators were tailing him, and so he calmed his fears with beer and diet pills.

Heaven and Moses only know what he was offered under the table, but there was enough on top. After choosing Maryland, Malone posed for *Sports Illustrated*, sitting on the hood of a new Chrysler, acquired through a "lease-purchase" agreement.

Shortly after that, Malone accepted a straight-cash offer from the ABA's Utah Stars. Driesell did everything but lay down in front of Mo's Chrysler to keep him. Afterward he listed Mo in his brochure as one of the players he'd sent to the pros.

Thus, Malone became the first high school student to make the jump—and quite a jump it was.

Homesick and out of place in far-off Salt Lake City, he still averaged 19 points and 15 rebounds in 1974–75 for the Stars, who promptly folded. He was dispersed to the Spirits of St. Louis only to see the entire ABA fold, whereupon he became a Portland Trail Blazer.

For a month, anyway.

"We were teammates when we first started out in the NBA," says Bill Walton. "He was there a month and they wouldn't play him. They didn't want to pay a backup guy $350,000. He was coming off the bench behind myself. He was making $350,000 at the time, most of it deferred, and they still didn't want to pay him, so they traded him for a first-round draft choice.

"They traded him to Buffalo and kept Robin Jones. The Blazers' director of player personnel said, 'On the whole, Robin Jones is a better basketball player than Moses Malone. Moses may do one or two things better, but on the whole, Robin is a better player.'

"And then after they traded him to Buffalo for a first-round draft choice, Buffalo turned around six days later and traded him to Houston for two first-round draft choices."

It was not so much that Malone became a star in Houston. He'd always been one; it was just that no one knew it.

The 220-pounder from Petersburg was now a 240-pounder from hell. Tough guys didn't look forward to messing with him, and even the lordly Kareem Abdul-Jabbar—no man to back down from a challenge—winced at the sight of this primal force.

"Moses had everything," Walton says. "He had the heart and passion of a Cowens, he had the quickness of a McAdoo, he had the power of an Unseld. Was not a player who was skilled in the fundamentals. Was not a player who had great coaching early in his career.

"Moses, like Artis [Gilmore], never bought into the fact that there were rules in basketball, in terms of traveling or three seconds or double dribble or offensive fouls. They were so tough and so physical.

"Moses was relentless, like Cowens, in his pursuit of the ball. He was a lot like the players are today. When you watch basketball today, so much of it is guys just throwing it up and then attacking the offensive boards, and whoever can push and shove the most and jump the highest dunks it back in.

"Moses was not a high jumper. He was not a big-time jumper, but he was so quick and relentless—he would do what Dennis Rodman and Shawn Kemp would do later."

- Born: March 23, 1955, in Petersburg, Virginia
- College: None
- 6´10´´/260 pounds
- Selected out of high school in the third round of the 1974 ABA Draft by the Utah Stars
- Member of ABA All-Rookie Team in 1975
- Voted NBA Most Valuable Player in 1979, 1982, and 1983
- Member of four All-NBA First Teams (1979, 1982, 1983, 1985), four All-NBA Second Teams (1980, 1981, 1984, 1987), one NBA All-Defensive First Team (1983), and one NBA All-Defensive Second Team (1979)
- Holds NBA career records for offensive rebounds with 6,731, and consecutive games without a disqualification with 1,212 (January 7, 1978, through 1994–95 season)
- Holds NBA single-season record for offensive rebounds with 587 (1979) and single-game record for offensive rebounds with 21 (February 11, 1982, vs. Seattle)
- Holds NBA single-game playoff record for offensive rebounds with 15 (April 21, 1977, vs. Washington)
- Member of Philadelphia 76ers NBA championship team in 1983
- Named NBA Finals Most Valuable Player in 1983
- Finished with combined ABA/NBA averages of 20.3 points and 12.3 rebounds per game
- Voted One of the 50 Greatest Players in NBA History in 1996

"THERE ARE CERTAIN FORCES IN NATURE YOU CAN'T STOP, AND HE IS ONE OF THEM."

—KURT RAMBIS

Malone's physical style commanded respect from the best of the big men—even the league's top dog, Abdul-Jabbar.

With NBA players' accuracy increasing and the number of shots diminishing, rebound totals dropped sharply. But on a percentage basis, Malone's best seasons compared with Chamberlain's. When Moses pulled down 17.6 a game in 1978–79, it represented 38 percent of the Rockets' total. When Wilt averaged 27.2 in 1960–61, it was 36 percent of the Warriors' total.

By the spring of 1982, Malone was a two-time NBA MVP. The Rockets, however, under the gun financially, traded him to the 76ers, who were willing to pay him $2.2 million a year. He moved east and, in short order, won his third MVP and led the Sixers to the 1983 title. In a rare burst of "quotability"—he usually growled at the press until it ran away—he predicted three playoff sweeps in 1983, or as he put it, "Fo', fo', fo'." The 76ers went 12–1, still the postseason record.

Malone was now in the spotlight, whether he liked it or not. Shy by nature, speaking rapidly with a rural Southern accent, he was hard for friends to

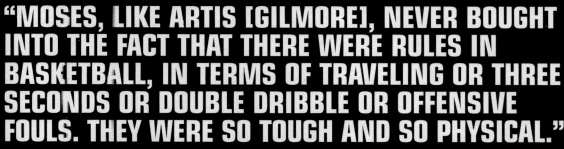

ABA Regular-Season Record

Season	Team	G	Min.	2-Point FGM	FGA	Pct.	3-Point FGM	FGA	Pct.	FTM	FTA	Pct.	Reb.	Ast.	Pts.	Averages RPG	APG	PPG
'74–'75	Utah	83	3,205	591	1,034	.572	0	1	.000	375	591	.635	1,209	82	1,557	14.6	1.0	18.8
'75–'76	St. Louis	43	1,168	251	488	.514	0	2	.000	112	183	.612	413	58	614	9.6	1.3	14.3
Totals		126	4,373	842	1,522	.553	0	3	.000	487	774	.629	1,622	140	2,171	12.9	1.1	17.2

ABA Playoff Record

Season	Team	G	Min.	2-Point FGM	FGA	Pct.	3-Point FGM	FGA	Pct.	FTM	FTA	Pct.	Reb.	Ast.	Pts.	Averages RPG	APG	PPG
'74–'75	Utah	6	235	51	80	.638	0	0	...	34	51	.667	105	9	136	17.5	1.5	22.7

ABA All-Star Game Record

	G	Min	2-Point FGM	FGA	Pct.	3-Point FGM	FGA	Pct.	FTM	FTA	Pct.	Reb.	Ast.	Pts.
Totals	1	20	2	3	.667	0	0	...	2	5	.400	10	0	6	

NBA Regular-Season Record

Season	Team	G	Min.	FGM	FGA	Pct.	FTM	FTA	Pct.	Rebounds Off.	Def.	Tot.	Ast.	St.	Blk.	TO	Pts.	Averages RPG	APG	PPG
'76–'77	Buff.-Hou.	82	2,506	389	810	.480	305	440	.693	*437	635	1,072	89	67	181	...	1,083	13.1	1.1	13.2
'77–'78	Houston	59	2,107	413	828	.499	318	443	.718	*380	506	886	31	48	76	220	1,144	15.0	0.5	19.4
'78–'79	Houston	82	*3,390	716	1,325	.540	599	811	.739	*587	857	1,444	147	79	119	326	2,031	*17.6	1.8	24.8
'79–'80	Houston	82	3,140	778	1,549	.502	563	*783	.719	573	617	1,190	147	80	107	300	2,119	14.5	1.8	25.8
'80–'81	Houston	80	3,245	806	1,545	.522	609	*804	.757	*474	706	*1,180	141	83	150	.308	2,222	*14.8	1.8	27.8
'81–'82	Houston	81	*3,398	945	1,822	.519	630	*827	.762	*558	630	*1,188	142	76	125	294	2,520	*14.7	1.8	31.1
'82–'83	Philadelphia	78	2,922	654	1,305	.501	*600	*788	.761	*445	*749	*1,194	101	89	157	264	1,908	*15.3	1.3	24.5
'83–'84	Philadelphia	71	2,613	532	1,101	.483	545	727	.750	352	598	950	96	71	110	250	1,609	*13.4	1.4	22.7
'84–'85	Philadelphia	79	2,957	602	1,284	.469	*737	*904	.815	385	646	*1,031	130	67	123	286	1,941	*13.1	1.6	24.6
'85–'86	Philadelphia	74	2,706	571	1,246	.458	*617	*784	.787	339	533	872	90	67	71	261	1,759	11.8	1.2	23.8
'86–'87	Washington	73	2,488	595	1,311	.454	570	692	.824	340	484	824	120	59	92	202	1,760	11.3	1.6	24.1
'87–'88	Washington	79	2,692	531	1,090	.487	543	689	.788	372	512	884	112	59	72	249	1,607	11.2	1.4	20.3
'88–'89	Atlanta	81	2,878	538	1,096	.491	561	711	.789	386	570	956	112	79	100	245	1,637	11.8	1.4	20.2
'89–'90	Atlanta	81	2,735	517	1,077	.480	493	631	.781	*364	448	812	130	47	84	232	1,528	10.0	1.6	18.9
'90–'91	Atlanta	82	1,912	280	598	.468	309	372	.831	271	396	667	68	30	74	137	869	8.1	0.8	10.6
'91–'92	Milwaukee	82	2,511	440	929	.474	396	504	.786	320	424	744	93	74	64	150	1,279	9.1	1.1	15.6
'92–'93	Milwaukee	11	104	13	42	.310	24	31	.774	22	24	46	7	1	8	10	50	4.2	0.6	4.5
'93–'94	Philadelphia	55	618	102	232	.440	90	117	.769	106	120	226	34	11	17	59	294	4.1	0.6	5.3
'94–'95	San Antonio	17	149	13	35	.371	22	32	.688	20	26	46	6	2	3	11	49	2.7	0.4	2.9
Totals		1,329	45,071	9,435	19,225	.491	8,531	11,090	.769	6,731	9,481	16,212	1,796	1,089	1,733	3,804	27,409	12.2	1.4	20.6

NBA Playoff Record

Season	Team	G	Min.	FGM	FGA	Pct.	FTM	FTA	Pct.	Rebounds Off.	Def.	Tot.	Ast.	St.	Blk.	TO	Pts.	Averages RPG	APG	PPG
'76–'77	Houston	12	518	81	162	.500	63	91	.692	84	119	203	7	13	21	...	225	16.9	0.6	18.8
'78–'79	Houston	2	78	18	41	.439	13	18	.722	25	16	41	2	1	8	8	49	20.5	1.0	24.5
'79–'80	Houston	7	275	74	138	.536	33	43	.767	42	55	97	7	4	16	22	181	13.9	1.0	25.9
'80–'81	Houston	21	955	207	432	.479	148	208	.712	125	180	305	35	13	34	59	562	14.5	1.7	26.8
'81–'82	Houston	3	136	29	67	.433	14	15	.933	28	23	51	10	2	2	6	72	17.0	3.3	24.0
'82–'83	Philadelphia	13	524	126	235	.536	86	120	.717	70	136	206	20	19	25	40	338	15.8	1.5	26.0
'83–'84	Philadelphia	5	212	38	83	.458	31	32	.969	20	49	69	7	3	11	21	107	13.8	1.4	21.4
'84–'85	Philadelphia	13	505	90	212	.425	82	103	.796	36	102	138	24	17	22	23	262	10.6	1.8	20.2
'86–'87	Washington	3	114	21	47	.447	20	21	.952	15	23	38	5	0	3	8	62	12.7	1.7	20.7
'87–'88	Washington	5	198	30	65	.462	33	40	.825	22	34	56	7	3	4	15	93	11.2	1.4	18.6
'88–'89	Atlanta	5	197	32	64	.500	40	51	.784	27	33	60	9	7	4	11	105	12.0	1.8	21.0
'90–'91	Atlanta	5	84	4	20	.200	13	14	.929	16	15	31	3	2	1	2	24	6.2	0.6	4.2
Totals		94	3,796	750	1,566	.479	576	756	.762	510	785	1,295	136	84	151	215	2,077	13.8	1.4	22.1

NBA All-Star Game Record

	G	Min.	FGM	FGA	Pct.	FTM	FTA	Pct.	Rebounds Off.	Def.	Tot.	Ast.	PF	Dq.	St.	Blk.	TO	Pts.
Totals	11	271	44	98	.449	40	67	.594	44	64	108	15	26	0	9	6	19	128

Combined ABA and NBA Regular-Season Records

G	Min.	FGM	FGA	Pct.	FTM	FTA	Pct.	Rebounds Off.	Def.	Tot.	Ast.	St.	Blk.	TO	Pts.	Averages RPG	APG	PPG
1,455	49,444	10,277	20,750	.495	9,018	11,864	.760	7,382	10,452	17,834	1,936	1,199	1,889	4,264	29,580	12.3	1.3	20.3

"MOSES, LIKE ARTIS [GILMORE], NEVER BOUGHT INTO THE FACT THAT THERE WERE RULES IN BASKETBALL, IN TERMS OF TRAVELING OR THREE SECONDS OR DOUBLE DRIBBLE OR OFFENSIVE FOULS. THEY WERE SO TOUGH AND SO PHYSICAL."

—BILL WALTON

understand. Away from the press, though, he was bubbly and popular with teammates.

He was 28 when the 76ers won their title, a nine-year veteran, aging fast. His shooting percentage had already started falling, almost annually. He couldn't do little things, like passing out of the post or increasing his shooting range, to cut corners. Basically, he still went to the rack; sometimes it just took him longer to get there.

The 76ers, frustrated at his stubbornness, traded him to the Washington Bullets in 1986. Two seasons later, he signed with the Atlanta Hawks as a free agent. He remained a double-figures scorer and rebounder until 1990, when he was 35. He hung on

five years after that, chasing his last seasons as tenaciously as he pursued the ball on the rim.

"I always called him James Brown, the hardest-working man in show business," says Doc Rivers, a teammate in Atlanta. "He just worked.

"God, he was great for me and for all the younger guys. He was the first guy at practice. He rode the bike for 15 minutes before practice, or the Stairmaster. He never, ever missed a practice. There was nobody that outworked him."

In 1995 Malone retired after 21 seasons in two leagues and with nine teams, one of whom (the 76ers) he played for twice, a terror weapon no longer but a legend fo'ever. ■

Chief Among His Peers

"He's probably the best medium-range shooting big man in the history of the game."

—BILL WALTON

Despite a slow start, Robert Parish's drive and intensity led him to a Hall-of-Fame career.

ROBERT PARISH

WHEN ROBERT PARISH JOINED THE GOLDEN STATE WARRIORS, PLAYERS WERE OLD AT 30, ANCIENT AT 35, AND BROADCASTER MATERIAL AFTER THAT. IF THE FANS HAD BEEN ASKED TO PREDICT WHICH OF THE SEVENTIES WARRIORS WOULD PLAY INTO HIS FORTIES, THEY'D HAVE USED UP A LOT OF GUESSES BEFORE THEY GOT TO THE MAN WHO WOULD BE CHIEF

Around the Warriors, the question wasn't how long Parish would play, but how long they were stuck with him.

"What's interesting about Parish," says Bill Walton, a foe for years and a teammate in Boston, "is how slow he started his career. And really, at the beginning of his career, people thought he wasn't going to make it. People thought he was a bust, a washout. Rick Barry was dogging him so bad at Golden State that he couldn't even get into the game.

"And he had those bone spur surgeries, and they traded him to Boston—and straight to the Hall of Fame."

It was a long and winding road, indeed, that led Parish from Shreveport, Louisiana, through Northern California and disrepute to Massachusetts and fame. And then, in the early nineties when the story seemed over and he conceded, "I'm definitely winding down," he instead went onward to stints in Charlotte and Chicago.

Former Bulls GM Jerry Krause, a longtime admirer who signed Parish for his final season in 1996 when he was 43, once said of him, "A body like his comes along once in a century." But this was just as much an act of will.

Parish had a wonderfully lean, fit, athletic body, and he never had a major injury. He played through lots of minor ones, maintaining his hunger all the while, which was a great irony because his biggest problem in Golden State was his perceived indifference.

He was a small-town kid, embarrassed to be so much taller than everyone else, reluctant to play basketball, leery of going far from home to showcase himself. He got his famous No. 00 because his high school was out of jerseys with numbers on them.

Squirming through a feverish recruiting battle, Parish chose Centenary, a tiny Methodist college in Shreveport with 750 students. It was no basketball factory, but to admit Parish the school, creatively, had to project Parish's ACT score into an acceptable SAT mark. With all the big-time losers in the recruiting race complaining, it was little surprise that the NCAA investigated the deal and turned it thumbs-down.

Parish was told he could transfer and be eligible—the NCAA, of course, wanted him—and Centenary would get two years' probation. Or he could stay and it would be four years—his entire career—with no postseason play, no TV games, and no statistics on the national lists.

Parish stayed and became the mystery man of the seventies, the player everyone heard about but no one saw.

The eighth pick in the 1976 draft, he joined the Warriors and quickly proved he was no legend, all too human, a shy, silent, homesick young man with an impassive demeanor and a flowing style that was easy to take for laziness.

It wasn't all misperception. Parish would later acknowledge that he thought of himself as lacking drive, too quiet to lead anyone anywhere, even, as he told *Sports Illustrated*'s Alex Wolff, "kind of lazy."

"I thought he was just a seven-foot piece of crap, frankly, from what I'd seen," says the *Boston Globe*'s Bob Ryan, "loping around, taking that jump shot, didn't seem to care."

Actually, Parish was getting better but the Warriors were getting worse, so who noticed the improvement?

One of the few was Bill Fitch, the Celtics coach, who'd seen Parish at Centenary and thought he was overmatched in Golden State, where he was expected to score, rebound, and block shots.

The Celtics, overrun in the 1980 Eastern finals by the 76ers' twin giants, Darryl Dawkins and Caldwell Jones, were looking for two good big men and got them. Red Auerbach swung the deal that would be voted

- Born: August 30, 1953, in Shreveport, Louisiana
- College: Centenary
- 7´1´´/244 pounds
- Named first-team All-American by *The Sporting News* in 1976
- Averaged 21.6 points and 16.9 rebounds per game in college
- Holds NBA career records for seasons with 21, games with 1,611, and defensive rebounds with 10,117
- Ranks in the top 10 in NBA history in rebounds (14,715), blocked shots (2,361), and minutes (45,704)
- Averaged 14.5 points and 9.3 rebounds per game in the NBA
- Holds NBA career playoff record for offensive rebounds with 571
- Member of All-NBA Second Team in 1982 and All-NBA Third Team in 1989
- Played in nine NBA All-Star Games
- Recorded a triple-double on March 29, 1987, against the Philadelphia 76ers
- Holds Boston Celtics career record for blocked shots with 1,703 (1980–81 through 1993–94)
- Member of three Boston Celtics NBA championship teams (1981, 1984, 1986) and one Chicago Bulls NBA championship team (1997)
- Voted One of the 50 Greatest Players in NBA History in 1996

"A BODY LIKE HIS COMES ALONG ONCE IN A CENTURY."
—FORMER BULLS GENERAL MANAGER JERRY KRAUSE

When all was said and done, Parish had earned three championship rings in Boston and one more in Chicago.

the most lopsided in league history: Parish and the Warriors' No. 3 pick (which went for Kevin McHale) for the Celtics' No. 1 pick (which went for Joe Barry Carroll).

Joe Barry, the bust that Parish was supposed to be, would be rechristened "Just Breathing," although it took a while to figure out how lopsided the trade was.

The Celtics planned to break in Parish gradually, behind veteran Dave Cowens. Suddenly, during the 1980 exhibition season, Cowens quit, informing stunned players and coaches on a team bus in Terre Haute, Indiana.

"He goes up to Parish," says Ryan, who was on the bus, "and he tells him, 'I know you can do the job.' And

I'm thinking, 'Who you kidding?' That night, Parish starts the game in Evansville, and he gets five fouls the first quarter. Fitch leaves him out there to die."

Fitch, a taskmaster from the old school, drove Parish mercilessly for weeks, so hard that he says Robert "never had much time for me" after that. By Thanksgiving, however, Parish looked pretty much like the player he'd be ever after.

The Celtics had enough scorers; they just needed him to play defense, run the court—which he did better than any of his peers and proved particularly hard on Kareem Abdul-Jabbar—and take good shots. They won 62 games in 1980–81, edged the 76ers in

Collegiate Record

Season	Team	G	Min.	FGM	FGA	Pct.	FTM	FTA	Pct.	Reb.	Ast.	Pts.	RPG	APG	PPG
'72–'73	Centenary	27	885	285	492	.579	50	82	.610	505	25	620	18.7	0.9	23.0
'73–'74	Centenary	25	841	224	428	.523	49	78	.628	382	34	497	15.3	1.4	19.9
'74–'75	Centenary	29	900	237	423	.560	74	112	.661	447	43	548	15.4	1.5	18.9
'75–'76	Centenary	27	939	288	489	.589	93	134	.694	486	48	669	18.0	1.8	24.8
Totals		108	3,565	1,034	1,832	.564	266	406	.655	1,820	150	2,334	16.9	1.4	21.6

NBA Regular-Season Record

Season	Team	G	Min.	FGM	FGA	Pct.	FTM	FTA	Pct.	Off.	Def.	Tot.	Ast.	St.	Blk.	TO	Pts.	RPG	APG	PPG
'76–'77	Golden St.	77	1,384	288	573	.503	121	171	.708	201	342	543	74	55	94	...	697	7.1	1.0	9.1
'77–'78	Golden St.	82	1,969	430	911	.472	165	264	.625	211	469	680	95	79	123	201	1,025	8.3	1.2	12.5
'78–'79	Golden St.	76	2,411	554	1,110	.499	196	281	.698	265	654	916	115	100	217	233	1,304	12.1	1.5	17.2
'79–'80	Golden St.	72	2,119	510	1,006	.507	203	284	.715	247	536	783	122	58	115	225	1,223	10.9	1.7	17.0
'80–'81	Boston	82	2,298	635	1,166	.545	282	397	.710	245	532	777	144	81	214	191	1,552	9.5	1.8	18.9
'81–'82	Boston	80	2,534	669	1,235	.542	252	355	.710	288	578	866	140	68	192	221	1,590	10.8	1.8	19.9
'82–'83	Boston	78	2,459	619	1,125	.550	271	388	.698	260	567	827	141	79	148	185	1,509	10.6	1.8	19.3
'83–'84	Boston	80	2,867	623	1,140	.547	274	368	.745	243	614	857	139	55	116	184	1,520	10.7	1.7	19.0
'84–'85	Boston	79	2,850	551	1,016	.542	292	393	.743	263	577	840	125	56	101	186	1,394	10.6	1.6	17.6
'85–'86	Boston	81	2,567	530	966	.549	245	335	.731	246	524	770	145	65	116	187	1,305	9.5	1.8	16.1
'86–'87	Boston	80	2,995	588	1,057	.556	227	309	.735	254	597	851	173	64	144	191	14,063	10.6	2.2	17.5
'87–'88	Boston	74	2,312	442	750	.589	177	241	.734	173	455	628	115	55	84	154	1,061	8.5	1.6	14.3
'88–'89	Boston	80	2,840	596	1,045	.570	294	409	.719	342	654	996	175	79	116	200	1,486	12.5	2.2	18.6
'89–'90	Boston	79	2,396	505	871	.580	233	312	.747	259	537	796	103	38	69	169	1,243	10.1	1.3	15.7
'90–'91	Boston	81	2,441	485	811	.598	237	309	.767	271	585	856	66	66	103	153	1,207	10.6	0.8	14.9
'91–'92	Boston	79	2,285	468	874	.535	179	232	.772	219	486	705	70	68	97	131	1,115	8.9	0.9	14.1
'92–'93	Boston	79	2,146	416	777	.535	162	235	.689	246	494	740	61	57	107	120	994	9.4	0.8	12.6
'93–'94	Boston	74	1,987	356	725	.491	154	208	.740	141	401	542	82	42	96	108	866	7.3	1.1	11.7
'94–'95	Charlotte	81	1,352	159	372	.427	71	101	.703	93	257	350	44	27	36	66	389	4.3	0.5	4.8
'95–'96	Charlotte	74	1,086	120	241	.498	50	71	.704	89	214	303	29	21	54	50	290	4.1	0.4	3.9
'96–'97	Chicago	43	406	70	143	.490	21	31	.677	42	47	89	22	6	19	28	161	2.1	0.5	3.7
Totals		1,611	45,704	9,614	17,914	.537	4,106	5,694	.721	4,598	10,117	14,715	2,180	1,219	2,361	3,183	23,334	9.1	1.4	14.5

NBA Playoff Record

Season	Team	G	Min.	FGM	FGA	Pct.	FTM	FTA	Pct.	Off.	Def.	Tot.	Ast.	St.	Blk.	TO	Pts.	RPG	APG	PPG
'76–'77	Golden St.	10	239	52	108	.481	17	26	.654	43	60	103	11	7	11	...	121	10.3	1.1	12.1
'80–'81	Boston	17	492	108	219	.493	39	58	.672	50	96	146	19	21	39	44	255	8.6	1.1	15.0
'81–'82	Boston	12	426	102	209	.488	51	75	.680	43	92	135	18	5	48	39	255	11.3	1.5	21.3
'82–'83	Boston	7	249	43	89	.483	17	20	.850	21	53	74	9	5	9	17	103	10.6	1.3	14.7
'83–'84	Boston	23	869	139	291	.478	64	99	.646	76	172	248	27	23	41	45	342	10.8	1.2	14.9
'84–'85	Boston	21	803	136	276	.493	87	111	.784	57	162	219	31	21	34	50	359	10.4	1.5	17.1
'85–'86	Boston	18	591	106	225	.471	58	89	.652	52	106	158	25	9	30	44	270	8.8	1.4	15.0
'86–'87	Boston	21	734	149	263	.567	79	103	.767	59	139	198	28	18	35	38	377	9.4	1.3	18.0
'87–'88	Boston	17	626	100	188	.532	50	61	.820	51	117	168	21	11	19	38	250	9.9	1.2	14.7
'88–'89	Boston	3	112	20	44	.455	7	9	.778	6	20	26	6	4	2	6	47	8.7	2.0	15.7
'89–'90	Boston	5	170	31	54	.574	17	18	.944	23	27	50	13	5	7	12	79	10.0	2.6	15.8
'90–'91	Boston	10	296	58	97	.598	42	61	.689	33	59	92	6	8	7	16	158	9.2	0.6	15.8
'91–'92	Boston	10	335	50	101	.495	20	28	.714	38	59	97	14	7	15	9	120	9.7	1.4	12.0
'92–'93	Boston	4	146	31	57	.544	6	7	.857	13	25	38	5	1	6	6	68	9.5	1.3	17.0
'94–'95	Charlotte	4	71	6	11	.545	2	5	.400	4	5	9	1	0	3	1	14	2.3	0.3	3.5
'96–'97	Chicago	2	18	1	7	.143	0	0	...	2	2	4	0	0	3	0	2	2.0	0.0	1.0
Totals		184	6,177	1,132	2,239	.506	556	770	.722	571	1,194	1,765	234	145	309	365	2,820	9.5	1.3	15.3

NBA All-Star Game Record

	G	Min.	FGM	FGA	Pct.	FTM	FTA	Pct.	Off.	Def.	Tot.	Ast.	PF	Dq.	St.	Blk.	TO	Pts.
Totals	9	142	36	68	.529	14	21	.667	16	37	53	8	15	0	4	8	10	86

"HE HAD THE ABILITY TO PLAY HURT. HE HAD THE ABILITY TO PLAY WITHIN A TEAM STRUCTURE AND NEVER GET HIS MIND OUT OF WHACK IF HE COULDN'T GO OUT AND GET THE BIG STATS ONE NIGHT. HE'D JUST DO WHAT HE COULD DO. THAT'S WHY HE SURVIVED."

—BILL FITCH

a seven-game Eastern finals, and won the first of their three titles in the eighties.

Parish's lope and his hook became part of Celtics lore. After seeing *One Flew Over the Cuckoo's Nest*, teammate Cedric Maxwell named him "Chief," after the regal, slow-moving Chief Bromden. That was it forever after.

In Parish's first 11 Celtics seasons, he shot between 54 percent and 59 percent. His scoring average was whatever they needed. One season, he took as few as 11 shots a game.

At age 36 he had his best rebounding year (12.5), and shot 57 percent from the floor and 72 percent from the line. At 37 he was an All-Star with 10.5

rebounds, and shot 58 percent from the floor and 75 percent from the line.

"Never in my wildest dreams did I think Parish would be playing now," Fitch said at the time. "I mean, I would have bet everything I owned and everything I was going to make.

"Because the guy had foot problems. He had knee problems. But he had the ability to play hurt. He had the ability to play within a team structure and never get his mind out of whack if he couldn't go out and get the big stats one night because he was playing hurt. He'd just do what he could do. That's why he survived.

"Now for whatever reasons, he's ended up being a real chief." ■

THE | EIGHTIES

Kevin McHale

Bill Laimbeer

Ralph Sampson

Hakeem Olajuwon

Patrick Ewing

David Robinson

One game changed basketball. It wasn't an NBA game, nor was it played in the eighties. It was the last NCAA championship game of the seventies, the finals between Magic Johnson's Michigan State and Larry Bird's Indiana State, a matchup that seized popular imagination and led to the highest TV ratings any basketball game had ever garnered—or would for the rest of the century.

It was the NBA's good fortune that both players turned pro the following season, went to glamour teams, and turned out to be superstars in every sense of the word. Johnson, in particular, was a spokesman and salesman for the game, living proof that even if these players were highly paid, they still enjoyed playing—did it with verve and flair and without compromise. Bird, the self-styled "hick from French Lick," went from surly to droll. Michael Jordan arrived in 1984. The NBA's golden period was at hand.

It was at this time that people began to suggest that great centers had become passé. Lots of fine newcomers arrived—Ralph Sampson, Hakeem Olajuwon, and Patrick Ewing within three years, followed by David Robinson—but their teams never seemed to win.

Of course, by the grace of the draft, Sampson joined a Rockets team that had won 14 games the season before, Olajuwon joined a Rockets team that had won 29, Ewing joined a Knicks team that had won 24, and Robinson joined the Spurs, who had just won 21.

Old distinctions were crumbling. Johnson, the point guard who played center in the last game of the 1980 NBA Finals, was 6´9´´, 220 as a rookie, 235 when he retired. In the fifties, he might have played center all the time—if the world had been ready for one who ran the fast break. Bird was roughly the same size as Johnson, but he had such superb skills that the Celtics ran their offense through him as if he were their point guard.

Despite anti–big guy sentiment, no one won anything without them. Johnson played with Abdul-Jabbar. Bird played with three future Hall-of-Fame big men: McHale, Robert Parish, and, briefly, Bill Walton.

When the decade started, the NBA was a decided number three among American pro team sports. (When Johnson starred at center in Game 6 of the NBA Finals, it wasn't even on live TV.) By the decade's end, it was heating up fast. With profit would come challenges.

80s

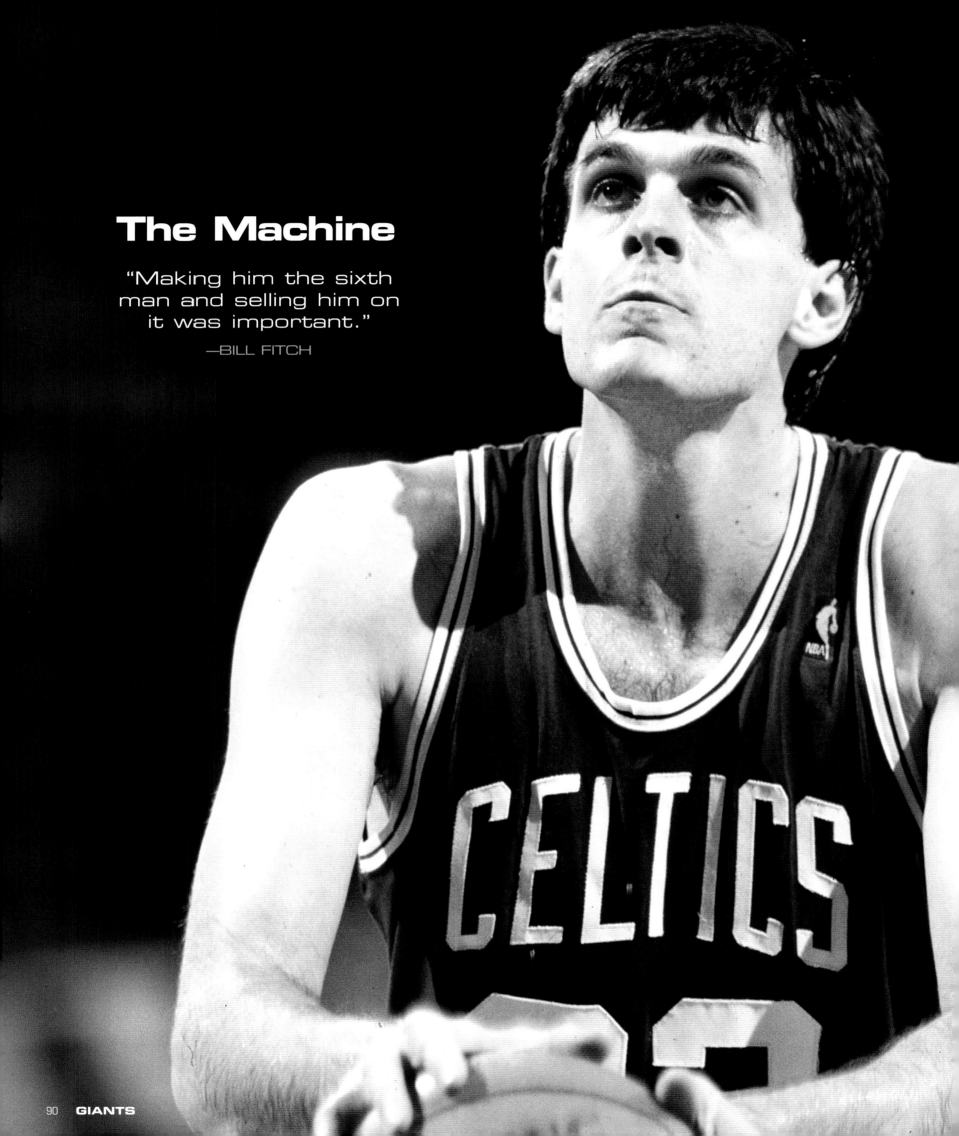

The Machine

"Making him the sixth man and selling him on it was important."

—BILL FITCH

14 KEVIN MCHALE

HE WASN'T A CENTER. FOR MUCH OF HIS CAREER, HE WASN'T EVEN A STARTER. WHAT KEVIN MCHALE WAS WAS ONE OF THE GREATEST LOW-POST TECHNICIANS WHO EVER LIVED, A WALKING CLINIC WITH A SEEMINGLY UNENDING REPERTOIRE OF MOVES THAT MADE HIM A CULT FIGURE AMONG HIS PEERS.

"McHale was the second-best low-post player I ever played against," says Bill Walton. "Kareem was the best."

To have been in the Atlantic Division in the eighties was to have studied footage of McHale backward and forward, trying to figure out how he did it. As Knicks coach, Rick Pitino used to run tapes of McHale. John Gabriel, later Orlando GM, then a young executive in Philadelphia, said the 76ers did it. Pete Newell borrowed McHale techniques and passed them on at his summer camp.

McHale was unique, 6´10´´ with coat-hanger shoulders, long arms, and perfect technique. He did everything that coaches howled at the other guys to do their whole careers—keep the ball up, block a right-hander's shot with your left hand—and did it from the get-go.

If his game suggested thousands of hours of work, he was anything but a grind. He was as irrepressible as Larry Bird was intense, making him the only Celtic with the talent, personality, and spirit to challenge the team leader. Although McHale and Bird coexisted easily enough and avoided outright rivalry, they were different.

"Larry thought Kevin didn't work hard enough," says the Boston Globe's Bob Ryan. "Kevin thought Larry needed a life."

McHale busted chops. That, as much as playing basketball, was what he did. He laughed, wisecracked, and played practical jokes constantly, challenging Bill Fitch, the crusty authoritarian coach, and Red Auerbach, the living legend GM. McHale threatened to sign with an Italian team when he didn't like the Celtics' offer coming out of college in 1980. Four years later, he threatened to sign with the hated Knicks as a free agent.

In a Celtics-worshipping town, his independence didn't make him the more beloved. When he flirted with the Knicks in 1983, the Globe ran a cartoon of him with a pig's snout, wallowing in dollar bills, captioned, "The Real McHale." Seventy percent of the respondents in a Globe poll wanted him traded.

"With Kevin," says Bill Walton, a teammate for two seasons, "basketball was a social event. To him there was just a time to go to the gym and have fun with all the guys. With Larry and Magic [Johnson] and Michael [Jordan], it was much more life and death, they just had to win. With Kevin, it was, 'Hey, I'm here, I'm going to do my absolute best but before the game, after the game, during the game, hey, I'm going to be yapping, I'm going to be talking, I'm going to be having fun.'"

McHale was his very own person, and a rare one it was. Born and raised in Hibbing,

McHale's transition from the college game to the NBA was quicker and easier than that of most players.

- Born: December 19, 1957, in Hibbing, Minnesota
- College: Minnesota
- 6′10″/225 pounds
- Grew from 5′9″ to 6′10″ during his career at Hibbing High School
- Averaged 15.2 points and 8.5 rebounds per game in college
- Member of one All-NBA First Team (1987), three NBA All-Defensive First Teams (1986, 1987, 1988), three NBA All-Defensive Second Teams (1983, 1989, 1990), and NBA All-Rookie Team (1981)
- Averaged 17.9 points and 7.3 rebounds during his NBA career
- Shot 79.8 percent from the free throw line in his career; made the NBA's top five in free throw accuracy in 1989–90 at 89.3 percent
- Appeared in seven NBA All-Star Games
- Won the NBA Sixth Man Award in 1984 and 1985, becoming the first repeat winner
- Member of three Boston Celtics NBA championship teams (1981, 1984, 1986)
- Had his No. 32 retired by the Celtics on January 30, 1994
- Voted One of the 50 Greatest Players in NBA History in 1996
- Inducted into the Naismith Memorial Basketball Hall of Fame in 1999

"HE WAS A CLUTCH PLAYER, A CLUTCH SHOOTER FROM THE VERY BEGINNING. HE HAD MORE BIG FOURTH QUAR- TERS AS A ROOK- IE THAN BIRD AND COWENS PUT TOGETHER."

—BILL WALTON

Minnesota, Bob Dylan's hometown, he was an unreconstructed liberal in a milieu as apolitical as a video arcade. He was outspoken and irreverent. He talked the talk but unfailingly walked the walk.

The Celtics got the news right away. Rookies weren't supposed to give the lordly Celtics a hard time but to sign quickly for whatever Red thought was fair. Instead, McHale and his agent flew to Milan and opened negotiations with an Italian team.

Red's offer shot up and McHale flew home, joining the Celts late—as he would be throughout his career.

"He flies all night, lands at the airport," says Ryan. "They send him right to Hellenic College. It's a night scrimmage; everyone else has been in camp three or four days. Bill Fitch, of course, is just dying to get his hands on this kid and teach him a lesson. He's already announced his 'Let him eat spaghetti' line— got a lot of laughs out of that.

"Gospel truth, this is like a Hollywood movie. They start the scrimmage and Bill's going to have this kid's tongue licking the floor. All we see is this kid hitting turnaround jump shots, dunking the ball, and blocking shots with either hand. Putting on a show.

"Kevin was never a rookie. The thing about him, as much as any player, he was never a rookie. He had more big fourth quarters as a rookie than Bird and Cowens put together. He was a clutch player, a clutch shooter from the very beginning. And he drove Fitch

Collegiate Record

Season	Team	G	Min.	FGM	FGA	Pct.	FTM	FTA	Pct.	Reb.	Ast.	Pts.	RPG	APG	PPG
'76–'77	Minnesota	27	...	133	241	.552	58	77	.753	218	36	324	8.1	1.3	12.0
'77–'78	Minnesota	26	...	143	242	.591	54	77	7.01	192	27	340	7.4	1.0	13.1
'78–'79	Minnesota	27	...	202	391	.517	79	96	.823	259	33	483	9.6	1.2	17.9
'79–'80	Minnesota	32	...	236	416	.567	85	107	.794	281	28	557	8.8	0.9	17.4
Totals		112	...	714	1,290	.553	276	357	.773	950	124	1,704	8.5	1.1	15.2

NBA Regular-Season Record

Season	Team	G	Min.	FGM	FGA	Pct.	FTM	FTA	Pct.	Off.	Def.	Tot.	Ast.	St.	Blk.	TO	Pts.	RPG	APG	PPG
'80–'81	Boston	82	1,645	355	666	.533	108	159	.679	155	204	359	55	27	151	110	818	4.4	0.7	10.0
'81–'82	Boston	82	2,332	465	875	.531	187	248	.754	191	365	556	91	30	185	137	1,117	6.8	1.1	13.6
'82–'83	Boston	82	2,234	483	893	.541	169	269	.717	215	338	553	104	34	192	159	1,159	6.7	1.3	14.1
'83–'84	Boston	82	2,577	587	1,055	.556	336	439	.765	208	402	610	104	23	126	150	1,511	7.4	1.3	18.4
'84–'85	Boston	79	2,653	605	1,062	.570	355	467	.760	229	483	712	141	28	120	157	1,565	9.0	1.8	19.8
'85–'86	Boston	68	2,397	561	978	.574	326	420	.776	171	380	551	181	29	134	149	1,448	8.1	2.7	21.3
'86–'87	Boston	77	3,060	790	1,307	*.604	428	512	.836	247	516	763	198	38	172	197	2,008	9.9	2.6	26.1
'87–'88	Boston	64	2,390	550	911	*.604	346	434	.797	159	377	536	171	27	92	141	1,446	8.4	2.7	22.6
'88–'89	Boston	78	2,876	661	1,211	.546	436	533	.818	223	414	637	172	26	97	196	1,758	8.2	2.2	22.5
'89–'90	Boston	82	2,722	648	1,181	.549	393	440	.893	201	476	677	172	30	157	183	1,712	8.3	2.1	20.9
'90–'91	Boston	68	2,067	504	912	.553	228	275	.829	145	335	480	126	25	146	140	1,251	7.1	1.9	18.4
'91–'92	Boston	56	1,398	323	634	.509	134	163	.822	119	211	330	82	11	59	82	780	5.9	1.5	13.9
'92–'93	Boston	71	1,656	298	649	.459	164	195	.841	95	263	358	73	16	59	92	762	5.0	1.0	10.7
Totals		971	30,118	6,830	12,334	.554	3,634	4,554	.798	2,358	4,764	7,122	1,670	344	1,690	1,893	17,335	7.3	1.7	17.9

NBA Playoff Record

Season	Team	G	Min.	FGM	FGA	Pct.	FTM	FTA	Pct.	Off.	Def.	Tot.	Ast.	St.	Blk.	TO	Pts.	RPG	APG	PPG
'80–'81	Boston	17	296	61	113	.540	23	36	.639	29	30	59	14	4	25	15	146	3.5	0.8	8.5
'81–'82	Boston	12	344	77	134	.575	40	53	.755	41	44	85	11	5	27	16	194	7.1	0.9	16.2
'82–'83	Boston	7	177	34	62	.548	10	18	.556	15	29	42	5	3	7	10	78	6.0	0.7	11.1
'83–'84	Boston	23	702	123	244	.504	94	121	.777	62	81	143	27	3	35	38	340	6.2	1.2	14.8
'84–'85	Boston	21	837	172	303	.568	121	150	.807	74	134	208	32	13	46	60	465	9.9	1.5	22.1
'85–'86	Boston	18	715	168	290	.579	112	141	.794	51	104	155	48	8	43	48	448	8.6	2.7	24.9
'86–'87	Boston	21	827	174	298	.584	96	126	.762	66	128	194	39	7	30	54	444	9.2	1.9	21.1
'87–'88	Boston	17	716	158	262	.603	115	137	.839	55	81	136	40	7	30	39	432	8.0	2.4	25.4
'88–'89	Boston	3	115	20	41	.488	17	23	.739	7	17	24	9	1	2	4	57	8.0	3.0	19.0
'89–'90	Boston	5	192	42	69	.609	25	29	.862	8	31	39	13	2	10	14	110	7.8	2.6	22.0
'90–'91	Boston	11	376	78	148	.527	66	80	.825	18	54	72	20	5	14	14	228	6.5	1.8	20.7
'91–'92	Boston	10	306	65	126	.516	35	44	.795	21	46	67	13	5	5	9	165	6.7	1.3	16.5
'92–'93	Boston	4	113	32	55	.582	12	14	.857	9	20	29	3	2	7	5	76	7.3	0.8	19.0
Totals		169	5,716	1,204	2,145	.561	766	972	.788	456	797	1,253	274	65	281	326	3,182	7.4	1.6	18.8

NBA All-Star Game Record

	G	Min.	FGM	FGA	Pct.	FTM	FTA	Pct.	Off.	Def.	Tot.	Ast.	PF	Dq.	St.	Blk.	TO	Pts.
Totals	7	125	24	48	.500	12	14	.857	13	24	37	8	21	0	1	12	5	61

"HE BECAME THE MOST DIFFICULT LOW-POST PLAYER TO DEFEND—ONCE HE MADE THE CATCH—IN THE HISTORY OF THE LEAGUE."

—HUBIE BROWN

nuts. He could take anything Fitch dished out, and he didn't care."

Fitch remembers McHale arriving with a turnaround jump shot but without that incredible repertoire. Kevin taught himself the rest. He had a whole series of moves and countermoves, turning right for the jump hook, or, if cut off, pivoting back to the left for his famous up-and-under, or, if nothing else worked out, fading back for his jumper with the picture-perfect high release.

McHale never shot with his left hand—because he didn't have to. He seldom passed out of the pivot—because he didn't have to. His buddy, Danny Ainge, called him a black hole: the ball goes in and never comes out.

"It's funny," replied McHale. "I get up to the rim and I never see Danny's face."

In 1986–87 McHale averaged 26 points a game for half a season and wound up making the All-NBA First Team, beating out Dominique Wilkins, Karl Malone, and Charles Barkley. He also became the only player in history to shoot 60 percent from the floor and 80 percent from the foul line.

Midway through that season, though, Cleveland's Larry Nance stepped on McHale's foot, injuring it. He played well after that, but the people who saw him every day say he was never the same.

Nevertheless, in 1983–84 he averaged 18.4 points per game while shooting 55 percent from the floor and 83 percent from the line.

At the end of his career, he was even trying three-pointers. In his first six years, he had shot a total of 20 of them and made one. However, he shot 33 percent from the arc in 1989–90 and 41 percent the next season. It was as though there was nothing he couldn't learn to do.

Says Ryan: "Larry's thing was Kevin didn't work hard, but where did Larry think those moves came from? Kevin stayed after practice all the time."

Hobbled by foot injuries, McHale retired in 1993. In his last Boston Garden game, he hit his first five shots, scored 17 points, and took 11 rebounds.

He was picked for the All-Rookie team, was a Sixth Man Award winner (twice), an All-Defensive First Teamer (three times), and a Second Teamer (three more times)—a McHale real enough for the ages.

McHale is currently the vice president of basketball operations for his hometown Timberwolves, and in 1999 he was elected to the Basketball Hall of Fame. ∎

"He was one of the most underrated centers who ever lived because everyone hated his guts."

—BILL WALTON

He didn't win any popularity contests, but Bill Laimbeer did get his hands on two consecutive championship trophies.

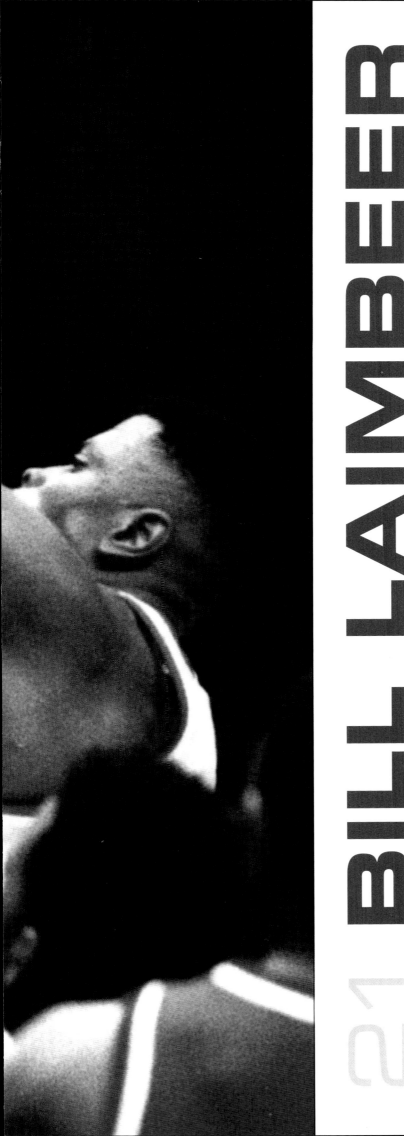

21 BILL LAIMBEER

Then there was Bill Laimbeer, who was in a class all by himself.

Of all the "projects" who ever made it beyond "white stiff," only George Mikan had more impact, and that was in a simpler, less athletic day with no one his own size to push back. Laimbeer, who wasn't close to being the biggest guy around and had few other obvious gifts, was the most highly evolved project who ever paid off down the line.

Of course, it isn't basketball he's best remembered for but villainy. In Atlanta, the Hawks mascot once chainsawed a life-sized Laimbeer doll, to cheers.

The Lakers' Mychal Thompson, who went against his Pistons in the 1988 and 1989 NBA Finals, called him "captain of the all-dirty team. Captain, coach, owner, and commissioner."

"He was one of the most underrated centers who ever lived," muses Bill Walton, "because everyone hated his guts."

Not that it made Laimbeer a whit more beloved. Even in his heyday, players around the league disagreed about whether he was a menace to society or just a hard-nosed guy who'd do whatever needed to be done.

The answer was probably somewhere in between. In the 1987 Eastern finals, Laimbeer must have thought Larry Bird needed to be pulled to the floor—because that was what he did, with a takedown worthy of the World Wrestling Federation. The next game, with just the pretext of a little elbow, Robert Parish came up behind Laimbeer and started pummeling the back of his head, knocking him to the floor. Parish received congratulations from coast to coast.

In the 1988 Eastern finals, the teams hooked up again, literally and figuratively. The Pistons took a 3–2 lead. Laimbeer warned that the Celtics were like snakes whose heads had to be cut off. To make his point, he brought a sickle to Game 6, which the Pistons won.

Pure hate flowed between Detroit and Boston. During one series, Johnny Most, the famed announcer whose rhetoric waxed and waned according to the threat to the Celtics dynasty, likened Laimbeer and running-mate-in-mayhem Rick Mahorn to prehistoric life-forms. This was just Most being Most, but the NBA thought it played so well that Johnny was invited to reprise his act on the *Today Show*.

"All the fans know is me as a player," said Laimbeer, amused. "They don't know me as a person. It's the image I project. As long as people in Detroit appreciate me, what do I care about people in Boston and Milwaukee, places like that?

"I don't have the physical capabilities to play any other way. I'm not a leaper. I'm definitely not fast. So I have to do what I have to do. Most NBA players like to go from this spot to this spot and do their little thing. They don't like somebody always running into them."

Laimbeer had little in common with his peers. They tended to be black, from humble circumstances. He emerged from the mean streets of suburbia.

Laimbeer could have been the boy next door, provided you could afford the prices in Palos Verdes, California, where he attended high school. His father was an executive with Owens-Illinois. When Bill's NBA salary reached $150,000, he joked that he was the only NBA player whose dad made more than he did.

Highly competitive, Laimbeer preferred golf, turning reluctantly to basketball only after spurting from 6´4´´ as a freshman to 6´10´´ as a junior.

"I don't really like basketball," he said. "The accident was, I grew. But if I'm going to do something, I'm going to do it well. If I was going to be a basketball player, I'd identify a way to be a good one."

With Laimbeer, there were lots of surprises. His best friend on the Pistons would be Isiah Thomas, a refugee from the west side of Chicago whose childhood was as hard as Laimbeer's was privileged. Laimbeer said he taught Isiah things like how to eat lobster. Thomas taught Laimbeer that everyone doesn't grow up eating lobster.

Laimbeer played at Notre Dame, where Digger Phelps favored the Midwestern big-sides-of-beef style. He averaged only 7.4 points a game for three years (his average

HIGHLIGHTS: BILL LAIMBEER

- Born: May 19, 1957, in Boston
- College: Notre Dame
- 6′11″/260 pounds
- Averaged 7.4 points and 6.3 rebounds per game in college
- Led the NBA in rebounding with 13.1 per game in 1985–86 and ranked second with 12.4 per game in 1984–85
- Ranked third in the NBA in free throw percentage at 89.4 in 1986–87
- Averaged 12.9 points and 9.7 rebounds per game during his NBA career
- Posted a career free throw percentage of 83.7
- Ranks 10th in NBA history in personal fouls with 3,633
- Member of Detroit Pistons NBA championship teams in 1989 and 1990
- Ranks second in defensive rebounds for a five-game NBA Finals series with 55 (1990 vs. Portland)
- Shares NBA Finals single-game record for points in an overtime period with nine (June 7, 1990, vs. Portland)
- Holds Detroit Pistons career record for rebounds with 9,430 (1981–82 through 1993–94)

"I DON'T FIGHT. I AGITATE, THEN WALK AWAY."
—BILL LAIMBEER

There was never any doubt: during much of the eighties, you were definitely going to get banged up when you went up against Laimbeer and the Pistons.

actually declined all three seasons) but was drafted by the Cavaliers in the third round of the 1979 draft on the basis of his size and the certainty that someone would always need a backup center.

The Cavaliers were pleased when he chose to play in Italy, which allowed Laimbeer to gain experience off of Cleveland's books. Unlike Phelps, the Italians didn't mind if Laimbeer shot occasionally. He averaged 21 points, came home a year later, made the Cavs, and was quickly sent to Detroit in a little-noted four-player deal.

In Laimbeer's first full season in Detroit, he averaged 13 points and was the league's third-leading rebounder at 12.1 a game. He couldn't get far off his tiptoes, but with bulk, great hands, savvy, and desire, he stayed among the top 10 rebounders for the balance of the eighties.

Coach Chuck Daly, a defensive ace, arrived in Detroit in 1983. Mahorn, a big-bottomed bopper, arrived two years later. Mahorn's gift to modern

warfare was the pick that stuns. One night he knocked three 76ers guards out of the game—Mo Cheeks, Andrew Toney, and Clint Richardson—although he said he wasn't sure how to score it since Richardson came back.

Improbable or not, the Pistons climbed the ladder to the stars and, just as remarkably, stayed there two years running.

"The Pistons," says Walton, "are one of the few teams that ever won anything without a dominating player on their front line because they were willing to go beyond what was normally done in athletic competition."

Calling themselves the "Raiders of basketball" (and avidly hawking theme merchandise), the Pistons lost in the 1988 NBA Finals after a late foul call on Laimbeer put Kareem Abdul-Jabbar on the line to bring the Lakers from one point down and avoid elimination in Game 6. The call was a ticky-tack one,

Collegiate Record

Season	Team	G	Min.	FGM	FGA	Pct.	FTM	FTA	Pct.	Reb.	Ast.	Pts.	RPG	APG	PPG
'76-'77	Owens Tech.								Did not play.						
'75-'76	Notre Dame	10	190	32	65	.492	18	23	.783	79	10	82	7.9	1.0	8.2
'77-'78	Notre Dame	29	654	97	175	.554	42	62	.677	190	31	236	6.6	1.1	8.1
'78-'79	Notre Dame	30	614	78	145	.538	35	50	.700	164	30	191	5.5	1.0	6.4
Totals		69	1,458	207	385	.538	95	135	.704	433	71	509	6.3	1.0	7.4

Italian League Record

Season	Team	G	Min.	FGM	FGA	Pct.	FTM	FTA	Pct.	Reb.	Ast.	Pts.	RPG	APG	PPG
'79-'80	Brescia	29	...	258	465	.555	97	124	.782	363	...	613	12.5	...	21.1

NBA Regular-Season Record

Season	Team	G	Min.	FGM	FGA	Pct.	FTM	FTA	Pct.	Off.	Def.	Tot.	Ast.	St.	Blk.	TO	Pts.	RPG	APG	PPG
'80-'81	Cleveland	81	2,460	337	670	.503	117	153	.765	266	427	693	216	56	78	132	791	8.6	2.7	9.8
'81-'82	Clev.-Det.	80	1,829	265	536	.494	184	232	.793	234	383	617	100	39	64	121	718	7.7	1.3	9.0
'82-'83	Detroit	82	2,871	436	877	.497	245	310	.790	282	711	993	263	51	118	176	1,119	12.1	3.2	13.6
'83-'84	Detroit	82	2,864	553	1,044	.530	316	365	.866	329	674	*1,003	149	49	84	151	1,422	12.2	1.8	17.3
'84-'85	Detroit	82	2,892	595	1,177	.506	244	306	.797	295	718	1,013	154	69	71	129	1,438	12.4	1.9	17.5
'85-'86	Detroit	82	2,891	545	1,107	.492	266	319	.834	305	*770	*1,075	146	59	65	133	1,360	*13.1	1.8	16.6
'86-'87	Detroit	82	2,854	506	1,010	.501	245	274	.894	243	712	955	151	72	69	120	1,263	11.6	1.8	15.4
'87-'88	Detroit	82	2,897	455	923	.493	187	214	.874	165	667	832	199	66	78	136	1,110	10.1	2.4	13.5
'88-'89	Detroit	81	2,640	449	900	.499	178	212	.840	138	638	776	177	51	100	129	1,106	9.6	2.2	13.7
'89-'90	Detroit	81	2,675	380	785	.484	164	192	.854	166	614	780	171	57	84	98	981	9.6	2.1	12.1
'90-'91	Detroit	82	2,668	372	778	.478	123	147	.837	173	564	737	157	38	56	98	904	9.0	1.9	11.0
'91-'92	Detroit	81	2,234	342	727	.470	67	75	.893	104	347	451	160	51	54	102	783	5.6	2.0	9.7
'92-'93	Detroit	79	1,933	292	574	.509	93	104	.894	110	309	419	127	46	40	59	687	5.3	1.6	8.7
'93-'94	Detroit	11	248	47	90	.522	11	13	.846	9	47	56	14	6	4	10	108	5.1	1.3	9.8
Totals		1,068	33,956	5,574	11,198	.498	2,440	2,916	.837	2,819	7,581	10,400	2,184	710	965	1,594	13,790	9.7	2.0	12.9

NBA Playoff Record

Season	Team	G	Min.	FGM	FGA	Pct.	FTM	FTA	Pct.	Off.	Def.	Tot.	Ast.	St.	Blk.	TO	Pts.	RPG	APG	PPG
'83-84	Detroit	5	165	29	51	.569	18	20	.900	14	48	62	12	4	3	12	76	12.4	2.4	15.2
'84-85	Detroit	9	325	48	107	.449	36	51	.706	36	60	96	15	7	7	16	132	10.7	1.7	14.7
'85-86	Detroit	4	168	34	68	.500	21	23	.913	20	36	56	1	2	3	8	90	14.0	0.3	22.5
'86-87	Detroit	15	543	84	163	.515	15	24	.625	30	126	156	37	15	12	20	184	10.4	2.5	12.3
'87-88	Detroit	23	779	114	250	.456	40	45	.889	43	178	221	44	18	19	30	273	9.6	1.9	11.9
'88-89	Detroit	17	497	66	142	.465	25	31	.806	26	114	140	31	6	8	19	172	8.2	1.8	10.1
'89-90	Detroit	20	667	91	199	.457	25	29	.862	41	170	211	28	23	18	16	222	10.6	1.4	11.1
'90-91	Detroit	15	446	66	148	.446	27	31	.871	42	80	122	19	5	12	17	164	8.1	1.3	10.9
'91-92	Detroit	5	145	17	46	.370	5	5	1.000	5	28	33	8	4	1	5	41	6.6	1.6	8.2
Totals		113	3,735	549	1,174	.468	212	259	.819	257	840	1,097	195	84	83	143	1,354	9.7	1.7	12.0

NBA All-Star Game Record

	G	Min.	FGM	FGA	Pct.	FTM	FTA	Pct.	Off.	Def.	Tot.	Ast.	PF	Dq.	St.	Blk.	TO	Pts.
Totals	4	45	13	20	.650	2	3	.667	3	8	11	2	7	0	2	2	1	28

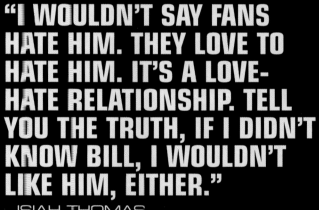

"I WOULDN'T SAY FANS HATE HIM. THEY LOVE TO HATE HIM. IT'S A LOVE-HATE RELATIONSHIP. TELL YOU THE TRUTH, IF I DIDN'T KNOW BILL, I WOULDN'T LIKE HIM, EITHER."
—ISIAH THOMAS

but Laimbeer, so hated for his on-court histrionics and weepy looks, wouldn't say a word about it.

"We don't complain about fouls," he said later. "Fouls are part of the game. They [officials] blow it, it's a foul."

A year later, the Bad Boys took out the injured Lakers 4-0. A year after that, they won three straight at Portland to finish off the Trail Blazers 4-1. Laimbeer was such a force inside—taking charges and gumming up the Blazers offense—that the next season Dallas coach Richie Adubato showed his team a Laimbeer highlight film.

In later years, Laimbeer appeared in a series of Fila TV ads, in which he taught the next Pistons star, Grant Hill, old Pistons tricks like head-butting and snarling into cameras. Here's the scary part: that wasn't an actor. Bill Laimbeer was as real as it gets.

In a move some found shocking, Laimbeer was named the head coach of the WNBA's Detroit Shock in 2002 ∎

What Might Have Been

Sampson was the first big man who really had little man's skills.

Though Ralph Sampson's knees cut his career short, he still took the Rockets from a 14-win record to the NBA Finals in just three seasons.

22 RALPH SAMPSON

He was too good and too dedicated and too stubborn. He may not have fit anyone's preconceptions of how 7´4´´ centers played, but he was a great college player and a fine professional whose Houston Rockets, 14–68 when he joined them, made the NBA Finals within three seasons of his arrival.

Least of all did he deserve his knees grinding to a halt, turning the most graceful of big men into a teetering colossus. He had his moments—the College Player of the Year awards, the 1985 All-Star MVP, the improvised shot to oust the Lakers in the 1986 Western finals—and he made a few million dollars. However, he needed more time than fate gave him to prove he could do it his way.

"He had the ability to revolutionize the game," says Calvin Murphy, whose Rockets career was ending just as Sampson's was starting. "He was a seven-footer who could play the guard position. He was the kind of guy that little men fear because he could make them obsolete. He was an innovator of the game. If you'll remember, he went to the All-Star Game and played the big forward and was the MVP. . . .

"He was definitely, definitely a talent. Ralph would come down to my basketball camp in Connecticut. He worked as hard as anybody who's ever played this game. He was dedicated to excellence. Remember now, he was the MVP of the college ranks, so he knew the pressure on him to be great. And for him not to be great was not his fault at all because he put in the hours to make it happen.

"This is eyewitness news: when I would close my gym down, Ralph would turn the lights back on 'cause he was still in there working out. Not just shooting the ball. I'm talking about jump-roping, calisthenics, and all the things that are necessary to have some longevity in the game."

Sampson was a transition figure in more ways than one. Kareem Abdul-Jabbar, it was said, was so talented, he could have played even if he hadn't been 7´2´´, although it's hard to picture a 6´6´´ forward making a living with a hook shot. Sampson, however, was the first big man who really had little man's skills. He could bring the ball up against pressure. He could play facing the hoop. He could do a little of everything. . . .

Or just enough to make everyone around him crazy.

"Ralph was the College Player of the Year, three or four years," says Bill Fitch, his coach in Houston. "At 7´3´´, and a real 7´3´´, he was very graceful. The crowd would immediately look at this good-looking kid, but he was very thin. He never really became a good outside shooter—but he looked good taking it."

It wasn't just Sampson's style that was new.

In the days when the great players at the prestige schools customarily stayed four years, the pros began courting him early—right after his freshman year when Boston GM Red Auerbach begged him to enter the draft and then cried like a rejected lover when Sampson said he was staying in school. ("If he were an intellectual genius and was planning on being a surgeon," quoth Auerbach, "then I'd buy it.")

As brilliant a prospect as he was, Sampson had one problem: he was rail thin, and he wasn't the long-suffering Kareem

- Born: July 7, 1960, in Harrisonburg, Virginia
- College: Virginia
- 7´4´´/235 pounds
- Led his high school team to the state championship in 1978 and 1979
- Turned down offers to play professional basketball during all four years of college to pursue a degree
- Honored as the College Player of the Year by UPI, AP, and U.S. Basketball Writers Association in 1981, 1982, and 1983
- Won the Naismith Award in 1981, 1982, and 1983
- Earned the Wooden Award in 1982 and 1983
- Voted College Player of the Year by the National Association of Basketball Coaches in 1982 and 1983
- Ranks fourth in rebounds by an NCAA Division I freshman with 381 (1979–80) and ranks 23rd in Division I history in career rebounds with 1,511
- Led University of Virginia to 112 wins after it had recorded 66 victories in the previous four years
- Led Virginia to third place in the NCAA Tournament in 1981
- Averaged 19.9 points per game as an NBA rookie in 1983–84
- Ranked fifth in the NBA in rebounding (11.1) and third in blocks per game (2.40) in 1983–84
- Helped lead the Houston Rockets, who had won just 14 games in 1982–83, to the NBA Finals in 1986
- Member of four NBA All-Star teams

"HE HAD THE ABILITY TO REVOLUTIONIZE THE GAME. HE WAS THE KIND OF GUY THAT LITTLE MEN FEAR BECAUSE HE COULD MAKE THEM OBSOLETE. HE WAS AN INNOVATOR OF THE GAME."

—CALVIN MURPHY

Sampson, one of the most celebrated college players of all time, is shown here battling fellow future NBA star Sam Perkins.

kind of center who'd hang in there and take a beating to get his shot off.

Sampson fought coaches who wanted him to master one deadly shot like Abdul-Jabbar's hook. Ralph fancied himself a jack-of-all-trades. Or as Professor Robert Rotella, who had him in a course called "The Psychology of the Gifted Athlete" at UVA, put it in a daintily academic turn of phrase to *Sports Illustrated*'s Alex Wolff: "To some degree, he finds simply going into the low post and throwing in a hook shot uninteresting."

Sampson's biographer, Roland Lazenby, once noted, "Maybe this experiment is just Ralph's way of justifying playing soft." But more than many realized or conceded, Sampson was coming on as a pro player.

Hakeem Olajuwon arrived in Houston a year later, a star from day one, but when the two faced off against the Celtics in the 1986 NBA Finals, Fitch—whom Sampson fought every inch of the way and ripped after leaving Houston—says Ralph was still the better player.

Not that playing in a Finals turned out well, either.

Sampson wasn't the first to take a pratfall in the limelight and get mugged by the press. However, his treatment after laying a two-point egg in Game 1 and

getting ejected for fighting little Jerry Sichting in Game 5 was memorable, with "loser" and "sissy" and "dog biscuits" thrown around until you couldn't tell the stories in the Boston press from the banners in the stands.

Sampson was emotional, he didn't like rough play, and he wasn't good with the press. Aside from that, he handled it OK.

Nevertheless, he was 26, a three-year pro with career averages of 21 points and 11 rebounds, and—with his characteristic devotion—might well have fought back, except his knees were already going.

The Rockets watched it happen for two years before peddling him to the Warriors' Don Nelson, who called him the "modern-day center." Within two years, Nelson sent Sampson next door to Sacramento, where the truth finally became painfully obvious all around.

"He was getting his knee aspirated about every six weeks when he was at Virginia," Fitch says. "They started getting more and more blood out of it.

"It was just a slow process. He got to the point where he couldn't really stop and put weight on it. It really affected his game. He became more of a one-legged player than anybody ever surmised. When we

Collegiate Record

Season	Team	G	Min.	FGM	FGA	Pct.	FTM	FTA	Pct.	Reb.	Ast.	Pts.	Averages RPG	APG	PPG
'79–'80	Virginia	34	...	221	404	.547	66	94	.702	381	...	508	11.2	...	14.9
'80–'81	Virginia	33	...	230	413	.557	125	198	.631	378	...	585	11.5	...	17.7
'81–'82	Virginia	32	...	198	353	.561	110	179	.615	366	...	506	11.4	...	15.8
'82–'83	Virginia	33	...	250	414	.604	126	179	.704	386	...	629	11.7	...	19.1
Totals		132	...	899	1,584	.568	416	650	.640	1,511	...	2,228	11.4	...	16.9

NBA Regular-Season Record

Season	Team	G	Min.	FGM	FGA	Pct.	FTM	FTA	Pct.	Off.	Def.	Tot.	Ast.	St.	Blk.	TO	Pts.	RPG	APG	PPG
'83–'84	Houston	82	2,693	716	1,369	.523	287	434	.681	293	820	913	163	70	197	294	1,720	11.1	2.0	21.0
'84–'85	Houston	82	3,086	753	1,499	.502	303	448	.676	227	626	853	224	81	168	326	1,809	10.4	2.7	22.1
'85–'86	Houston	79	2,864	624	1,280	.488	241	376	.641	258	621	879	283	99	129	285	1,491	11.1	3.6	18.8
'86–'87	Houston	43	1,326	277	566	.489	118	189	.624	88	284	372	120	40	58	126	672	8.7	2.8	15.6
'87–'88	Hou.-G.S.	48	1,653	299	582	.438	149	196	.760	140	322	462	122	41	88	171	749	9.6	2.5	15.6
'88–'89	Golden St.	61	1,086	164	365	.449	62	95	.653	105	202	307	77	31	65	90	393	5.0	1.3	6.4
'89–'90	Sacramento	26	417	43	129	.372	12	23	.522	11	73	84	28	14	22	34	109	3.2	1.1	4.2
'90–'91	Sacramento	25	348	34	93	.366	5	19	.263	41	70	111	17	11	17	27	74	4.4	0.7	3.0
'91–'92	Washington	10	108	9	28	.310	4	6	.667	11	19	30	4	3	8	10	22	3.0	0.4	2.2
Totals		455	13,591	2,924	6,012	.486	1,181	1,786	.681	1,174	2,837	4,011	1,038	390	752	1,363	7,039	8.8	2.3	15.4

NBA Playoff Record

Season	Team	G	Min.	FGM	FGA	Pct.	FTM	FTA	Pct.	Off.	Def.	Tot.	Ast.	St.	Blk.	TO	Pts.	RPG	APG	PPG
'84–'85	Houston	5	193	43	100	.430	19	37	.514	25	58	83	7	2	8	17	106	10.8	1.4	21.2
'85–'86	Houston	20	741	136	301	.518	86	118	.729	66	149	215	80	30	35	71	399	10.8	4.0	19.9
'86–'87	Houston	10	330	75	146	.514	35	43	.814	27	61	88	21	2	12	31	186	8.8	2.1	18.6
'88–'89	Golden St.	3	43	9	22	.409	2	4	.500	6	8	14	1	1	2	4	20	4.7	0.3	6.7
Totals		38	1,307	283	569	.497	142	202	.703	124	276	400	109	35	57	123	711	10.5	2.9	18.7

NBA All-Star Game Record

	G	Min.	FGM	FGA	Pct.	FTM	FTA	Pct.	Off.	Def.	Tot.	Ast.	PF	Dq.	St.	Blk.	TO	Pts.
Totals	3	66	21	33	.636	7	10	.700	5	14	19	2	13	0	2	1	6	49

"HE COULD MAKE THE OUTLET PASS ON THE FAST BREAK AS WELL AS ANY PLAYER WHO HAS EVER PLAYED THE GAME."
—BILL FITCH

made the trade with Golden State, he went out there and it just increased.

"I used to see it in practice. Olajuwon and Ralph would be pretty equal. And then as the session went along, the worse that knee got. It wasn't really a good match.

"When we played out there the first time, everybody's looking to see, Olajuwon versus Sampson, and it was no contest. By then, Ralph had become a one-legged player."

Healthy, Sampson had been underrated. He missed three games in his first three seasons, averaging 35 minutes. However, he played only 50 games once after the 1986 Finals. In 1988–89, his first full season with the Warriors, he averaged only 17 minutes.

After that, the going only got tougher. Characteristically, he tried to fight his way back, but his knees failed him.

After a 10-game stint with the Washington Bullets, he retired for good in 1992 at the age of 32. Some men post numbers, some hang banners, some have to be content with a brief role in a highlight reel and the ability to go home, look in the mirror, and say, "I gave it my best shot." That was Ralph Sampson. ■

Out of Africa

"He has, without a doubt, the
quickest feet and the
greatest ability to create
a shot with those quick feet
of anybody I've seen."

—PETE NEWELL

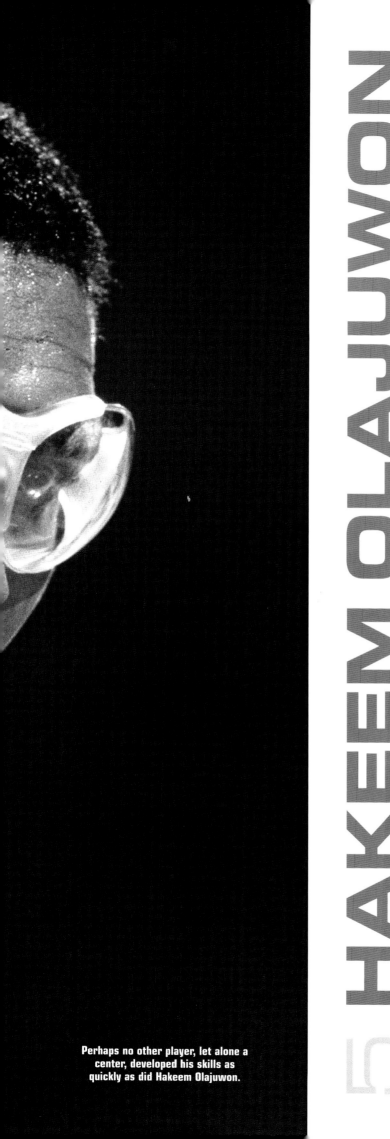

Perhaps no other player, let alone a center, developed his skills as quickly as did Hakeem Olajuwon.

5 HAKEEM OLAJUWON

WHO SAID: "YOU MUST WORK TO ESTABLISH A PROFESSIONAL CODE OF CONDUCT. WHEN YOU GET INTO CALLING NAMES AND TRYING TO EMBARRASS YOUR OPPONENT AFTER A GAME, THAT IS WRONG. IT SHOWS YOUR OWN INSECURITY. I UNDERSTAND PROMOTING THE FLASHY PLAYS. SPORTS IS ENTERTAINMENT. BUT VIOLENCE AND TALK ARE NOT ENTERTAINMENT."

Gandhi? The Maharishi? Or Hakeem Olajuwon?

Who said: "I know what sport is for. If you are sitting at a dinner table with people from different nationalities, it's very difficult to discuss politics, to discuss religion. You get into fights. Sports should be something everybody can discuss and have fun. Everybody has his favorite team, favorite players. Sports should promote peace among peoples."

Buddha? Mother Teresa? Or Hakeem Olajuwon?

It was Olajuwon, known as "the Dream," who arrived in the United States from Lagos, Nigeria, at age 17—having discovered basketball a year before—to show everyone how to play this game, and how games should be played in general.

He would attain an uncommon artistry, a rare maturity, and preeminence among his peers. In their day, Wilt Chamberlain and Bill Russell never resolved the question of who was best. But Olajuwon dominated his chief rivals—Patrick Ewing, David Robinson, even the massive, 10-years-younger Shaquille O'Neal—in head-on playoff matchups as the Rockets posted two of the most improbable championships in NBA history.

Olajuwon's serenity was even harder won. Always intelligent and sweet-tempered, he learned the game in what seemed a blinding flash. He learned the lifestyle quickly, too, turning into an Americanized me-first mercenary.

"People forget how much Olajuwon had to learn when he came in," says Bill Fitch, his first pro coach. "People said he was greedy and selfish. Well, he was to a certain extent."

"He was a young man who just wanted to get the ball, throw it on the floor, and run up and down," says Robert Reid, a teammate for Olajuwon's first five seasons.

"I remember a time when I was playing point Dream's rookie year. He said in his accent, 'Boh-bee, gimme the ball, mon.' I said, 'But Dream, you've got four guys hanging on you.' He said, 'That's OK, I dunk on all of them.'

"He was getting scarred up a bit. In Dream's mind, if you didn't get upset or play as hard as he did, he felt you were leaving something. . . . I can remember a couple times, if I missed Dream if he was open down low or if I threw a ball away, he would scold and get mad and you would argue with him."

In between blowups, however, Olajuwon was something. He had boundless energy and athleticism to match. In the 1986 Western finals, in which the young Rockets slew Kareem Abdul-Jabbar and the Lakers, an admiring Pat Riley noted, ironically:

"Nobody's gotten to him and distorted his mind. Centers in this league are supposed to pace themselves. Nobody's told him to pace himself. He's irrepressible. He just never stops playing. He pursues the basketball and pursues the basketball. You can't block him out. He's so persistent and so strong. He just comes through people."

In the ensuing years, however, what was supposed to be a dynasty unraveled. Three Rockets guards were lost to substance abuse problems. Ralph Sampson's knees deteriorated. Fitch traded Ralph and was himself fired.

The time came, as it always does, when the blame was laid at the doorstep of the remaining giant. In 1991, when the Rockets went 15–2 with Olajuwon out, callers to talk radio began wondering how much they needed Hakeem.

Not yet mellow, Olajuwon wondered how much he needed Houston.

"Sure, they could always trade me," he said. "You know how long that would take

- Born: January 21, 1963, in Lagos, Nigeria
- College: Houston
- 7´0´´/255 pounds
- Named NCAA Tournament Outstanding Player in 1983
- Named first-team All-American by *The Sporting News* in 1984
- Averaged 13.3 points and 10.7 rebounds per game in college
- Led NCAA Division I with a 67.5 field-goal percentage, 13.5 rebounds per game, and 5.6 blocks per game in 1983–84
- Selected first overall in the 1984 NBA Draft by the Houston Rockets
- Averaged 21.8 points and 11.1 rebounds per game in his NBA career
- Scored 26,946 points in his NBA career
- Holds the NBA record for career blocked shots with 3,830
- Became the first player in NBA history to total both 2,000 career blocks and 2,000 career steals in 1999
- Led the NBA with 4.59 blocks per game in 1989–90, 3.95 per game in 1990–91, and 4.17 per game in 1993
- Named NBA Most Valuable Player in 1994
- Voted NBA Defensive Player of the Year in 1993 and 1994
- Won the NBA's IBM Award for all-around contributions to his team's success in 1993
- Member of six All-NBA First Teams (1987, 1988, 1989, 1993, 1994, 1997), three All-NBA Second Teams (1986, 1990, 1996), three All-NBA Third Teams (1991, 1995, 1998), five All-NBA Defensive First Teams (1987, 1988, 1990, 1993, 1994), four NBA All-Defensive Second Teams (1985, 1991, 1996, 1997), and NBA All-Rookie Team (1985)
- Member of Houston Rockets NBA championship teams in 1994 and 1995
- Named NBA Finals Most Valuable Player in 1994 and 1995
- Shares records for blocked shots in an NBA Finals game with 8 (June 5, 1986, vs. Boston) and blocked shots in an NBA playoff game with 10 (April 29, 1990, vs. Los Angeles Lakers)
- Holds Houston Rockets franchise records for points (26,511), rebounds (13,382), steals (2,088), and blocked shots (3,830)
- Member of the gold medal–winning U.S. Olympic team in 1996
- Voted One of the 50 Greatest Players in NBA History in 1996

"IT HASN'T BEEN EASY BUT IT'S BEEN FUN."

—HAKEEM OLAJUWON

Olajuwon arrived from Nigeria and starred at the University of Houston before the Rockets made him the first pick overall in the 1984 NBA Draft.

the Rockets? I'd be gone like that. The Rockets would get two or three players and probably some money. And I know that I'd get more money. So I guess everybody could be happy. I could be happy with more money if that's what everybody wants."

Olajuwon added that if hard work wasn't good enough for the man in the street, "He can go to hell."

A year later, the Rockets tried to trade him to the Lakers after critics accused Olajuwon of malingering to get a new contract and Hakeem called owner Charlie Thomas "a coward." The deal didn't go through only because of a salary cap complication.

Things, however, were changing. Owner and player made peace. Owner sold the team. Player mellowed, a process heightened by his reconversion to Islam. Olajuwon changed the spelling of his first name (until then, it had been Akeem). During the monthlong Ramadan holiday, he fasted all day, even on game days.

Moreover, he was converted to passing the basketball. His game rose to another level. By this time, he had post moves the equal of the master technician, Kevin McHale. Combined with his grace, agility, and quickness, these moves made him as beautiful as he was unstoppable.

"Hakeem has the best footwork of any center I've seen," says Pete Newell. "I give soccer credit for that. He'd played a lot more soccer than basketball before he came to Houston, and he developed his game off his footwork. He has, without a doubt, the quickest feet and the greatest ability to create a shot with those quick feet of anybody I've seen."

The Rockets started the 1993–94 season 18–1 and finished 58–24, and then began a remarkable playoff run. After defeating Portland in the opening series, they lost the first two games on their home court to the defending Western champion Suns, then—after both local newspapers ran "CHOKE CITY"

Collegiate Record

Season	Team	G	Min.	FGM	FGA	Pct.	FTM	FTA	Pct.	Reb.	Ast.	Pts.	RPG	APG	PPG
'80–'81	Houston						Did not play.								
'81–'82	Houston	29	529	91	150	.607	58	103	.563	179	11	240	6.2	0.4	8.3
'82–'83	Houston	34	932	192	314	.611	88	148	.595	388	29	472	11.4	0.9	13.9
'83–'84	Houston	37	1,260	249	369	.675	122	232	.526	500	48	620	13.5	1.3	16.8
Totals		100	2,721	532	833	.639	268	483	.555	1,067	88	1,332	10.7	0.9	13.3

NBA Regular-Season Record

Season	Team	G	Min.	FGM	FGA	Pct.	FTM	FTA	Pct.	Off.	Def.	Tot.	Ast.	St.	Blk.	TO	Pts.	RPG	APG	PPG
'84–'85	Houston	82	2,914	677	1,258	.538	338	551	.613	*440	534	974	111	99	220	234	1,692	11.9	1.4	20.6
'85–'86	Houston	68	2,467	625	1,188	.526	347	538	.645	333	448	781	137	134	231	195	1,597	11.5	2.0	23.5
'86–'87	Houston	75	2,760	677	1,332	.508	400	570	.702	315	543	858	220	140	254	228	1,755	11.4	2.9	23.4
'87–'88	Houston	79	2,825	712	1,385	.514	381	548	.695	302	657	959	163	162	214	243	1,805	12.1	2.1	22.8
'88–'89	Houston	82	3,024	790	1,556	.508	454	652	.696	338	*767	*1,105	149	213	282	275	2,034	*13.5	1.8	24.8
'89–'90	Houston	82	3,124	806	1,609	.501	382	536	.713	299	*850	*1,149	234	174	*376	316	1,995	14.0	2.9	24.3
'90–'91	Houston	56	2,062	487	959	.508	213	277	.769	219	551	770	131	121	221	174	1,187	13.8	2.3	21.2
'91–'92	Houston	70	2,636	591	1,177	.502	328	428	.766	246	599	845	157	127	304	187	1,510	12.1	2.2	21.6
'92–'93	Houston	82	3,242	848	1,603	.529	444	570	.779	283	785	1,068	291	150	*342	262	2,140	13.0	3.5	26.1
'93–'94	Houston	80	3,277	894	*1,694	.528	388	542	.716	229	726	955	287	128	297	271	2,184	11.9	3.6	27.3
'94–'95	Houston	72	2,853	798	1,545	.517	406	537	.756	172	603	775	255	133	242	237	2,005	10.8	3.5	27.8
'95–'96	Houston	72	2,797	768	1,494	.514	397	548	.724	176	608	784	257	113	207	247	1,936	10.9	3.6	26.9
'96–'97	Houston	78	2,852	727	1,426	.510	351	446	.787	173	543	716	236	117	173	281	1,810	9.2	3.0	24.3
'97–'98	Houston	47	1,633	306	633	.483	160	212	.755	116	344	460	143	84	96	126	772	9.8	3.0	16.4
'98–'99	Houston	50	1,784	373	725	.514	195	272	.717	106	372	478	88	82	123	139	945	9.5	1.5	18.9
'99–'00	Houston	44	1,049	193	421	.458	69	112	.616	65	209	274	61	41	70	73	455	6.2	1.4	10.3
'00–'01	Houston	58	1,545	283	568	.498	123	198	.621	124	307	431	72	70	88	81	689	7.1	1.2	11.9
'01–'02	Toronto	61	1,378	194	418	.464	47	84	.512	98	268	366	66	74	90	98	435	6.0	1.1	7.1
Totals		1,238	44,222	10,749	20,991	.512	5,423	7,621	.712	4,034	9,714	13,748	3,058	2,162	3,830	3,667	26,946	11.1	2.5	21.8

NBA Playoff Record

Season	Team	G	Min.	FGM	FGA	Pct.	FTM	FTA	Pct.	Off.	Def.	Tot.	Ast.	St.	Blk.	TO	Pts.	RPG	APG	PPG
'84–'85	Houston	5	187	42	88	.477	22	46	.478	33	32	65	7	7	13	11	106	13.0	1.4	21.2
'85–'86	Houston	20	766	205	387	.530	127	199	.638	101	135	236	39	40	69	43	537	11.8	2.0	26.9
'86–'87	Houston	10	389	110	179	.615	72	97	.742	39	74	113	25	13	43	36	292	11.3	2.5	29.2
'87–'88	Houston	4	162	56	98	.571	38	43	.884	20	47	67	7	9	11	9	150	16.8	1.8	37.5
'88–'89	Houston	4	162	42	81	.519	17	25	.680	14	38	52	12	10	11	10	101	13.0	3.0	25.3
'89–'90	Houston	4	161	31	70	.443	12	17	.706	15	31	46	8	10	23	11	74	11.5	2.0	18.5
'90–'91	Houston	3	129	26	45	.578	14	17	.824	12	32	44	6	4	8	8	66	14.7	2.0	22.0
'92–'93	Houston	12	518	123	238	.517	62	75	.827	52	116	168	57	21	59	45	308	14.0	4.8	25.7
'93–'94	Houston	23	989	267	514	.519	128	161	.795	55	199	254	98	40	92	83	664	11.0	4.3	28.9
'94–'95	Houston	22	929	306	576	.531	111	163	.681	44	183	227	98	26	62	69	725	10.3	4.5	33.0
'95–'96	Houston	8	329	75	147	.510	29	40	.725	17	56	73	31	15	17	29	179	9.1	3.9	22.4
'96–'97	Houston	16	629	147	249	.590	76	104	.731	46	128	174	54	33	41	46	370	10.9	3.4	23.1
'97–'98	Houston	5	190	39	99	.394	24	33	.727	9	45	54	12	5	16	13	102	10.8	2.4	20.4
'98–'99	Houston	4	123	23	54	.426	7	8	.875	5	24	29	2	5	3	5	53	7.3	0.5	13.3
'01–'02	Toronto	5	86	12	22	.545	4	6	.667	9	10	19	2	7	4	6	28	3.8	0.4	5.6
Totals		145	5,749	1,504	2,847	.528	743	1,034	.718	471	1,150	1,621	458	245	472	424	3,755	11.2	3.2	25.9

NBA All-Star Game Record

	G.	Min.	FGM	FGA	Pct.	FTM	FTA	Pct.	Off.	Def.	Tot.	Ast.	PF	Dq.	St.	Blk.	TO	Pts.
Totals	12	270	45	110	.400	26	50	.520	38	56	94	17	30	1	15	22	25	106

"HE'S IRREPRESSIBLE. HE JUST NEVER STOPS PLAYING. HE PURSUES THE BASKETBALL AND PURSUES THE BASKETBALL. YOU CAN'T BLOCK HIM OUT. HE'S SO PERSISTENT AND SO STRONG. HE JUST COMES THROUGH PEOPLE."

—PAT RILEY

headlines—they rallied to win it, then beat Utah in the Western Conference finals.

In the NBA Finals, they fell behind the Knicks 3–2, won Game 6 after Olajuwon deflected John Starks' potential championship-winner in the closing seconds, then closed it out in Game 7. For the series, Hakeem outscored Patrick Ewing 188–132.

A year later, the Rockets staged an even wilder coup, coming from 2–1 behind to beat the Jazz, from 3–1 behind to beat the Suns, then conquering the Spurs and sweeping the Magic in the Finals. Along the way, Hakeem buried David Robinson, who'd been billed as "Mr. MVP" on the cover of

Sports Illustrated, 212–143, and outscored O'Neal, everyone's heir apparent, 131–112.

Olajuwon won the MVP award in 1994, becoming the first center to capture the award since Moses Malone in 1983.

"I think I've had a wonderful career," Olajuwon said. "I don't look at the bad; I look at the good. The good way overrides the bad. It hasn't been easy but it's been fun."

In 2001 Olajuwon was traded to the Toronto Raptors, closing out a Rockets career in which he set just about every franchise scoring and rebounding record. He is still the NBA's career leader in blocked shots. ∎

Prisoner of Seventh Avenue

"One of the greatest centers to play the game."
—MARK JACKSON

Patrick Ewing was a hero to many in New York, but his inability to win a championship for the Knicks cast a shadow over his brilliant career.

PATRICK EWING

WHAT THEY SAW WAS ALL THEY GOT. THE PLAYER WHO CAME IN WITH A REPUTATION OF BEING A KLUTZ ON OFFENSE TURNED INTO ONE OF THE GREATEST SHOOTING BIG MEN OF ALL TIME.

Once upon a time in the busy kingdom of New York, there lived a giant possessed of such power and grace, the villagers chose him to represent them in games against the other villages. The giant was shy and soft-spoken and hated standing out in crowds. However, he was good at games and liked the coins they paid him by the cartload.

Unfortunately, the other New York players weren't as good, and New York always lost. Other giants claimed the brass ring, some of them less accomplished, like the wicked Bill Laimbeer from the duchy of Detroit, the creaky Bill Cartwright, and the surfing Luc Longley of Chicago.

Because New York was the biggest village of all, this failure to win the big one was difficult to accept. The villagers sometimes wept and cursed their giant, although he was powerless to do more.

He tried not to hold it against them. He knew their lives were hard, living all packed in on top of each other, and they got crazy about their games.

They besieged him with their entreaties.

He never knew what to say.

In few careers, perhaps not even Wilt Chamberlain's, were the expectations placed on great centers shown as clearly as with Ewing's.

When the Knicks drew him with the first pick in the first lottery in 1985, there were knowing winks that the league office had stacked the deck. He averaged 20 points as a rookie and that much or more for the next 12 seasons. He was a career 50 percent shooter. By his fifth season, he was a top-10 rebounder and shot-blocker annually.

Unfortunately, the Knicks had a problem: everything else.

In Ewing's first six seasons, they had five coaches (Hubie Brown, Bob Hill, Rick Pitino, Stu Jackson, and John MacLeod) and several general managers, presidents, and ownership groups, leaving a single constant—Patrick—to shoulder the blame.

Patrick was Pat Riley's centerpiece in the glory days of the early nineties, but they finished one win short of a title. Ewing was outplayed by Hakeem Olajuwon in the 1994 NBA Finals, and Riley took it on the lam a year later. Thus, the era isn't remembered fondly in Gotham.

Two years and two more coaches (Don Nelson and Jeff Van Gundy) later, Ewing teed off on Madison Square Garden fans. "Whenever something goes wrong, they jump off the bandwagon," he said. "They're annoying me. It's been like that for 12 years, and I'm fed up with it." The fans started booing him.

"Of all the guys I've ever played with, he's the guy I feel the worst for," says former teammate Doc Rivers. "Most of the guys you don't feel bad for. An NBA athlete, you feel great for.

"Patrick Ewing might be the only guy you don't feel great for. The heat he took, in a

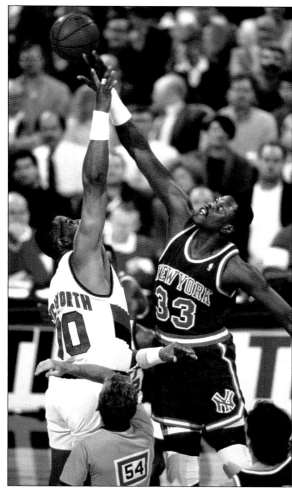

- Born: August 5, 1962, in Kingston, Jamaica
- College: Georgetown
- 7´0´´/240 pounds
- Named College Player of the Year by *The Sporting News* in 1985
- Won the Naismith Award in 1985
- Named first-team All-American by *The Sporting News* in 1985 and second-team in 1983 and 1984
- Averaged 15.3 points and 9.2 rebounds per game in college while shooting 62.0 percent from the field
- Member of NCAA championship team in 1984
- Voted NCAA Tournament Most Outstanding Player in 1984
- Member of gold medal–winning U.S. Olympic teams in 1984 and 1992
- Selected first overall in the 1985 NBA Draft by the New York Knicks
- Voted NBA Rookie of the Year in 1986
- Named to the All-NBA First Team in 1990 and All-NBA Second Team in 1988, 1989, 1991, 1992, 1993, and 1997
- Earned NBA All-Defensive Second Team honors in 1988, 1989, and 1992
- Named an NBA All-Star 11 times, including a span of 10 straight seasons from 1988 to 1997
- Holds NBA Finals single-series record for blocked shots with 30 (1994 vs. Houston) and shares NBA Finals single-game record for blocked shots with 8 (June 17, 1994, vs. Houston)
- Led the Knicks in scoring and blocked shots in every season from 1985–86 to 1996–97 and led the team in rebounds eight times
- Holds New York Knicks career records for games (1,039), minutes (37,586), points (23,665), field goals made (9,260), field goals attempted (18,224), free throws made (5,126), free throws attempted (6,904), rebounds (10,759), steals (1,061), and blocks (2,758)
- Voted One of the 50 Greatest Players in NBA History in 1996
- The Knicks retired his No. 33 jersey on February 28, 2003

"HE HAS THE HEART OF A CHAMPION. WHEN YOU THOUGHT ABOUT NEW YORK, YOU THOUGHT OF PATRICK EWING."

—MICHAEL JORDAN

Ewing dominated the college game during his four years at Georgetown and then became the NBA's first-ever lottery pick in 1985.

city that is usually a very knowledgeable city . . . for whatever reason, they didn't accept Patrick Ewing."

If Ewing's image was one of being aloof, in real life he was pleasant and unassuming. Born in Jamaica, he moved to Boston when he was 11. He had a heavy accent and towered awkwardly above everyone.

"Everyone looked at me like some kind of freak," he told the *Boston Globe*'s Jackie MacMullan. "The older guys taunted me. They told me I would never be anything. They said I would never learn the game.

"At first, I couldn't understand why they said those things. But I got used to it. And I learned not to let what anyone said affect me."

Ewing was an average student, but his high school coach, Mike Jarvis, drafted a list of requirements for colleges recruiting him: Patrick had to be given untimed tests and allowed to tape lectures. The list became public, leading to a

common misperception: Patrick can't read. That became the chant around the Big East whenever Ewing's Georgetown Hoyas played.

Ewing spent four stormy years at Georgetown. Taunts from opposing fans crossed the line into racism. Coach John Thompson's program, which had once been merely protective of Patrick, closed around Ewing and was derided as Hoya Paranoia.

Patrick became the college game's leading villain. Once at Boston College, he fought 5´10´´ Michael Adams.

"I couldn't believe it when I got to the NBA and I finally talked to him," Adams said. "He was a totally different person. Calm. Very nice. I told him, 'Man, you had me fooled.'"

Ewing's image softened after he turned pro, or faded. Still shy, and preferring Thompson's cocoon-like approach, he made himself unavailable to the press on off days.

Collegiate Record

Season	Team	G	Min.	FGM	FGA	Pct.	FTM	FTA	Pct.	Reb.	Ast.	Pts.	Averages RPG	APG	PPG
'81–'82	Georgetown	37	1,064	183	290	.631	103	167	.617	279	23	469	7.5	0.6	12.7
'82–'83	Georgetown	32	1,024	212	372	.570	141	224	.629	325	26	565	10.2	0.8	17.7
'83–'84	Georgetown	37	1,179	242	368	.658	124	189	.656	371	31	608	10.0	0.8	16.4
'84–'85	Georgetown	37	1,132	220	352	.625	102	160	.638	341	48	542	9.2	1.3	14.6
Totals		143	4,399	857	1,382	.620	470	740	.635	1,316	128	2,184	9.2	0.9	15.3

NBA Regular-Season Record

Season	Team	G	Min.	FGM	FGA	Pct.	FTM	FTA	Pct.	Rebounds Off.	Def.	Tot.	Ast.	St.	Blk.	TO	Pts.	Averages RPG	APG	PPG
'85–'86	New York	50	1,771	386	814	.474	226	306	.739	124	327	451	102	54	103	172	998	9.0	2.0	20.0
'86–'87	New York	63	2,206	530	1,053	.503	296	415	.713	157	398	555	104	89	147	229	1,356	8.8	1.7	21.5
'87–'88	New York	82	2,546	656	1,183	.555	341	476	.716	245	431	676	125	104	245	287	1653	8.2	1.5	20.2
'88–'89	New York	80	2,896	727	1,282	.567	361	484	.746	213	527	740	188	117	281	266	1,815	9.3	2.4	22.7
'89–'90	New York	82	3,165	922	1,673	.551	502	648	.775	235	658	893	182	78	327	278	2,347	10.9	2.2	28.6
'90–'91	New York	81	3,104	845	1,645	.514	464	623	.745	194	711	905	244	80	258	291	2,154	11.2	3.0	26.6
'91–'92	New York	82	3,150	796	1,525	.522	377	511	.738	228	693	921	156	88	245	209	1,970	11.2	1.9	24.0
'92–'93	New York	81	3,003	779	1,550	.503	400	556	.719	191	*789	980	151	74	161	265	1,959	12.1	1.9	24.2
'93–'94	New York	79	2,972	745	1,503	.496	445	582	.765	219	666	885	179	90	217	260	1,939	11.2	2.3	24.5
'94–'95	New York	79	2,920	730	1,452	.503	420	560	.750	157	710	867	212	68	159	256	1,886	11.0	2.7	23.9
'95–'96	New York	76	2,783	678	1,456	.466	351	461	.761	157	649	806	160	68	184	221	1,711	10.6	2.1	22.5
'96–'97	New York	78	2,887	665	1,342	.488	439	582	.754	175	659	834	156	69	189	269	1,751	10.7	2.0	22.4
'97–'98	New York	26	848	203	403	.504	134	186	.720	59	206	265	28	16	58	77	540	10.2	1.1	20.8
'98–'99	New York	38	1,300	247	568	.435	163	231	.706	74	303	377	43	30	100	99	657	9.9	1.1	17.3
'99–'00	New York	62	2,035	361	775	.466	207	283	.685	140	464	604	58	36	84	142	929	9.7	0.9	15.0
'00–'01	Seattle	79	2,107	294	684	.430	172	251	.685	124	461	585	92	53	91	151	760	7.4	1.2	9.6
'01–'02	Orlando	65	901	148	333	.444	94	134	.701	60	203	263	35	22	45	65	390	4.0	0.5	6.0
Totals		1,183	40,594	9,702	19,241	.504	5,392	7,289	.740	2,752	8,855	11,607	2,215	1,136	2,894	3,537	24,815	9.8	1.9	21.0

NBA Playoff Record

Season	Team	G	Min.	FGM	FGA	Pct.	FTM	FTA	Pct.	Rebounds Off.	Def.	Tot.	Ast.	St.	Blk.	TO	Pts.	Averages RPG	APG	PPG
'87–'88	New York	4	153	28	57	.491	19	22	.864	16	35	51	10	6	13	11	75	12.8	2.5	18.8
'88–'89	New York	9	340	70	144	.486	39	52	.750	23	67	90	20	9	18	15	179	10.0	2.2	19.9
'89–'90	New York	10	395	114	219	.521	65	79	.823	21	84	105	31	13	20	27	294	10.5	3.1	29.4
'90–'91	New York	3	110	18	45	.400	14	18	.778	2	28	30	6	1	5	11	50	10.0	2.0	16.7
'91–'92	New York	12	482	109	239	.456	54	73	.740	33	100	133	27	7	31	23	272	11.1	2.3	22.7
'92–'93	New York	15	604	165	322	.512	51	80	.638	43	121	164	36	17	31	39	382	10.9	2.4	25.5
'93–'94	New York	25	1,032	210	481	.437	123	163	.755	88	205	293	65	32	76	83	547	11.7	2.6	21.9
'94–'95	New York	11	399	80	156	.513	48	70	.686	17	89	106	27	6	25	30	209	9.6	1.9	19.0
'95–'96	New York	8	328	65	137	.474	41	63	.651	11	74	85	15	1	25	30	172	10.6	1.9	21.5
'96–'97	New York	9	357	88	167	.527	27	42	.643	26	69	95	17	3	22	27	203	10.6	1.9	22.6
'97–'98	New York	4	132	20	56	.357	16	27	.593	9	23	32	5	3	5	10	56	8.0	1.3	14.0
'98–'99	New York	11	347	58	135	.430	28	36	.778	14	82	96	6	7	8	10	144	8.7	0.5	13.1
'99–'00	New York	14	461	71	170	.418	62	89	.697	29	104	133	6	16	20	27	204	9.5	0.4	14.6
'01–'02	Orlando	4	67	8	25	.320	10	17	.588	5	17	22	4	1	4	2	26	5.5	1.0	6.5
Totals		139	5,207	1,104	2,353	.469	597	831	.718	337	1,098	1,435	275	122	303	345	2,813	10.3	2.0	20.2

NBA All-Star Game Record

	Min.	FGM	FGA	Pct.	FTM	FTA	Pct.	Rebounds Off.	Def.	Tot.	Ast.	PF	Dq.	St.	Blk.	TO	Pts.
Totals	190	44	82	.537	18	26	.692	15	45	60	7	27	0	11	16	23	106

"UNFORTUNATELY, HE DIDN'T WIN A CHAMPIONSHIP. BUT HE CONDUCTED HIMSELF LIKE A CHAMPION AND PUT MORE INTO TRYING TO WIN A CHAMPIONSHIP THAN ANYONE."

—JEFF VAN GUNDY

In a metropolis that idolized celebrities, this handsome, recognizable star went years with no major endorsements. The bright lights of Manhattan may as well have been on the moon. During the season, he lived across the Hudson River in suburban Fort Lee, New Jersey, and commuted. During the summer, he went "home" to Georgetown, where he and his Hoya successors, Alonzo Mourning and Dikembe Mutombo, had homes near the campus.

"I always thought he was cold," said Rivers, who joined the Knicks in 1992. "But he's not that at all. He's very open with the team, laughing all the time. People assumed I knew him because I play in the league, but you don't."

"What Patrick is going to have to do to be remembered, to be considered great, is win," Riley once told *Sports Illustrated*'s Rick Reilly. "That's how he's been slotted: For you, Patrick, the ultimate criteria, because you're not open to us, because we don't know anything about your private life, will be on the court. You've got to win.

"The headline I hope to see for Patrick the day he wears that ring is 'FINALLY.'"

Riley said that before the 1994 NBA Finals, in which the Knicks lost to Houston in seven games. They returned to the Finals in 1999 only to lose to San Antonio in five games (and Ewing missed that Series with an injury). Ewing lasted one more season in New York before playing out the final two years of his career unceremoniously in Seattle and Orlando.

But time heals all wounds, even in New York. Upon his return to Madison Square Garden in a Magic uniform in 2001, Ewing was visibly touched by a three-minute ovation for all he had done for so long. It was a lovely moment and a deserved one. ■

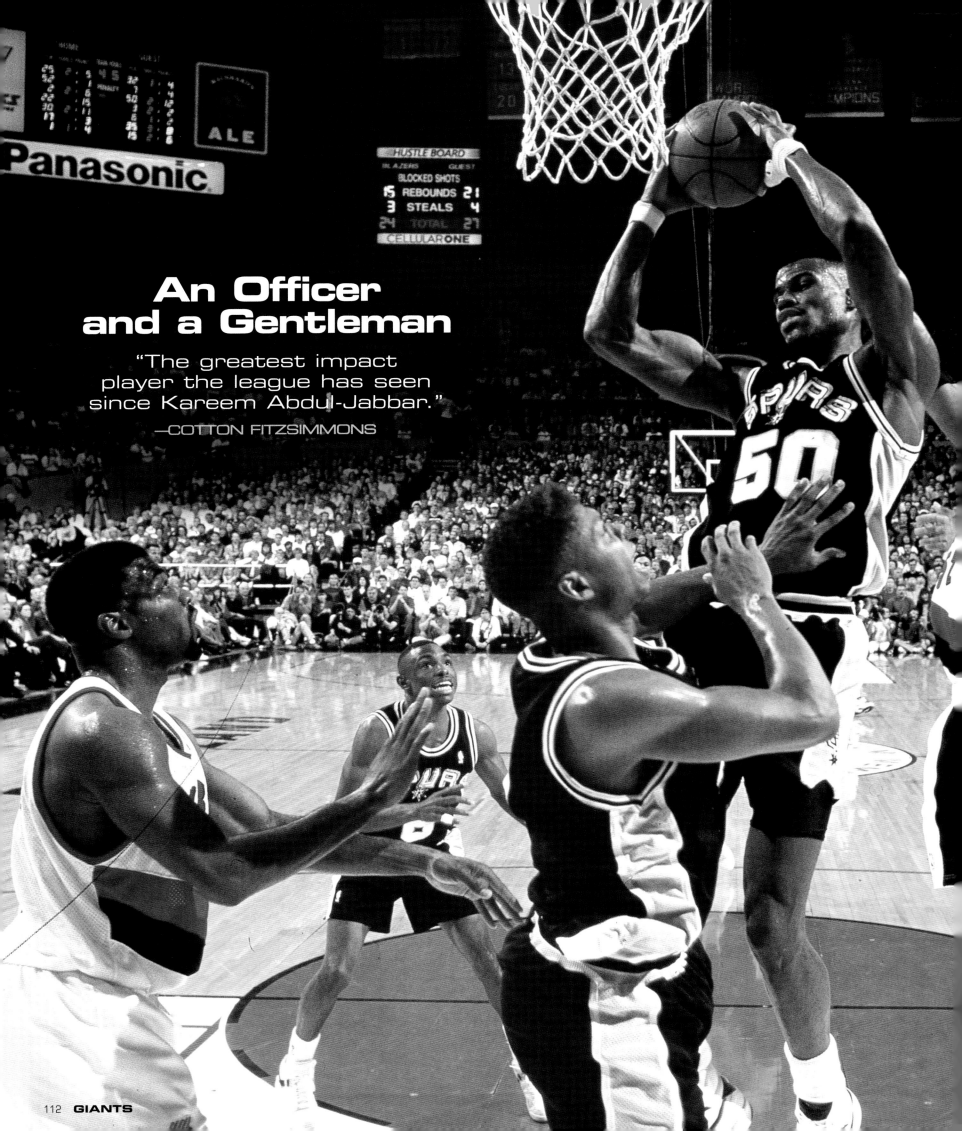

An Officer and a Gentleman

"The greatest impact player the league has seen since Kareem Abdul-Jabbar."

—COTTON FITZSIMMONS

By helping the Spurs to NBA titles in 1999 and 2003, David Robinson secured his place as one of the greatest centers in league history.

DAVID ROBINSON

AT FIRST, WHEN THEY SAID DAVID ROBINSON WAS TOO GOOD TO BE TRUE, THEY MEANT IT AS A COMPLIMENT.

He was a Renaissance man: gifted, hardworking, whip-smart, a whiz at several musical instruments, a computer hacker, articulate, and pleasant. When *Sports Illustrated* profiled him in 1996, it posed him as a 7´1´´ angel.

Of course, Robinson was then up to six seasons, one MVP trophy, and nothing resembling a championship. His San Antonio Spurs had been knocked out of the first round of the playoffs three times, the second round twice, and the third round once, and David's postseason performances hadn't lived up to the ones he had posted during the regular season.

Now there were people, including teammates and peers, who said he was too angelic or just not interested enough.

"Athletic ability, he's the best I've ever seen or ever played with," says Doc Rivers, a teammate in 1995 when the Spurs surrendered their home-court advantage to the Rockets and lost in the West finals. "He's more athletically gifted than Dominique [Wilkins]. Can run faster than most guards. Can jump higher than about anybody in the league. He has a 'God's gift' body. I think the only thing he doesn't have yet is an understanding for the game and a passion for the game.

"He was asked to play basketball. The first time he ever played, he was asked. In high school, the coach asked him to come out his junior year and he actually said no. The guy said, 'Why don't you give it a try?' He tried out and made it and then the best player got hurt, and that was the only reason he played."

True enough, David Robinson wasn't like the other guys.

He wasn't from the inner city. He didn't grow up on a playground dreaming of being the next Bill Russell. His childhood was more like Bill Gates' than Russell's.

A fine student, raised in a solid middle-class family in Manassas, Virginia—his parents later wrote a book, *Raising an MVP: Most Valuable Person and Player*—he didn't have the slightest inclination to be a sports star until he began to grow. As Rivers explained, the basketball coach at Osbourn Park High School approached him.

After the ensuing tug-of-war, Robinson did OK but not well enough to think it would be anything more than another of his many extracurricular activities. He was 6´6´´, 175 when he left Osbourn Park. Without giving it a second thought, he accepted an appointment to the Naval Academy, committing himself to five years' active duty after graduation.

Only after he sprouted another seven inches, and went from pretty good to great, did everyone begin to reconsider.

The navy, which needed good publicity more than a 7´1´´ ensign, cut his tour to two years so he could play in the NBA. The Spurs considered themselves privileged to take him with the first pick in the 1987 draft, even knowing they'd have to wait.

So the prodigy was unloosed upon the NBA, and the NBA shivered. Robinson was a 25-points-a-game scorer, a top-10 rebounder, and a devastating shot-blocker almost from the day he showed up. In his first seven seasons, he was All-NBA First Team four times.

If the test of a great player is making his teammates better, he did that, too. The season before he arrived, the Spurs had won 21 games. In his rookie year (he was, of course, the runaway Rookie of the Year in 1990), they leapt to 56—the biggest jump in NBA history at the time.

- Born: August 6, 1965, in Key West, Florida
- College: Navy
- 7´1´´/250 pounds
- Voted College Player of the Year by *The Sporting News* in 1987
- Won the Naismith Award and Wooden Award in 1987
- Named first-team All-American by *The Sporting News* in 1986 and 1987
- Holds NCAA Division I single-season records for total blocks with 207 (1986)
- Shares NCAA Division I single-game record for blocked shots with 14 (January 4, 1986, vs. UNC Wilmington)
- Selected first overall in the 1987 NBA Draft by the San Antonio Spurs
- Named NBA Rookie of the Year in 1990
- Won the NBA Most Valuable Player Award in 1995
- Voted NBA Defensive Player of the Year in 1992
- Earned the NBA's IBM Award for all-around contributions to his team's success in 1990, 1991, 1994, 1995, and 1996
- Member of four All-NBA First Teams (1991, 1992, 1995, 1996), two All-NBA Second Teams (1994, 1998), four All-NBA Third Teams (1990, 1993, 2000, 2001), four NBA All-Defensive First Teams (1991, 1992, 1995, 1996), four NBA All-Defensive Second Teams (1990, 1993, 1994, 1998), and NBA All-Rookie Team (1990)
- Holds San Antonio Spurs career records for points (20,790), rebounds (10,497), blocked shots (2,954), and free throws made (6,035)
- Member of two gold medal–winning U.S. Olympic teams (1992, 1996) and one bronze medal–winning U.S. Olympic team (1988)
- Voted One of the 50 Greatest Players in NBA History in 1996

IF THE TEST OF A GREAT PLAYER IS MAKING HIS TEAMMATES BETTER, HE DID THAT, TOO.

Robinson evoked memories of another highly athletic, left-handed big man—Bill Russell.

"The greatest impact player the league has seen since Kareem Abdul-Jabbar," said then-Suns coach Cotton Fitzsimmons, ticking off such also-rans as Jordan, Magic Johnson, and Larry Bird. "They're all MVPs," said Fitzsimmons. "This guy is more."

If those were the expectations, Robinson would have to dominate or disappoint. It was the latter.

Not that it was all his fault, or even mostly his fault. In happier circumstances, he might have been the second coming of Abdul-Jabbar or, to choose another model, Russell, to whom he bore more resemblance.

Like Russell, Robinson was left-handed, possessed of superior quickness and athleticism, a stellar defender, and fond of luring big men out of the lane on offense and then driving past them.

But Robinson, who had so much good fortune in everything else, had buzzard's luck in the NBA. He didn't join a good team, like Russell's Celtics. The Spurs were so bedraggled, even Larry Brown hadn't been able to save them, posting the only losing season in his 17-year coaching career, 21–61 in 1988–89.

Nor was there a sharpie like Red Auerbach running things. Instead, there was a parade of owners, presidents, general managers, and coaches. In 10 drafts after the Robinson no-brainer in 1987, the Spurs took only three players who were still with them 10 years later. Two, Sean Elliott and Vern Maxwell, were traded and reacquired for peanuts.

Thus began their series of playoff pratfalls: the 1990 second-round loss to Portland after finishing first in the Midwest Division; the 1994 first-round upset by the Jazz; the loss to Houston in the 1995 West finals when Olajuwon (getting defensive help) outscored Robinson (trying to play Hakeem straight-up and getting burned to the consistency of charcoal) 212–143.

"David needs another bad guy on the team, where Shaq [Orlando center Shaquille O'Neal] doesn't," said Rivers in 1995. "Shaq is the bad guy.

"David doesn't have the body. They talk about his toughness; David doesn't have the body to be the tough guy. It's one thing to ask Charles Oakley,

Collegiate Record												Averages			
Season	Team	G	Min.	FGM	FGA	Pct.	FTM	FTA	Pct.	Reb.	Ast.	Pts.	RPG	APG	PPG
'83–'84	Navy	28	...	86	138	.623	42	73	.575	111	6	214	4.0	0.2	7.6
'84–'85	Navy	32	...	302	469	.644	152	243	.626	370	19	756	11.6	0.6	23.6
'85–'86	Navy	35	...	294	484	.607	208	331	.628	455	24	796	13.0	0.7	22.7
'86–'87	Navy	32	...	350	592	.591	202	317	.637	378	33	903	11.8	1.0	28.2
Totals		127	...	1,032	1,683	.613	604	964	.627	1,314	82	2,669	10.3	0.6	21.0

NBA Regular-Season Record										Rebounds										Averages		
Season	Team	G	Min.	FGM	FGA	Pct.	FTM	FTA	Pct.	Off.	Def.	Tot.	Ast.	St.	Blk.	TO	-	Pts.		RPG	APG	PPG
'87–'88	San Ant.							Did not play—in military service.														
'88–'89	San Ant.							Did not play—in military service.														
'89–'90	San Ant.	82	3,002	690	1,300	.531	613	837	.732	303	680	983	164	138	319	257		1,993		12.0	2.0	24.3
'90–'91	San Ant.	82	3,095	754	1,366	.552	592	777	.762	335	728	*1,063	208	127	*320	270		2,101		*13.0	2.5	25.8
'91–'92	San Ant.	68	2,564	592	1,074	.551	393	561	.701	261	568	829	181	158	*305	182		1,578		12.2	2.7	23.1
'92–'93	San Ant.	82	3,211	676	1,348	.501	561	766	.732	229	727	956	301	127	264	241		1,916		11.7	3.7	23.4
'93–'94	San Ant.	80	3,241	840	1,658	.507	*693	*925	.749	241	614	855	381	139	265	253		*2,383		10.7	4.8	*29.8
'94–'95	San Ant.	81	3,074	788	1,487	.530	*656	847	.775	234	643	877	236	134	262	233		2,238		10.8	2.9	27.6
'95–'96	San Ant.	82	3,019	711	1,378	.516	*626	*823	.761	319	*681	*1,000	247	111	271	190		2,051		12.2	3.0	25.0
'96–'97	San Ant.	6	147	36	72	.500	34	52	.654	19	32	51	8	6	6	8		106		8.5	1.3	17.7
'97–'98	San Ant.	73	2,457	544	1,065	.511	485	660	.735	239	536	775	199	64	192	202		1,574		10.6	2.7	21.6
'98–'99	San Ant.	49	1,554	268	527	.509	239	363	.658	148	344	492	103	69	119	108		775		10.0	2.1	15.8
'99–'00	San Ant.	80	2,557	528	1,031	.512	371	511	.726	193	577	770	142	97	183	164		1,427		9.6	1.8	17.8
'00–'01	San Ant.	80	2,371	400	823	.486	351	470	.747	208	483	691	116	80	197	122		1,151		8.6	1.5	14.4
'01–'02	San Ant.	78	2,303	341	672	.507	269	395	.681	191	456	647	94	86	140	104		951		8.3	1.2	12.2
'02–'03	San Ant.	64	1,677	197	420	.469	152	214	.710	160	346	506	64	52	111	83		544		7.9	1.0	8.5
Totals		987	34,271	7,365	14,221	.518	6,035	8,201	.735	3,083	7,414	10,497	2,441	1,388	2,954	2,417		20,790		10.6	2.5	21.1

NBA Playoff Record										Rebounds								Averages		
Season	Team	G	Min.	FGM	FGA	Pct.	FTM	FTA	Pct.	Off.	Def.	Tot.	Ast.	St.	Blk.	TO	Pts.	RPG	APG	PPG
'89–'90	San Ant.	10	375	89	167	.533	65	96	.677	36	84	120	23	11	40	24	243	12.0	2.3	24.3
'90–'91	San Ant.	4	166	35	51	.686	33	38	.868	11	43	54	8	6	15	15	103	13.5	2.0	25.8
'92–'93	San Ant.	10	421	79	170	.465	73	110	.664	29	97	126	40	10	36	25	231	12.6	4.0	23.1
'93–'94	San Ant.	4	146	30	73	.411	20	27	.741	13	27	40	14	3	10	9	80	10.0	3.5	20.0
'94–'95	San Ant.	15	623	129	289	.446	121	149	.812	57	125	182	47	22	39	56	380	12.1	3.1	25.3
'95–'96	San Ant.	10	353	83	161	.516	70	105	.667	37	64	101	24	15	15	24	236	10.1	2.4	23.6
'97–'98	San Ant.	9	353	57	134	.425	61	96	.635	41	86	127	23	11	30	25	175	14.1	2.6	19.4
'98–'99	San Ant.	17	600	87	180	.483	91	126	.722	36	132	168	43	28	40	40	265	9.9	2.5	15.6
'99–'00	San Ant.	4	155	31	83	.373	32	42	.762	17	38	55	10	7	12	8	94	13.8	2.5	23.5
'00–'01	San Ant.	13	409	78	159	.472	66	95	.695	39	114	153	22	17	31	28	216	11.8	1.7	16.6
'01–'02	San Ant.	4	81	9	19	.474	0	4	.000	6	17	23	5	3	3	2	18	5.8	1.3	4.5
'02–'03	San Ant.	23	538	64	118	.542	52	78	.667	46	108	154	21	18	31	24	179	6.7	0.9	7.8
Totals		123	4,221	768	1,604	.479	684	966	.708	367	934	1,301	280	151	312	280	2,221	10.5	2.3	18.0

NBA All-Star Game Record								Rebounds								
	G	Min.	FGM	FGA	Pct.	FTM	FTA	Pct.	Off.	Def.	Tot.	Ast.	PF	Dq.	St.	Blk.	TO	Pts.
Totals	11	184	50	85	.588	41	59	.694	22	40	62	8	21	0	13	13	11	141

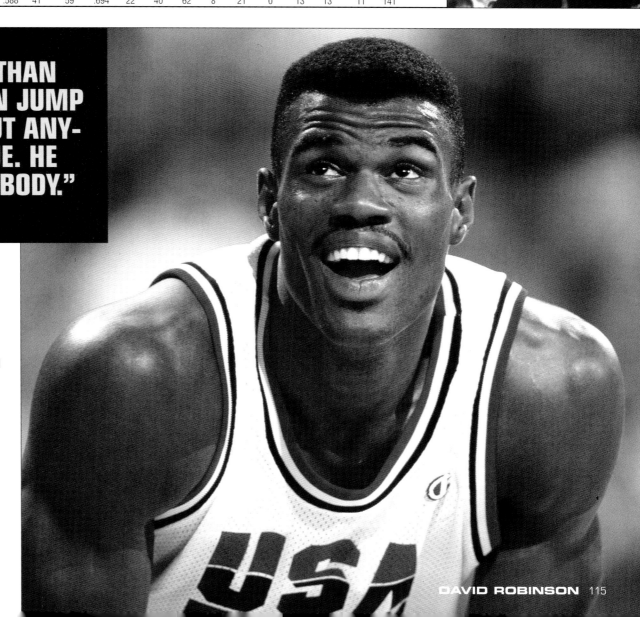

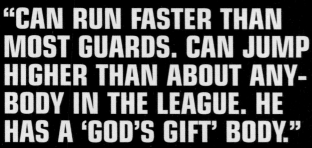

"CAN RUN FASTER THAN MOST GUARDS. CAN JUMP HIGHER THAN ABOUT ANYBODY IN THE LEAGUE. HE HAS A 'GOD'S GIFT' BODY."
—DOC RIVERS

Charles Barkley, Dennis Rodman, the Shaqs, to be the tough guy. It's another thing to ask Olive Oyl to be the tough guy.

"David Robinson plays hard; he just physically doesn't have the body to be banging. So he shouldn't play that game. He should try to take guys away from the bucket and use his finesse and his speed."

As it turned out, all David Robinson needed was someone a lot like David Robinson. When Tim Duncan was drafted by the Spurs in 1997, Robinson's game improved—and so did the Spurs. Within two years, the Spurs were in the NBA Finals, where they defeated the Knicks in five games to win the 1999 championship.

Robinson was at times dominant, recording eight double-doubles during that postseason and scoring in double figures in every postseason game. He answered the call—and put to rest whatever doubts existed about his overall game. ■

THE | NINETIES

AND THE NEXT CENTURY

Shaquille O'Neal

Alonzo Mourning

Tim Duncan

It was the day of the "megastar." In the wake of the PR genius of Magic Johnson and the commercial genius of Michael Jordan, young NBA players found themselves arriving in the league as multimillionaires before they had proved they could play at that level.

The decade introduced Shaquille O'Neal, as much an evolutionary stride as Russell, Chamberlain, and Abdul-Jabbar. O'Neal was 7´1´´, 300 pounds, with 11 percent body fat.

Young players now had clout, whether they had earned it or not, and it had its impact. Given the number of great centers in the seventies and eighties, one might have expected as many or more in the nineties, but there were actually fewer.

More and more young players didn't want to be centers. Despite all the criticism he took, O'Neal knew what he was. He played in the hole and gave as good as he got, if not better, as did the lionhearted Alonzo Mourning.

The gifted, Mourning-sized Chris Webber made it clear that he was a power forward, which he played in the style of his childhood hero, not Wilt Chamberlain or Kareem Abdul-Jabbar, but Magic Johnson.

Whichever positions they chose, the players got bigger and bigger. By the nineties, the average player was 6´8´´, 220. The average "big man"—centers and power forwards—was probably 6´10´´ or 6´11´´ and weighed 250 pounds or so.

The NBA included some real giants such as 7´7´´ Romanian-born Gheorge Muresan, 7´6´´ Shawn Bradley, and, in 2002, China's 7´5´´ Yao Ming. Power forwards were now auxiliary centers, a trend that dated back to the eighties when they ran as large as the 6´11´´ Kevin McHale and the 7´4´´ Ralph Sampson.

Sampson and Hakeem Olajuwon were greeted with great fanfare in the eighties, but by the nineties massive front lines were so common as to be unnoticed. The Pacers, for example, started 7´4´´ Rik Smits, 6´11´´ Dale Davis, and 6´10´´ Derrick McKey, while the Spurs had 7´1´´ David Robinson, 7´0´´ Tim Duncan, and 6´8´´ Robert Bowen.

Duncan, like McHale and Sampson before him—but to an even greater degree—has been so spectacular in the role of auxiliary center that a list of all-time greats would be incomplete without him. If he continues to play at the level he played at during his first six seasons, he will go down as one of the truly elite big men in the history of the game.

The Timberwolves had 6´11´´ Dean Garrett, 6´10´´ Tom Gugliotta, and 7´0´´ Kevin Garnett. Garnett was another trendsetter who arrived right out of high school not yet fully grown, and was skilled enough to play out on the floor. He was classified as a "small forward," as were 6´11´´ Marcus Camby and 6´10´´ Shareef Abdur-Rahim.

There may not be more great centers now than before, but there are more giants than you can count.

90s
AND THE NEXT CENTURY

A Wilt for the Nineties

"Scary."

—BILL LAIMBEER

Following in the footsteps of former Lakers Abdul-Jabbar and Chamberlain, Shaquille O'Neal has been the NBA's dominant big man since entering the league in 1992.

SHAQUILLE O'NEAL

SHAQUILLE O'NEAL CALLED HIMSELF A ROLE MODEL ON HIS CD SHAQ DIESEL. YES, HIS CD. HE'S HAD SEVERAL. SOME EVEN SHIPPED GOLD, AS THEY SAY IN THE MUSIC BIZ.

Then there's his movie career. Don't send him any more basketball scripts. His people are worried about him being typecast, as they say in the movie biz.

There's his life story, published when he was 21, breaking the old rule: have the life, then write the story.

By the nineties a megastar wasn't confined to one sport. He might play two, or branch out into other areas of the entertainment biz, which was what athletes said they really were. Then there was the enormous money to be made in commercial endorsements.

Of course, only a few stars were of this rank, but Shaquille O'Neal was one from the day he showed up. Even in a game populated by giants, he represented another dimension. By mid-decade the NBA listed 29 seven-footers, and the average NBA player was 6′8′′, big enough to have been a center in the George Mikan days. When Wilt Chamberlain broke in, the NBA featured just one seven-footer, Walter Dukes, and only three more players over 6′9′′.

As a 20-year-old rookie in 1992, Shaq was a legitimate 7′1′′, measured in stocking feet at Chicago's predraft camp. He weighed 303 pounds. He had 11 percent body fat. He was a tremendous athlete who could run and jump.

"The NBA ain't ready for this kid," said Indiana Pacers President Donnie Walsh. "This is like Wilt coming into the league."

Said Miami's Rony Seikaly after playing against him in an exhibition: "He's 20 years old? Give me a break."

It was going to get worse. By O'Neal's fifth season, he'd be up to 330. He was awesome to behold. The great menace, Bill Laimbeer, winding up his career, laughingly called him "scary." A few years later, Marcus Camby, a 220-pound rookie, collided with Shaq. "I thought," said Camby afterward, 'Man, I can't be doing this.'"

Shaq had other things going: an outgoing personality—he was the one who came up with that "Bambi meets Terminator" description of himself—a nice smile, a crowd-pleasing game, and a cool name that even rhymed.

The world fell into his lap like an overripe plum.

His first NBA contract was for seven seasons at $40 million. He had a five-year, $10 million hookup with Reebok. In his first season, he earned an estimated $10 million in endorsements, a level Michael Jordan took years to reach.

Even after Shaq's departure years later, Magic general manager John Gabriel would marvel at how well the young man handled everything. At work, he was responsible and hardworking, with one flaw: although he shot thousands of them and worked with myriad coaches, he couldn't make free throws.

After work, though, he was all kid.

After signing his first pro contract, he celebrated by taking friends to a water park. At closing time, he offered the owner $5,000 to stay open for them.

In Orlando, he would ask the 12-year-old in the mansion next door to take his motorboat out to create a wake for his jet ski. Shaq and his friends had paint gun fights. Once, he tried bungee jumping from a tower in a park in Portland, noting he was careful: "I tied the rope around my waist," he said, "not my leg." He wasn't the kind of

- Born: March 6, 1972, in Newark, New Jersey
- College: Louisiana State
- 7´1´´/301 pounds
- Named first-team All-American by *The Sporting News* in 1991 and 1992
- Averaged 21.6 points and 13.5 rebounds per game in college
- Led NCAA Division I with 14.7 rebounds per game in 1991 and 5.2 blocks per game in 1992
- Selected first overall in the 1992 NBA Draft by the Orlando Magic following his junior year of college
- Named NBA Rookie of the Year in 1993
- Named NBA Player of the Week in his first week as a rookie in 1992, averaging 25.8 points, 16.4 rebounds, and 3.4 blocked shots
- Led the NBA in scoring with 29.3 points per game in 1994–95 and 29.7 in 1999–00
- Led the NBA in field goal percentage in 1993–94, 1997–98, 1998–99, 1999–00, 2000–01, and 2001–02
- Member of five All-NBA First Teams (1998, 2000, 2001, 2002, 2003), two All-NBA Second Teams (1995, 1999), three All-NBA Third Teams (1994, 1996, 1997), and three NBA All-Defensive Second Teams (2000, 2001, 2003)
- Selected for nine NBA All-Star Games
- Voted MVP of the 2000 NBA All-Star Game after tallying 22 points and nine rebounds
- Member of Los Angeles Lakers NBA championship teams in 2000, 2001, and 2002, earning the NBA Finals Most Valuable Player award each year
- Holds Orlando Magic career records for rebounds with 3,691 and blocked shots with 824 (1992–93 to 1995–96)
- Member of the gold medal–winning U.S. Olympic team in 1996 and gold medal–winning World Championship team in 1994
- Voted One of the 50 Greatest Players in NBA History in 1996
- Named MVP of the All-Star Game, regular season, and playoffs in 2000

"NONE OF THE GREAT CENTERS HAD SHAQ'S MOVES AND COUNTERS, AND NONE OF THEM, INCLUDING WILT, HAD HIS STRENGTH."

—PETE NEWELL

O'Neal towered over the Nets in the 2002 Finals, winning his third straight NBA Finals MVP award.

youngster to worry that a 300-pounder might be a lot for an elastic rope.

It would have been all but impossible to stay humble, and Shaq didn't. He got a Superman tattoo on one huge bicep, and another with the letters *TWISM*, for The World Is Mine.

Nor would you call him unspoiled. He measured his audience and cooperated accordingly. "I got four versions of the smile," he told *Gentlemen's Quarterly*'s Alan Richman. "I got the $1 million, the $2 million, the $4.6 million, and, if you're real good, the $8.8 million."

Imposing, gifted, and overexposed, it was inevitable he'd be caricatured as an indolent, starstruck disappointment, and he was. By his third season, there was so much flak that it had a name: "Shaq-bashing."

Of 21 coaches polled by *Sports Illustrated* that year, only nine named this 22-year-old monster with career averages of 25 points, 13.5 rebounds, and 58 percent from the floor the first player they'd start a

franchise with. One picked Alonzo Mourning, calling Shaq "a part-time basketball player."

By then, O'Neal had been to Pete Newell's big man's camp twice. Whenever the kindly Newell would hear that Shaq-Hollywood stuff, his blood pressure would rise.

"I think people who say that don't know much about basketball," Newell says. "They haven't seen him play much.

"If you look at his footwork, for a man that big, he shows you a lot of different moves. You've seen spin moves, you've seen step-back moves, you've seen power moves, you've seen jump shots. Every now and then he shows me a move I hadn't seen him use, and I know his game pretty good.

"I'm not a big dunk guy. I think that one of the problems we have with basketball today with big men, they don't learn how to shoot the ball in that 10-foot range because they don't practice it because they dunk everything. But he's a superior dunker

Collegiate Record

Season	Team	G	Min.	FGM	FGA	Pct.	FTM	FTA	Pct.	Reb.	Ast.	Pts.	RPG	APG	PPG
'89–'90	Louisiana St.	32	901	180	314	.573	85	153	.556	385	61	445	12.0	1.9	13.9
'90–'91	Louisiana St.	28	881	312	497	.628	150	235	.638	411	45	774	14.7	1.6	27.6
'91–'92	Louisiana St.	30	959	294	478	.615	134	254	.528	421	46	722	14.0	1.5	24.1
Totals		90	2,741	786	1,289	.610	369	642	.575	1,217	152	1,941	13.5	1.7	21.6

NBA Regular-Season Record

Season	Team	G	Min.	FGM	FGA	Pct.	FTM	FTA	Pct.	Off.	Def.	Tot.	Ast.	St.	Blk.	TO	Pts.	RPG	APG	PPG
'92–'93	Orlando	81	3,071	733	1,304	.562	427	721	.592	342	780	1,122	152	60	286	*307	1,893	13.9	1.9	23.4
'93–'94	Orlando	81	3,224	*953	1,591	*.599	471	850	.554	384	688	1,072	195	76	231	222	2,377	13.2	2.4	29.3
'94–'95	Orlando	79	2,923	*930	*1,594	.583	455	*854	.533	328	573	901	214	73	192	204	*2,315	11.4	2.7	*29.3
'95–'96	Orlando	54	1,946	592	1,033	.573	249	511	.487	182	414	596	155	34	15	155	1,434	11.0	2.9	26.2
'96–'97	L.A.	51	1,941	552	991	.557	232	479	.484	195	445	640	159	46	147	146	1,336	12.5	3.1	26.2
'97–'98	L.A.	60	2,175	670	1,147	.584	359	681	.527	208	473	681	142	39	144	175	1,699	11.4	2.4	28.3
'98–'99	L.A.	49	1,705	*510	885	*.576	269	498	.540	187	338	525	114	36	82	122	1,289	10.7	2.3	26.3
'99–'00	L.A.	79	3,163	956	1,665	.574	432	824	.524	336	742	1,078	299	36	239	223	2,344	13.6	3.8	29.7
'00–'01	L.A.	74	2,125	813	1,422	.572	499	972	.513	291	649	940	277	47	204	171	2,125	12.7	3.7	28.7
'01–'02	L.A.	67	2,419	712	1,229	.579	398	717	.555	235	480	715	200	41	137	171	1,828	10.7	3.0	27.2
'02–'03	L.A.	67	2,535	695	1,211	.574	451	725	.622	259	483	742	206	38	159	196	1,841	11.10	3.1	27.5
Totals		742	28,029	8,116	14,072	.577	4,242	7,832	.542	2,947	6,065	9,012	2,113	526	1,936	2,139	20,475	12.10	2.8	27.6

NBA Playoff Record

Season	Team	G	Min.	FGM	FGA	Pct.	FTM	FTA	Pct.	Off.	Def.	Tot.	Ast.	St.	Blk.	TO	Pts.	RPG	APG	PPG
'93–'94	Orlando	3	126	23	45	.511	16	34	.471	17	23	40	7	2	9	10	62	13.3	2.3	20.7
'94–'95	Orlando	21	805	195	338	.577	149	261	.571	95	155	250	70	18	40	73	539	11.9	3.3	25.7
'95–'96	Orlando	12	459	131	216	.606	48	122	.393	49	71	120	55	9	15	44	310	10.0	4.6	25.8
'96–'97	L.A.	9	326	89	173	.514	64	105	.610	38	57	95	29	5	17	22	242	10.6	3.2	26.9
'97–'98	L.A.	13	501	158	258	.612	80	159	.503	48	84	132	38	7	34	43	396	10.2	2.9	30.5
'98–'99	L.A.	8	315	79	155	.510	55	118	.466	44	49	93	18	7	23	18	213	11.6	2.3	26.6
'99–'00	L.A.	23	1,000	286	505	.566	135	296	.456	119	236	355	71	13	55	56	707	15.4	3.1	30.7
'00–'01	L.A.	16	676	191	344	.555	105	200	.525	91	156	247	51	7	38	57	487	15.4	3.2	30.4
'01–'02	L.A.	19	776	203	384	.529	135	208	.649	67	172	239	54	10	48	62	541	12.6	2.8	28.5
'02–'03	L.A.	12	481	121	226	.535	82	132	.621	64	115	179	44	7	34	35	324	14.8	3.7	27.0
Totals		136	5,465	1,476	2,644	.558	869	1,635	.531	631	1,118	1,749	437	85	313	420	3,821	12.9	3.2	28.3

NBA All-Star Game Record

	G	Min.	FGM	FGA	Pct.	FTM	FTA	Pct.	Off.	Def.	Tot.	Ast.	PF	Dq.	St.	Blk.	TO	Pts.
Totals	8	148	41	83	.494	21	44	.477	20	27	47	6	14	0	5	11	11	103

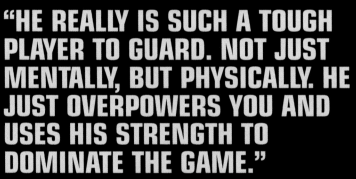

"HE REALLY IS SUCH A TOUGH PLAYER TO GUARD. NOT JUST MENTALLY, BUT PHYSICALLY. HE JUST OVERPOWERS YOU AND USES HIS STRENGTH TO DOMINATE THE GAME."

—DIKEMBE MUTOMBO

because he's so strong. You don't want to discourage this guy because he's so powerful. Why putt a two-foot putt if it's a gimme?"

Said Bill Walton at the time, who worked with Shaq while he was at Louisiana State: "Shaq's the only guy you could put with centers like Chamberlain and Kareem. He's only 24 years old. You look at where Wilt and Kareem were in their careers at 24. They were in their first or second seasons. Shaq's been in the league five years.

"He has the same problem Wilt has. He's so big and so strong, people think he can do anything. Even if he wins, it'll be, 'So what?'"

They never got to "So what?" in Orlando. The Magic reached the NBA Finals in Shaq's third season, 1994–95, with four starters 25 or younger, but they blew a 20-point lead to the Rockets in Game 1 and folded. A year later, Michael Jordan reasserted the Bulls dynasty, and that did it for Shaq in the East.

But in 1996 O'Neal signed with the Lakers for $120 million over seven years, the biggest sports contract ever, and helped lay the groundwork for one of the most successful dynasties in NBA history. With O'Neal as the centerpiece, the Lakers won three straight NBA championships.

The pressure on Shaq to win continues to increase, but then so will the opportunities on stage, screen, and television. Unlike Wilt, who seemed to have mixed feelings about standing out so far above the crowd, and Kareem, who disliked his public role, Shaq loves being Shaq.

"Oh, it's definitely a hard life," says Dennis Scott, his former Magic teammate. "We sit back and we talk about it all the time. But he definitely wouldn't trade it in for the whole world. He loves what he's doing. He loves the attention."

That's good. One way or another, he's always going to have it. ■

Alonzo Mourning's intensity more than made up for his small size compared to other NBA centers.

The Throwback

"He just fights you for everything. He blocks shots, he rebounds, he runs the floor. He just doesn't quit, and all his focus is on winning."

—JACK RAMSAY

ALONZO MOURNING

He really is a power forward. He just doesn't know it.

His listed height of 6´10´´ would make him one of the NBA's shorter starting centers, if he were that tall. At the 1992 Chicago predraft camp, they caught him at 6´9½´´ in stocking feet.

Not that Mourning ever worried about such things as size or versatility, or needed smaller players to push around when bigger ones were available.

"Zo is a warrior," says Jack Ramsay, a former commentator on Miami Heat telecasts. "Zo comes to play hard every night. He's not great as a low-post player. You wouldn't say he has a great shot or a great jump shot, but he can do all those things well.

"But he just fights you for everything. He blocks shots, he rebounds, he runs the floor. He just doesn't quit, and all his focus is on winning. I've watched him in games when he hasn't scored well but somebody else has—he's thrilled with the victory. And I've seen him score in the 30s and his team lose; he's very unhappy with that situation."

Mourning is a study in ferocity. Before a kidney disorder called focal glomerulosclerosis forced him to walk away from the game for the second time in three seasons prior to the start of the 2002–03 campaign, his special rival was none other than Shaquille O'Neal, to whom he spots at least three inches and about 70 pounds. They went 1–2 in the 1992 draft and warred ever after, a circumstance aggravated by the ebullient Charlotte Hornets crowing they'd have taken Zo with the first pick if they'd had it.

"I know Alonzo very well," says Shaq's friend, former Magic forward Dennis Scott. "We grew up in the same area. I tease him. I say, 'Big fellow's 7´1´´, 330 pounds. You're 260. He's agile, can put the ball on the floor. He'll dunk on you. He'll turn around and J [make a jump shot] on you.'

"Alonzo just laughs. He says, 'I'm gonna come out. He better bring it all.'"

Laughter, however, will not be what Mourning is remembered for. Bared teeth is closer to it.

Born and raised in Chesapeake, Virginia, he was 12 when his parents split up and left him with a family friend, Fannie Threet. By his senior year at Indian River High School, he was generally regarded as the top player of his class in the nation. He was the fourth prep ever to be invited to Olympic tryouts.

In 1988 he chose Georgetown, but without displaying the usual reverence toward coach John Thompson, whom he sometimes called "Big John" (before enrolling, anyway). By Mourning's sophomore season, Big John was increasingly worried about the young man's lifestyle. That year, Alonzo was summoned to federal court to describe his association with a convicted Washington, D.C., crack dealer.

Said Thompson later to *Sports Illustrated*'s Alex Wolff: "People ask what's wrong with Zo. . . . Sometimes we want to hold kids high when there's really a frightened child with the man's body."

Mourning's career seemed to stall, too. He had a controversy-filled sophomore year and a quiet junior season when recently arrived (and at 7´2´´, much bigger) Dikembe Mutombo replaced him on Thompson's pressing unit. Even after Mourning's breakout senior year, pro scouts debated about his offense and projected him as a power forward.

If he wasn't a classic center, he was the next best thing. As a rookie in 1992–93, he averaged 21 points and 10 rebounds and was fourth in the NBA in blocked shots. In the Hornets' first playoff appearance, he eliminated the Celtics with a 20-footer at the end of Game 4.

"He was kind of a new breed of a center," says Pete Newell. "He's a very good shotmaker facing the basket. He's very strong. He's very competitive, a very tough competitor. He doesn't like to lose and he lets you know it.

- Born: February 8, 1970, in Chesapeake, Virginia
- College: Georgetown
- 6′10′′/261 pounds
- Named second-team All-American by *The Sporting News* in 1990 and 1992
- Averaged 16.7 points and 8.6 rebounds per game in college
- Led NCAA Division I in blocked shots with 169 in 1989 and 160 in 1992
- Led NCAA Division I in blocks per game with 4.97 in 1989
- Named NBA Defensive Player of the Year in 1999 and 2000
- Named to the All-NBA First Team in 1999, All-NBA Second Team in 2000, NBA All-Defensive First Team in 1999 and 2000, and NBA All-Rookie First Team in 1993
- Has averaged 20.3 points and 9.8 rebounds per game in the NBA
- Selected for seven NBA All-Star Games (1994, 1995, 1996, 1997, 2000, 2001, 2002)
- Totaled 15 points and seven rebounds as a starter in the 2000 NBA All-Star Game
- Holds Charlotte Hornets career record for blocked shots with 684 (1992–93 to 1994–95)
- Member of Dream Team II, which won the gold medal at the 1994 World Championships

"HE'S ONE OF THE GREATEST CENTERS I EVER PLAYED WITH— PROBABLY THE GREATEST."

—SHAQUILLE O'NEAL

Mourning proved to be a tough assignment during the United States' gold-medal run at the 2000 Olympic Games in Sydney, Australia.

"Actually, I originally saw him as a power forward. He's giving away inches, size-wise. I don't know if he's 6′10′′, 6′9½′′. Night after night, he would give away size, sometimes weight."

It is sort of a reverse compliment, but people always carp about what Mourning doesn't do well (pass out of the post, play with his back to the basket) as if he were as big as the other elite centers. Nor does he concede much. In his first five seasons, he never finished outside the top five in blocks, swatting even more shots than Shaq.

By then, he was up to 261 pounds, with fearsome-looking arms and shoulders. In 1995 Mourning turned down the Hornets' $11 million offer, forcing the team to trade him. Dealt to Miami, he joined coach Pat Riley, a man as intense as he was. As for the sun and the beach, Zo couldn't have cared less.

"I don't care what else Miami has," said former teammate Scott Burrell. "If it has a good team and weight room, Zo will be happy."

The Heat tied the club record for victories in Mourning's first season and shattered it in his second. Heat games became emotional maelstroms with Zo as principal actor, operatic in his emotions, talking trash, scowling, frowning, raging, waving his arms, once even going into the stands in Miami, offended that so many expatriate New Yorkers were rooting for the visiting Knicks.

Some players may have played with as much emotion before, but few ever showed as much. Bill Walton once said he thought Mourning just did it to scare opponents. Mourning was surprised to hear it. It had never occurred to him. This was just . . . him.

"A lot of people," Mourning said in a rare peaceful moment, "they really don't know me. They say, 'Look at him, he's out there arguing with his teammates.' And it's not that. I'm my biggest critic. I get down on myself so much. This game is a very emotional game from that standpoint. . . .

"When the game's over, especially if we lose, I beat myself up. No question, I beat myself up in my

Collegiate Record

Season	Team	G	Min.	FGM	FGA	Pct.	FTM	FTA	Pct.	Reb.	Ast.	Pts.	Averages RPG	APG	PPG
'88–'89	Georgetown	34	962	158	262	.603	130	195	.667	248	24	447	7.3	0.7	13.1
'89–'90	Georgetown	31	937	145	276	.525	220	281	.783	265	36	510	8.5	1.2	16.5
'90–'91	Georgetown	23	682	105	201	.522	149	188	.793	176	25	363	7.7	1.1	15.8
'91–'92	Georgetown	32	1,051	204	343	.595	272	359	.758	343	53	681	10.7	1.7	21.3
Totals		120	3,632	612	1,082	.566	771	1,023	.754	1,032	138	2,001	8.6	1.2	16.7

NBA Regular-Season Record

Season	Team	G	Min.	FGM	FGA	Pct.	FTM	FTA	Pct.	Rebounds Off.	Def.	Tot.	Ast.	St.	Blk.	TO	Pts.	Averages RPG	APG	PPG
'92–'93	Charlotte	78	2,644	572	1,119	.511	495	634	.781	263	542	805	76	27	271	236	1,639	10.3	1.0	21.0
'93–'94	Charlotte	60	2,018	427	845	.505	433	568	.762	177	433	610	86	27	188	199	1,287	10.2	1.4	21.5
'94–'95	Charlotte	77	2,941	571	1,101	.519	490	644	.761	200	561	761	111	49	225	241	1,643	9.9	1.4	21.3
'95–'96	Miami	70	2,671	563	1,076	.523	488	712	.685	218	509	727	159	70	189	262	1,623	10.4	2.3	23.2
'96–'97	Miami	66	2,320	473	885	.534	363	565	.642	189	467	656	104	56	189	226	1,310	9.4	1.6	19.8
'97–'98	Miami	58	1,939	403	732	.551	309	465	.665	193	365	558	52	40	130	179	1,115	9.6	0.9	19.2
'98–'99	Miami	46	1,753	324	634	.511	276	423	.652	166	341	507	74	34	180	139	924	11.0	1.6	20.1
'99–'00	Miami	79	2,748	652	1,184	.551	414	582	.711	215	538	753	123	40	294	217	1,718	9.5	1.6	21.7
'00–'01	Miami	13	306	73	141	.518	31	55	.564	35	66	101	12	4	31	28	177	7.8	0.9	13.6
'01–'02	Miami	75	2,455	447	866	.516	283	431	.657	182	450	632	87	27	186	182	1,178	8.4	1.2	15.7
Totals		622	21,795	4,505	8,583	.525	3,582	5,079	.705	1,838	4,272	6,110	884	374	1,883	1,909	12,614	9.8	1.4	20.3

NBA Playoff Record

Sean	Team	G	Min.	FGM	FGA	Pct.	FTM	FTA	Pct.	Rebounds Off.	Def.	Tot.	Ast.	St.	Blk.	TO	Pts.	Averages RPG	APG	PPG
'92–'93	Charlotte	9	367	71	148	.480	72	93	.774	28	61	89	13	6	31	37	214	9.9	1.4	23.8
'94–'95	Charlotte	4	174	24	57	.421	36	43	.837	14	39	53	11	3	13	14	88	13.3	2.8	22.0
'95–'96	Miami	3	92	17	35	.486	20	28	.714	3	15	18	4	2	3	16	54	6.0	1.3	18.0
'96–'97	Miami	17	630	107	218	.491	86	155	.555	44	129	173	18	11	46	70	303	10.2	1.1	17.8
'97–'98	Miami	4	138	29	56	.518	19	29	.655	10	24	34	5	3	10	8	77	8.5	1.3	19.3
'98–'99	Miami	5	194	38	73	.521	32	49	.653	7	34	41	4	8	14	12	108	8.2	0.8	21.6
'99–'00	Miami	10	376	76	157	.484	64	96	.667	31	69	100	14	2	33	24	216	10.0	1.4	21.6
'00–'01	Miami	3	91	12	25	.480	11	19	.579	3	13	16	3	0	5	5	35	5.3	1.0	11.7
Totals		55	2,067	374	769	.486	340	512	.664	140	384	524	72	35	155	186	1,095	9.5	1.3	19.9

NBA All-Star Game Record

	G	Min.	FGM	FGA	Pct.	FTM	FTA	Pct.	Rebounds Off.	Def.	Tot.	Ast.	PF	Dq.	St.	Blk.	TO	Pts.
Totals	5	75	18	33	.545	4	6	.666	3	16	19	4	12	0	3	8	5	40

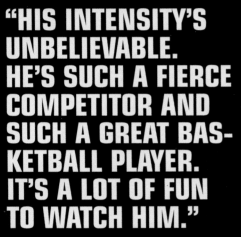

"HIS INTENSITY'S UNBELIEVABLE. HE'S SUCH A FIERCE COMPETITOR AND SUCH A GREAT BASKETBALL PLAYER. IT'S A LOT OF FUN TO WATCH HIM."

—VIN BAKER

head. I lay in bed and parts of the game just go straight through my mind. Constantly. Game situations, game situations, things I could have done differently.

"The thing about it, what's so good about the NBA, you've got a game either the next day or within a couple days' time, where you're able to get that one outta your mind and go on to the next one. Getting a win, regardless of how you do it, is so much more of a relief. You can sleep better, regardless of how many points you scored, how many turnovers you might have had, how many rebounds or blocked shots . . . a win is a win in this league. You play so many games in this league, that's what you fight for, regardless of how you do it. It's so much more of a stress reliever.

"I'm probably one of the worst losers on the planet."

There are players who want to win. There are players who need to win. Then there are some, like Alonzo Mourning, for whom anything else is intolerable. ∎

The Big Fundamental

"He's one of those almost-perfect players in terms of knowledge of the game. . . . He's so skilled, and he plays the game for the right reasons."

—JERRY WEST

With two MVP awards and two championships in his first six seasons, Tim Duncan stands to finish his career in very elite company.

TIM DUNCAN

"THE FANS AND MEDIA DON'T KNOW MUCH ABOUT HIM," SAN ANTONIO SPURS CENTER DAVID ROBINSON ONCE SAID OF TEAMMATE TIM DUNCAN. SO WHAT'S THERE TO KNOW ABOUT HIM?

He has a wizard tattooed on his chest and an abiding love for his PlayStation. And oh yeah, don't forget a drop-step post game that's decorated with an array of soft hooks and slams from the left block. When he steps out, he's got that face-up jumper that includes sweet banks from 19 feet and beyond. Plus he can take 'em off the dribble, and he's got a defensive presence that can stop penetrators in their tracks. His scouting report says he's got smarts (he skipped third grade and graduated with honors from high school in St. Croix, in the U.S. Virgin Islands) and his own special variety of leadership skills. He's even got a psychology degree from Wake Forest, which is good for getting in the heads of opponents or countering the mind-game tactics of Lakers coach Phil Jackson.

Taken all together, those characteristics are what made Shaquille O'Neal start calling Duncan "the Big Fundamental." They also help explain why Duncan claimed back-to-back honors as the NBA's Most Valuable Player in 2002 and 2003. The league hadn't had a back-to-back MVP since Michael Jordan did it in 1991–1992. Only eight players in the league's 56 years of operation have ever managed to achieve such status.

"He's so efficient in all the things he does," New Jersey Nets executive Willis Reed said of Duncan. "I just love his demeanor and how he handles himself."

"That's just my personality, my attitude," said Duncan. "I like to do what I do and I try to do it well. I let that speak for me."

That demeanor has also led to suggestions that Duncan could fit into any basketball era. He is perhaps the one modern player who could make a seamless transition to the old-school days of the league. According to Jerry West, Duncan would be right at home in the old school: "He's one of those almost-perfect players in terms of knowledge of the game. I enjoy a player like Tim more than almost any other player. He's so skilled, and he plays the game for the right reasons."

Among those "right reasons" is, of all things, a fear of sharks.

Back in the Virgin Islands, Duncan was a swimming prodigy until Hurricane Hugo destroyed the swimming pool where he trained as a youth intent on making the Olympics (he had competitive times as a 400-meter freestyler). It seems that with the pool gone, the only place Duncan could train was the ocean, and he wasn't too keen on swimming with sharks. So he opted for hoops, laced up his sneakers, and started working on his drop step.

At first, it wasn't a pretty sight. The early book on Timmy D. was that he was big, clumsy, and unable to dunk—a prime target for classmates' jokes. His coach figured he was too shy to be a hoopster.

"He never got angry," recalled a former classmate. "He just played harder."

And kept growing. It didn't take too long for the young seven-footer to attract the attention of American colleges, including Georgetown, Delaware, and Providence. However, his sister lived in Winston-Salem, North Carolina, so he chose Wake Forest.

Barely 17 when he arrived, Duncan spent the next four years fending off offers from the pros. He could have opted for the NBA Draft and its instant millions at any time during his four years with the Demon Deacons, but he hardly gave it a thought. He loved college life, but more important he was fulfilling a promise to his mother, who died when he was 14. He had told her that he would earn a college degree, so he did.

The result of this schooling was both a personal and competitive poise that many of his fellow players don't share. The time at Wake also helped fill holes in his repertoire. Duncan came into college with a reasonably good face-up game, but he added his post-up game while in school, where there was the time and space to work on it. As a result he graduated in four years, left Wake as the National College Player of the Year in 1997, and was promptly snapped up by San Antonio with the top pick in that year's draft.

With his arrival in the NBA he quickly picked up where he had left off in college. He led the Spurs to six wins in their first seven games.

"I can see why he went No. 1," Michael Jordan told reporters. "He has a lot of talent. He's matured. He's blossomed. He stayed those four years in college and his dividend is starting to show."

"I have seen the future and he wears No. 21," agreed Charles Barkley, then a forward for Houston. "He is better than I thought he was, and I was expecting good stuff."

That first season Duncan averaged 21.1 points, 11.9 rebounds, 2.7 assists, and 2.5 blocks per game. He shot .549 from the floor. He was a member of the All-NBA First Team,

- Born: April 25, 1976, in St. Croix, U.S. Virgin Islands
- College: Wake Forest
- 7´0´´, 260 pounds
- First player since Michael Jordan (1991–92) to win consecutive MVP awards
- Second player in NBA history to be named to both an All-NBA Team and an All-Defensive Team in each of his first five seasons (David Robinson was the first player to do so; he earned the honors in each of his first seven seasons)
- Named to the All-NBA First Team in all of his five seasons; first player since Larry Bird (and the seventh in NBA history) to be named All-NBA First Team in each of his first four seasons
- Earned a spot on the All-Defensive First Team each of the past four seasons after being named to the All-Defensive Second Team as a rookie in 1997–98
- Named the 1999 Finals MVP
- Named the 1998 Rookie of the Year
- Named co-MVP of the 2000 All-Star Game
- Selected as NBA Player of the Week eleven times and Player of the Month four times
- Named an All-Star in five straight seasons (no game was held in 1999); his career All-Star field-goal percentage (.625) ranks seventh in NBA history and is the best among active players
- Leads all players in the NBA in double-doubles over the past five seasons
- Ranks seventh among active players in playoff career scoring average, 23.9 points per game
- Played for the USA team in the 1999 Americas Qualifying Tournament in San Juan, Puerto Rico; was selected to play for the U.S. team in the 2000 Olympic Games but had to withdraw due to a knee injury

> ## "HE'S SO EFFICIENT IN ALL THE THINGS HE DOES. I JUST LOVE HIS DEMEANOR AND HOW HE HANDLES HIMSELF."
> —WILLIS REED

By staying at Wake Forest for four years, Duncan was able to make an immediate impact upon entering the NBA.

the All-Defensive Second Team, and the Western Conference All-Star Team. He swept the Rookie of the Month honors during all six months of the season and received 113 of a possible 116 Rookie of the Year votes.

The next season, which was shortened to 50 games due to labor troubles between the league and its players, Duncan averaged 21.7 points, 11.4 rebounds, 2.4 assists, and 2.52 blocks per game. He finished fifth in the NBA in rebounding, seventh in blocked shots, and seventh in scoring. He was ninth in minutes played and tenth in field-goal percentage. He was the only player ranked in the NBA's top 10 in scoring, rebounding, blocked shots, and field-goal percentage and was named to the NBA All-Defensive First Team. Most important, he led the Spurs to their first-ever NBA title, in six games over the New York Knicks, and was named the Most Valuable Player in the championship series.

All of this he accomplished on a remarkably even keel, according to Spurs coach Gregg Popovich. "He's not impressed with himself when he does something that's astounding. He's not depressed when he makes a mistake. He just keeps competing. He just keeps playing. He's got no MTV in him at all. Tim Duncan just wants to get better. He's not impressed with the hype."

Asked to explain his success, Duncan pointed to the team around him and his good fortune in being drafted by San Antonio. "It was a great situation for me," he said. "I knew I was going to a good team. They had a great player in David Robinson and lots of experience in Avery Johnson and Sean Elliott. I just wanted to find my niche and help make the team better. We had a chance to do some special stuff. I just wanted to fit in and go from there."

That great situation soon evolved into a challenge when the Spurs' roster suffered losses due to age and injury. Over the ensuing seasons it became apparent that Duncan was shouldering more and more of the burden. He did so without complaining, even as the Spurs fell victim to the Lakers, Shaq, and Kobe Bryant each year in the playoffs.

He averaged 25.5 points a game in 2001–02, good enough for his first league MVP award. In 2002–03 his numbers dropped to 23.3 points in 81 games, but he also averaged career bests of 12.9 rebounds, 3.9 assists, and 2.9 blocks per game, earning him his second straight MVP honor. When he scored his 10,000th point on March 21, 2003, against the Timberwolves, he became the 13th-fastest player in league history to record that many points and take 5,000 or more rebounds.

Collegiate Record

Season	Team	G	FGM	FGA	Pct.	FTM	FTA	Pct.	Reb.	Ast.	Pts.	Averages		
												RPG	APG	PPG
'93–'94	W. Forest	33	120	220	.545	82	110	.745	317	30	323	9.6	.9	9.8
'94–'95	W. Forest	32	208	352	.591	118	159	.742	401	67	537	12.5	2.0	16.8
'95–'96	W. Forest	32	228	411	.555	149	217	.687	395	93	612	12.3	2.9	19.1
'96–'97	W. Forest	31	234	385	.608	171	269	.636	457	98	645	14.7	3.1	20.8
Totals		128	790	1,368	.577	520	755	.689	1,570	288	2,117	12.3	2.3	16.5

NBA Regular-Season Record

Season	Team	G	Min.	FGM	FGA	Pct.	FTM	FTA	Pct.	Rebounds			Ast.	St.	Blk.	TO	Pts.	Averages		
										Off.	Def.	Tot.						RPG	APG	PPG
'97–'98	San Ant.	82	3,204	706	1,287	.549	319	482	.662	274	703	977	224	55	206	279	1,731	11.9	2.7	21.1
'98–'99	San Ant.	50	1,963	418	845	.495	247	358	.690	159	412	571	121	45	126	146	1,084	11.4	2.4	21.7
'99–'00	San Ant.	74	2,875	628	1,281	.490	459	603	.761	262	656	918	234	66	165	242	1,716	12.4	3.2	23.2
'00–'01	San Ant.	82	3,174	702	1,406	.499	409	662	.618	259	738	997	245	70	192	242	1,820	12.2	3.0	22.2
'01–'02	San Ant.	82	3,329	765	1,504	.508	560	701	.799	268	774	1,042	307	61	203	263	2,089	12.7	3.7	25.5
'02–'03	San Ant.	81	3,181	714	1,392	.513	450	634	.710	259	784	1,043	316	55	237	248	1,884	12.9	3.9	23.3
Totals		451	17,726	3,932	7,715	.510	2,444	3,440	.708	1,481	4,067	5,548	1,447	352	1,129	1,420	10,324	12.3	3.2	22.9

NBA Playoff Record

Season	Team	G	Min.	FGM	FGA	Pct.	FTM	FTA	Pct.	Rebounds			Ast.	St.	Blk.	TO	Pts.	Averages		
										Off.	Def.	Tot.						RPG	APG	PPG
'97–'98	San Ant.	9	374	73	140	.521	40	60	.667	20	61	81	17	5	23	25	186	9.0	1.9	20.7
'98–'99	San Ant.	17	733	144	282	.511	107	143	.748	55	140	195	48	13	45	52	395	11.5	2.8	23.2
'00–'01	San Ant.	13	526	120	246	.488	76	119	.639	55	134	189	50	14	35	13	317	14.5	3.8	24.4
'01–'02	San Ant.	9	380	82	181	.453	83	101	.822	28	102	130	45	6	39	36	248	14.4	5.0	27.6
'02–'03	San Ant.	24	1,020	218	412	.529	157	232	.677	96	274	370	127	15	79	76	593	15.4	5.3	24.7
Totals		72	3,034	637	1,261	.505	463	655	.706	253	710	963	286	53	221	240	1,739	13.4	3.9	24.1

NBA All-Star Game Record

		G	Min.	FGM	FGA	Pct.	FTM	FTA	Pct.	Rebounds			Ast.	PF	Dq.	St.	Blk.	TO	Pts.
										Off.	Def.	Tot.							
Totals		5	144	33	58	.569	7	7	1.000	20	48	68	12	7	0	4	4	12	73

"I HAVE SEEN THE FUTURE AND HE WEARS NO. 21. HE IS BETTER THAN I THOUGHT HE WAS, AND I WAS EXPECTING GOOD STUFF."

—CHARLES BARKLEY

Duncan's Spurs finished with 60 wins in 2002–03, knocked the Lakers off their throne, and captured their second NBA title in five years. He was 27 and had two championships and two MVP awards in six seasons. "I think I was probably as solid as I was last year," he said. "I think our team did better. I had to do a few different things this year. It's unbelievable. Every year I wanted to get a little bit better. Every year I wanted to add something to my game."

"Winning [the MVP award] two years in a row says a lot about his game," David Robinson told reporters. "He's not flashy. I get amazed by his game night in and night out."

Duncan proved to be so low-key and quiet that Robinson was right: fans really didn't know much about him. But they knew enough. If they watched the games, they knew he would soon display a perfect bank shot kissed off the glass from, say, 19 feet.

"I developed it in college," Duncan once explained. "I don't know who taught me. It was easy for me. I don't think anybody specified to me that that was a good shot or anything. It's just something that I felt comfortable with. I kept working on it."

Shaq, it seems, was also right on the money. "The Big Fundamental" is really all that fans need to know. ∎

- Born: September 12, 1980, in Shanghai, China
- College: None
- 7′5″, 296 pounds
- Averaged 23.5 points (on .641 percent shooting) and 15.4 rebounds in 122 games for the Shanghai Sharks of the China Basketball Association (CBA)
- Led the CBA with 14.5 rebounds and 5.3 blocks per game while averaging 21.3 points per game in 1999–00
- Won the CBA Most Valuable Player award in 2000–01 after finishing third in the league in scoring with 27.1 points per game
- Led the CBA with 19.4 rebounds and 5.5 blocks per game in 2000–01
- Averaged a career-high 32.6 points per game (on a career-best .708 percent shooting) with 19.0 rebounds and 4.8 blocks per game with the Sharks in 2001–02
- Led Shanghai to its first CBA championship in 2001–02, averaging 38.9 points, 20.2 rebounds, and 3.5 blocked shots in 10 playoff games
- Made the All-Tournament Team in the 2002 FIBA World Championship Games after posting team-leading averages of 21.0 points (on 75.3-percent shooting), 9.3 rebounds, and 2.3 blocked shots for China
- Selected first overall in the 2002 NBA Draft by the Houston Rockets
- Posted the highest field-goal percentage in NBA history over a six-game stretch (88.6), making 31 of 35 shots (November 9–21, 2002)
- Totaled 30 points and 16 rebounds on November 21, 2002, at Dallas for his first career double-double
- Made his first career NBA start on November 22, 2002, vs. Washington, scoring 18 points with eight rebounds and four blocked shots
- Selected as the Western Conference's starting center for the 2003 NBA All-Star Game

"HE HAS ALL THE TOOLS. HE CAN SHOOT. HE CAN DRIBBLE. HE'S NO SLOUCH."

—SHAQUILLE O'NEAL

The Next Superstar?

"He's a gift from God."

—ALLEN IVERSON

Yao Ming quieted the critics in his first NBA season by not only proving he belonged in the league, but also by dominating opposing veteran centers at times.

AFTERWORD: YAO MING

Never has there been as much fanfare and media attention surrounding a big man's NBA debut as that which was bestowed upon Chinese import Yao Ming during the 2002–03 season. And after a slow start that had the naysayers drawing comparisons to relatively giant busts such as Manute Bol and Gheorge Muresan, the 7´5´´, 296-pound Ming proved in his inaugural season that his destiny is far more likely to mirror that of an Olajuwon or a Ewing.

After averaging 23.5 points and 15.4 rebounds over five seasons with the Shanghai Sharks of the China Basketball Association, the 22-year-old Yao was selected by the Houston Rockets with the first overall pick in the 2002 draft. The Rockets, far removed from their glory days of the mid-nineties and strangers to the playoffs in the new millennium, were vilified by some for their dogged pursuit of the untested and unproven prospect. Critics claimed he was too skinny and perhaps too soft to withstand the punishment doled out throughout the course of an NBA season, and some predicted mediocrity for the young Asian superstar.

But by late November and throughout December Yao was putting up eye-popping numbers and playing as if he'd been in the league for years. Furthermore, his combination of size and skills made it obviously apparent that Yao's upside bordered on the sky's-the-limit realm.

"He's going to be a great player in this league," gushes Orlando All-Star Tracy McGrady. "Once he gets some games under his belt and gets comfortable with the game, he's going to be unbelievable. And he just takes a lot out of you. He's so big and hard to double-team because he can just look over the double-team and pass out of that with ease. He rebounds. Guys do a great job playing off him when he passes the ball. He's a handful, man."

Among Yao's breakout games in the opening months of the season were a 30-point, 16-rebound job against Dallas; a 29-point, 10-rebound, six-block effort in his rematch with the Pacers; and 27 points and 18 boards against Tim Duncan and the San Antonio Spurs.

"He's the best young player I've ever seen," says Dallas coach Don Nelson. "I told [Dallas owner] Mark Cuban [before the 2002 draft] if he ever wanted to win a whole bunch of championships, he needed to find a way to get him."

Yao's official arrival as one of the game's elite big men, however, would not come until his first face-to-face meeting with Shaquille O'Neal, unofficial club president. O'Neal had missed the teams' first meeting with an injury, and the worldwide interest in their January 17, 2003, confrontation reached epic proportions. Despite Yao's outstanding season up to that point, some speculated that the 350-pound O'Neal might humiliate the rookie.

Once again, Yao disappointed the skeptics, proving once and for all that he was more prodigy than pipe dream. He blocked O'Neal's first three shots of the game and finished with six blocks, 10 boards, and 10 points as the Rockets beat the defending champions 108–104 in overtime.

"Yao had some real nice opportunities, and he was able to get in under Shaq," said Lakers coach Phil Jackson, who had waited until this meeting to offer an opinion of the Chinese star. "Yao earned some credibility out there tonight."

"I thought he did a great job of reading defenses and finding ways to get to the free throw line and make some shots," said Rockets coach Rudy Tomjanovich. "But the great thing about this kid, he was talking about other players on our team: 'Well, that guy hasn't got a shot yet. Gotta get him involved.' The maturity of this kid has grown leaps and bounds this year. I thought he did a great job."

Said Yao of his own performance: "Shaq is a lot bigger and stronger than me. I had to respect him every second. If I didn't, he would get under the basket and we would be in a lot of trouble. It wore me out."

While Yao's appointment as one of the great big men of all time would be premature after just five seasons in China and one in the NBA, all indications are that he will not only live up to all the expectations but likely surpass them and go down as one of the elite. His pedigree is certainly there, having been born to a 6´4´´ mother and a 6´7´´ father, both of whom starred on China's national teams. He was enrolled in a basketball school at age 12 and was playing for his national team by 18.

Yao joined the Shanghai Sharks as a 17-year-old rookie, averaging 10 points and 8.3 rebounds per game, and was the CBA's Most Valuable Player within four years after raising his scoring average to 27.1 points per game. In short, his potential is virtually limitless, and he has responded to every situation thus far by exceeding all challenges placed in front of him.

Said Shaq about his new rival: "This was a good game for Yao. Yao Ming is my brother."

In other words, "Welcome to the club, kid." ∎

After five years without a true rival in China, Yao more than held his own in his first meeting with O'Neal.

STATISTICS: YAO MING

NBA Regular-Season Record

Season	Team	G	Min.	FGM	FGA	Pct.	FTM	FTA	Pct.	Off.	Def.	Tot.	Ast.	St.	Blk.	TO	Pts.	RPG	APG	PPG
'02–'03	Houston	82	2,382	401	805	.498	301	371	.811	196	479	675	137	31	147	173	1,104	8.2	1.7	13.5
Totals		82	2,382	401	805	.498	301	371	.811	196	479	675	137	31	147	173	1,104	8.2	1.7	13.5

NBA All-Star Game Record

G	Min.	FGM	FGA	Pct.	FTM	FTA	Pct.	Off.	Def.	Tot.	Ast.	PF	Dq.	St.	Blk.	TO	Pts.
1	17	1	1	1.000	0	0	.000	0	2	2	0	1	0	0	0	0	2

"HE'S THE BEST YOUNG PLAYER I'VE EVER SEEN."
—DON NELSON

THE DEMISE OF THE CENTER

College matchups between future Hall-of-Fame centers were prevalent in the days of Kareem Abdul-Jabbar and Elvin Hayes (above), and even into the eighties when Patrick Ewing (left) and Hakeem Olajuwon squared off. Nowadays we rarely see even one marquee college center come along each year, much less several.

The center may be the most important position in the history of basketball.

At the college basketball level, a great majority of the championship teams have been led by an outstanding center. During UCLA's remarkable string of NCAA championships, two centers—Kareem Abdul-Jabbar (then known as Lew Alcindor) and Bill Walton—were the leaders of six of those victorious teams. Bill Russell was the reason the University of San Francisco won consecutive championships in 1955 and 1956, and Alex Groza was the leader during Kentucky's championships in 1948 and 1949. Darrall Imhoff led the University of California–Berkeley to the 1959 championship. Until the eighties, the center position was the most important position in the college game.

At the NBA level, 20 of the 21 Most Valuable Player awards given out between the years 1959 and 1980 went to centers. Oscar Robertson was the only noncenter to receive the award, having edged out Wilt Chamberlain for MVP in 1964. I might add that between the years of 1959 and 1980, there were five additional centers who did not earn any MVP awards but who have since been inducted into the Hall of Fame: Elvin Hayes, Walt Bellamy, Wayne Embry, Bob Lanier, and Clyde Lovellett. I believe that proves the quality and depth of the post players during that period.

All of those great centers were born in America and went through our college basketball systems. Yet our programs have developed only a handful of great centers in the past two decades. Of those, Shaquille O'Neal is the only truly remarkable American center to emerge since the eighties.

To understand why, we have to go back to a rule change that was instituted in the early seventies that essentially defined what constitutes a legal screen. This rule brought with it a new arrangement of the five offensive players on the court and also changed the role of the post player.

Prior to this change, a legal screen had to be set three or more feet from the screened player. Any physical contact closer than three feet would result in a foul on the screener. Contact beyond three feet would result in a foul on the defender. But the new interpretation allowed the screener to set a screen directly on the opponent with only daylight between the two players. This change gave birth to the motion offense and, later, the flex offense.

For the most part, the motion offense is a five-player setup that changed the responsibilities of the post player. This offense did not possess the flexibility of the post offense and initially made it necessary for players to abandon a post or center position.

The role of the center was to set solid, aggressive down or side screens. A wide body was preferred. Defensively, the center was expected to be a strong rebounder and to protect the paint and basket area. The defensive demands on the center in the motion offense are not much different from those of the post-offense defender.

The most critical element of the motion and flex offenses has to do with the spacing of the offensive guards in relation to the post offensive style of spacing. In the early years of its adoption and increasing popularity, a two-guard front was standard. But today a great majority of the coaches who prefer motion and flex offenses rely on a one-guard front. The one-guard front offense puts the second guard below the extended foul line. This puts a fourth defender at or below the extended foul line.

Because of the massing of the four offensive players in the paint or basket area in this situation, a post player would be surrounded by teammates and their defenders. Backdoor cuts, drives to the basket, and limited movement by a ball-handling post player are but some of the changes which are then seen in post play and its movement off the ball.

Teaching the post offense—and the fundamentals so important to its success—is essentially progressive offensive teaching, as practically every drill is a component part of the whole. Teaching the fundamental rules requires repetition, proper technique, and an explanation of the "why" of what the athletes are doing. These drills are principally one-on-one, two-on-two, and three-on-three. Each drill relates to the five-player offenses.

The importance of developing individual passing, shooting, dribbling, and screen-setting skills requires more teaching time than putting together a motion or flex offense. These two offenses employ five players who have little use for individual drills or two-on-two drills. As a result, players are not exposed to the proper techniques that are taught in these offensive drills. While some drills are a part of motion-offense teaching, the many individual foot and passing drills are not. And, while motion is a good lateral offense, its success is impaired when facing an aggressive denial defense. Put simply, it is, in many ways, not a flexible offense.

These changes are at the heart of the problem causing the current drought in centers in the NBA. If a player who is not taught the offensive fundamentals at the high school level goes on to a college program that employs the one-guard offense, he will not be aware of the various types of shots and the mechanics of each shot. He is not being made aware of the many uses of the bounce pass, the post passes, the crosscourt

Pete Newell's big man camps continue to be the best training ground for NBA post players.

THE DEMISE OF THE CENTER

passes, and the dribble—all because these techniques are not emphasized or taught to any significant extent in motion and flex offenses. These are but some of the basics of the post offense, and they are a big part of NBA play—and yet our young athletes are not being taught these techniques.

Many of the players who receive this limited instruction at the high school and collegiate levels ultimately go into coaching themselves. Because they were not taught individual offensive skills, it's only logical that they are then in no position to teach such things themselves. The result is that, although we have been turning out thousands of coaches over the past two decades, very few of them are knowledgeable about the offensive fundamentals of the game.

In the recent 2002 World Games our international program displayed even more evidence of our present plight. A U.S. team of NBA players was defeated three times by countries that had never before come close to beating an American team. It should be noted that this U.S. team did not have a center who had been drafted into the NBA *as a center*. I do not state this as

a criticism of the selection process, but as a fact that exposes our dearth of post-type players. In 1960 my gold medal–winning U.S. Olympic team in Rome had four legitimate centers, two of whom are now in the Hall of Fame.

I have no miracle cure for solving this problem; what I do have is suggestions. None of these are simple solutions, nor are they knee-jerk responses to the problem that misread the real problem and its causes and cures. In my opinion, a quick answer is seldom the right answer.

First, I believe we must start at the high school level. In a sense, the problem started there, so maybe we can begin to correct it by looking at those programs. The most important pieces of the sport's programs throughout the country are our high school coaches and their players. We have to face facts, and those facts involve the problems our high schools have in regards to practice time as well as the education (or lack thereof) that our high school coaches have teaching the various fundamentals of the game.

The basketball community should push to create a summer system that teaches high school students the offensive basics and the importance of defense. The European and Asian basketball programs have been doing this with their young players. For example we now have Yao Ming in the NBA, a great Chinese center who exhibits foot skills and passing abilities that few centers in the NBA have shown during the past two decades. There's also Dirk Nowitzky, the Dallas Mavericks' German star, who plays a complete offensive game. These are players who have been taught the fundamentals at an early age.

Our present summer programs have talented high school–level players at camps that are funded by the shoe companies. These programs do not spend time teaching but instead have these kids playing as many as three games a day. Many high school coaches do not feel that these programs help their students, mainly because they compound bad habits. Somehow we must change this trend so that both our coaches and our young players are taught the fundamentals and the basics of the game.

Among the best sources for this kind of education are the numerous clinics held shortly after the season ends that last into September, until early practices begin. There has been a drastic change, I believe, in the formats and conduct seen at these clinics. Many of the clinics I attended early in my coaching career scheduled speakers for up to 20 hours of talk. Not every clinic was that demanding, but few expected less than six hours from speakers. As recently as the nineties coach Bob Knight and I had two-man clinics starting before 7:00 P.M. Friday that lasted until 10:00 or 10:30 P.M. The next day we would start before 9:00 A.M. and go until 4:00 or 5:00 P.M. I feel we taught those kids every aspect of the game—or at least we tried to.

Today clinics are much changed. A clinic will usually be a two- or three-day affair. As many as seven or eight different coaches will often appear. Their average speaking times will generally be only two hours, and seldom longer than three. A coach cannot cover the many fundamentals of offense and defense that quickly. The speakers are among our most successful coaches, and their names attract many younger coaches who want to learn, but little is actually taught because of the brevity of each speaking session.

We need to help our young coaches learn more about teaching the game. We need our more successful coaches and clinicians to share their knowledge with our high school coaches. Clinics should have fewer speakers, and these clinicians need to be given much more time to explain the game and how they teach it. Having a list of successful college coaches means little if they do not have the opportunity and time to express their thoughts fully. We must give back to the game—a game that has given us so much. A good first step would be to revise our present clinic formats.

I am confident that we will have dominant post players again. First we must bring offensive creativity back into the game. I also believe that when our younger coaches realize the personal satisfaction of teaching we will be making great strides toward these goals.

In my many years in the game, my greatest satisfaction as a coach was teaching. In my heart I truly believe that coaching is for today, but teaching is forever. ■

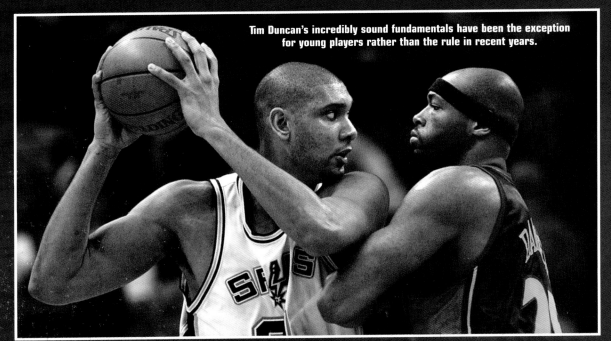

Tim Duncan's incredibly sound fundamentals have been the exception for young players rather than the rule in recent years.